Weapons Formed
Against Me

THE WOMAN WHO WALKED
THROUGH HELL

MARY ROSS

WEAPONS FORMED AGAINST ME
THE WOMAN WHO WALKED THROUGH HELL

iUniverse books may be ordered through booksellers or by contacting:

iUniverse
1663 Liberty Drive
Bloomington, IN 47403
www.iuniverse.com
1-800-Authors (1-800-288-4677)

ISBN: 978-1-4917-6696-5 (sc)
ISBN: 978-1-4917-6695-8 (e)

Library of Congress Control Number: 2015907920

Print information available on the last page.

iUniverse rev. date: 05/15/2015

Dedication & Acknowledgements

I dedicate this book to my Lord and Savior. I also dedicate these words to my development editor and friend, novelist Darnella Ford. Darnella has a great big heart and she gave me the encouragement and strength to write this book through her program *Journey to Worthy*. I love and respect this woman with all of my heart! Thank you Darnella! Also to Monique Lake, Darnella's sister, who lovingly gave her precious time to proofread my book. I appreciate the love! And to my endearing inspiration, songstress Natalie Cole. The lyrics to your songs *Keep Smiling, Annie Mae,* and *Thankful* literally saved my life and prevented me from committing suicide. That's my girl! I Love you, Natalie! I would also like to acknowledge Narvelle Edmonson, who also assisted me with proofreading the manuscript; and Eunice Brown who believed in me and gave me encouraged me to write this book. These two ladies were my inspiration where we all resided together in a transitional living house in Los Angeles, California. Patricia Madden, my best and dearest friend for life. Jonnie Muckelroy, my spiritual advisor and sister for life who always had my back.

Miss Leatrice Jones, a good hearted person who I love dearly. Deloris Baker, my long-time friend and "Auntie" who gave me respect and love all of the time. I also acknowledge Starleen Taylor, a brilliant woman! My brothers Kenneth Broaddus, my brother; and Luther Harold Broaddus (RIP) my brother for life. And Judith Broaddus, my mother figure. Susan Youngblood, who is also a dear friend who provided shelter from the cold. To Sharnette Lindsey, and Ruby Rankins who helped me enroll in California Institute and provided me with a roof over my head and friendship. To Lawrence D. Tate … thank you for showing me how a real true debonair man as supposed to act.Etheo Harvey who is the best damn case manager in the Skid Row area of Los Angeles. Patricia Hooper, who also gave me encouragement to write this book. Maurice Keyes I love you as if you were my own child. Connie Packnett, a childhood mother figure. Elizabeth Simmons-Watts, my favorite gym teacher and to Robert B. Burt, my first true boyfriend … you will always have a special place in my heart. And to Roman Mitchell, who helped me when I needed a roof over my head. And last but not least Wendell Harris who is a witty and funny man who kept me laughing through the bad times.

Epigraph

Cherish yours friends without childish tantrums and guilt ridden manipulation; let them have the freedom to be who they are

Table of Contents

Acknowledgments

Darnella Ford for her constant empowerment, encouragement and love at showing me that life is what you make of it and that I could thrive better when I learned to be dependent on me.

To singer Natalie Cole who helped me survive the hurt by her songs.

To my dysfunctional family. They made me learn how to forgive.

Foreword

A Real Life Journey To Worthy...

As an award winning novelist, I work with aspiring authors throughout the country. Almost two years ago, I traveled to Los Angeles' Skid Row to inspire and uplift the homeless. On these filthy streets, "hope" is a rare commodity; however, in the midst of a storm of despair, I met author Mary Ross, a woman who was living on Skid Row. Interestingly, for more than thirty years she dreamt of writing a book to tell her UNBELIEVABLE life story. Upon our meeting, Mary began attending my inspired lectures and shortly, thereafter; she asked if I would be willing to help her fulfill a lifelong dream of writing her biography, *Weapons Formed Against Me*. Reluctant to agree to such an undertaking, I told Mary if she was willing to put in some *real* work that I would work with her to assist in the development of her biography. All that I can truly say...is this author delivers!

Weapons Formed Against Me is a provocative, twisted, intensely bone crushing, and deeply disturbing memoir. This is the TRUE life story of Mary Ross, a young woman who was raised by a guardian who "tricked" Mary into believing she was her "mother" only to abuse, torment and ridicule Mary throughout her childhood. Her guardian "referred to as Hon" spent more than a decade perfecting her technique of torment and daily abuse that is simply BEYOND, BEYOND comprehension!!!! But THAT's not what makes this biography such a page-turner!!!! When Mary becomes a teenager she invents one of the most creatively genius, borderline demented plans to pay her abuser back…and it WORKS!!!! From where I stand, this is one of the most shocking tales of abuse AND revenge ever recorded! It will PULL you from one page to the next simply because you MUST know…*how in the world does it all end???* You simply MUST know!!!! I invite you to experience one woman's personal *Journey To Worthy* that will leave you utterly speechless in the end.

About Darnella Ford, Creator of Journey to Worthy

DARNELLA FORD is the author of five (5) bestselling novels and the recipient of the **BEST NEW VOICE OF 2003.** Her fifth novel, **FINDING ME,** was recently nominated for the **2010 STONEWALL LITERARY AWARD**. Known for her ability to create "unpretentious gritty masterpieces," Darnella has established a well-respected name for herself in the world of literature. However, in 2006, her life would profoundly change when Darnella traveled to Seattle and began a three-year course of study in Quantum Physics, Neuroscience and Neuro-Biology. Under the instruction of some of the most brilliant Physicists in the country, Darnella studied the profound world of energy/matter and how it all affects our daily lives. Deeply inspired by the changes she made in her own life—in 2008 Darnella created and launched *JOURNEY TO WORTHY,* a program of inspiration designed to expand awareness and transform lives. With its genesis rooted in the science of Quantum Physics, *Journey to Worthy* is based upon the principles of self-love and self-worth. In essence, *self-love* is the cornerstone of the program. In simple terms Darnella explains, "Whenever we take a trip...we always calculate the time it takes us to get from point A to point B. Well, the longest trip I ever took was the journey to my own worthiness!" Ingeniously, Darnella simplified the complex nature of science and began to do something unprecedented—she took Einstein's $E=MC^2$ to the inner city, mental health care facilities, prisons, and the classrooms of Compton. But she didn't stop there—she also took her program to Corporate America and to the affluent. With her unique teaching style, she created compelling presentations and began to affect change and initiate healing to all those who came in contact with her message—which simply states *YOU ARE WORTHY!!!*

JOURNEY TO WORTHY has garnished its own share of "fans" and the people who are touched by the program are changed forever. Under the umbrella of **JOURNEY TO WORTHY** are multiple programs with one of its standouts—a special presentation titled *"Beautiful"* which has been devoted to teenage women and explores the nature of "authentic beauty" as it relates to self-esteem and self-worth. It is Darnella's hope that a human being's understanding of their intrinsic "worth" will be as much a part of our culture as I-Phones, I-Pads and Facebook.

When all is said and done, Darnella insists that the most important aspect of ***JOURNEY TO WORTHY*** will always be "the people themselves" and to that end, "I have devoted the rest of my life to the profound knowing of truth and the ultimate experience of man's highest potential actualized in the material world." To learn more please visit www. journeytoworthy.org

Preface

I wrote this book to be of service to all who needs guidance and love in their life. People who feel like they are alone. Realize that you are never alone. You can take yourself out of any situation as long as you believe in yourself and never falter in your confidence. Go through life with an open mind and an open heart. I want this book to be of service to all people. I want to help someone grow and I want to pass the love that I received forward to you as the reader. And know that it is ok to cry.

Introduction

Hello my name is Mary Ross. I am the author of Weapons Formed Against Me. This is a gripping tale of torment dealt to an innocent child by a stranger she believed was her mother. But it was lies ... all lies. This is a tale of torture, danger, sexual abuse, twisted fates and a game of "payback" that you will *never* believe ... as told by the woman who walked through straight hell and lived to tell. Beaten, raped, starved, locked in a basement, tortured and left for dead ... I emerged *stronger*. This is my real life story. May it inspire you to live the very *best* you can.

Chapter 1

Life before Hell ...
the Good 'Ole Days

I was born under the sign of Gemini on June 4, 1961 in Kansas City, Missouri. As a child growing up, I lived on the well-manicured part of the block that was known as Olive Street. My parents were Ed and Hon, affectionately known as "mom." My folks were late bloomers at parenting, meaning that I was still in diapers, they were both their mid-sixties.

Ed was tall and lanky. He stood 6'3. Hon was short, round and fat reaching only 5'3. By the time I came along, both of my parents were retired. Dad was a very quiet man of Spanish descent. He loved sports, fishing, and smoking his non-filtered Pall Mall cigarettes. Mom, on the other hand, loved three things in life: eating, fishing, and watching the Kansas City Royals play ball on TV.

A retired registered nurse, and I always thought mom was the most beautiful woman I'd ever seen. Her complexion was as bright as a new copper penny. Her eyes were bluish-gray and reminded me of a tropical ocean wave on the eve of a sunset. She had long brown wavy hair that she dyed black to hide the gray. Some people said that mom was obsessed with beauty and youth. Her nationality was a mixture of Black and Spanish heritage.

As for me, I was an old child. I was a tall, lanky, naïve, big brown-eyed little girl who loved and trusted everybody. I was spoiled to death and every year when Christmas came, Mom and Dad bought me every toy that I had picked out from the Sears Catalogue. Mom spent hours getting me ready, and she was not satisfied until I looked like a princess out of a story book. I had long, brown wavy hair down to the middle of my back. Mom would sometimes press and curl it. I remember many days getting my "ears burned off" from the hot comb and curling irons. Mom tended to every detail of my care … from bathing to brushing teeth, fancy hairstyles and coordinating every piece of clothing that passed its way over my body!

Mom ran that house in fine fashion. She ruled with an iron fist, but did so with a smile on her face. She was a stickler for rules, and all was well as long as you followed the rules. During the weekdays, the house ran more like an assembly line than anything else:

Go to school.

Come home and change.

Do homework.

Watch TV.

Dinner.

Bed.

This was my life for years and a daily routine, which I was expected to follow. I would wake up in the morning to hear mom calling out my name. "Mary sweetheart … it's time for you to rise and shine my little darling," my mother would say every morning in a gleeful voice.

"Okay Mom I'm up," I would tell her in a sleepy voice.

"Let's get you into the bathtub, so I can give you a bath. I need to brush your teeth, and wash behind your ears, and scrub you up until you sparkle like the stars at night!" she said happily. Upon my arrival from school, I was always met with mother's cheerful voice. "Hello dear! Now let's get you out of those school clothes and have you change into some more suitable clothes, like your play clothes." Mom said as she gave a chuckle or two. "Do you have any homework today?" Mom would ask eagerly with concern in her voice.

"Yes Mom I do, and I'm getting ready to do it now."

"Good girl! When you are finished you can watch some TV, and I'll call when dinner is ready so you can wash up and eat."

I enjoyed outings at the park with my mother and early 4 a.m. fishing sessions.

Who in the world gets up that early to eat?

We did … that's who!

At the age of five, I was thrilled to start kindergarten. But it was the happiest and saddest time of my life. My father died that same year from lung cancer.

Neither I nor my mother attended the funeral.

I never knew why.

Mom also requested that I no longer call her mom, but Hon instead. This was what my dad used to call her. Perhaps it had a sentimental value to her, so I gave into her request.

Though again, I never knew why.

But this was only the beginning of the end … when my own personal wonderland was on the cusp of turning into a most unusual playground of torture and torment. The happiest place on earth was turning on its spine ... to a place called hell.

Within one year of my father's death, my life changed forever. My mother fell into an entirely different personality. One that I did not recognize. One that I came to fear. She began to linger between two different people, like a Dr. Jekyll AND Mr. Hyde scenario.

This troubled me so.

On one occasion when I asked Mom if I could have a friend visit me on a play date, she yelled at me angrily. "I do not allow children to come over to my house for any reason, and don't you ever ask me such a silly question again!" Then, two minutes later when my friend's mother phoned, she declined into an old, helpless, decrepit woman. "Hello Ms. Matthews ..." she said weakly. "Yes Mary told me about Jackie coming over to play with her. But you know my arthritis has been flaring up lately, and I can hardly get around the house."

When Hon began to change, I changed too. Gone was the carefree girl who was spoiled with love and fond affection. I emerged confused and anxiety-ridden over every little thing. I felt awkward and unsure of myself and my surroundings. I was intimidated and saddened. I felt alone and unloved. My once happy home was now in jeopardy of being a past life. My childhood was interrupted by the weapons that were formed against. And this is my real life story and descent into hell.

Chapter 2

Descent into Hell

In second grade and at the age of seven, the kids used to love to play with my hair. They called it dress up. They wanted to take down my braided hair and see how different styles looked on me. After trying out three or four different hairstyles, the girls would re-braid my hair like it was before. On one particular day, Mom had sent me to school with pretty ribbons that adorned my hair, and a solid colored blouse that matched my skirt. I wore white ankle-laced socks with my patent leather shoes and purse. I thought that my long, wavy, brown hair was cool because I would use it to gain friends.

But one day after coming home from school, my opinion of my hair being cool changed. As I was entering the house, Hon stopped me with a menacing glare. "Who has been playing in your damn hair?" she asked with conviction.

"One of my friends at school did. We were playing dress up, and she braided my hair," I so proudly replied back. And with that, I looked up to see Hon's hand rear back and slap me across my face, followed by a hard push that was so

5

forceful, it knocked me to the floor—where I landed with a big thud. Before I could regain my balance, I felt Hon ripping the ribbons out of my hair so hard that she yanked some of my own hair out. "What did I do?" I yelled back at her with anger.

"Why you bitch! You little cunt! You no good slut!" Hon yelled while hovering over my head. I had never heard these kinds of words before. What did they mean? I asked myself as I lay on the hardwood floor with my lip bleeding and patches of my pretty hair sitting on the ground beside me. "Get up off the goddamn floor and go change your fucking clothes!" She shouted in a bellowing voice. "I am about to beat the black off of your ass!" she promised.

"The black was already starting to come off," I thought to myself. But according to Hon, this was to be continued. Soon I began to hear the peculiar sound of her inner thighs rubbing together as she started to quickly follow behind me. I sensed her footsteps getting closer and closer until they were at my heels. Before I could go to my room to change my clothes, Hon had jerked my arm back. She swung me towards her and began to tear off my blouse. I watched in awe as the buttons flew off my shirt like tossed coins in a fountain. I dared not utter a single word, so in silence I sobbed, trying my best not to increase Hon's wrath.

Hon whaled on my body with a strong clenched fist. She kept punching and punching me until she took a moment to catch her breath. "Go outside to the back yard and get me three rosebush branches and bring them back to me, so I can make a switch!" she growled at me; Of course I did as I was told. I was way too afraid of her to challenge her authority. Tears started forming again and now they were streaming down my cheeks; mostly because I was embarrassed to walk outside in the backyard, bare-chested with just my shoes and skirt, as I hobbled to retrieve her weapon of choice. "Hurry the hell up!" she barked. "What's taking you so long? They better not be the smallest ones you could find either!" she threatened. After retrieving the branches, I started walking up the stairs which led to the kitchen door from the back yard.

When I reached the last step to enter the kitchen, Hon hit me on the back of my head with a mighty force, causing me to trip on the step. She found that to be amusing. It always seemed to me, that my pain was a joke to her that brought her joy. I reluctantly gave Hon the three rosebush branches. I remember clutching those branches, so tightly in my little hands, trying not to drop them, that some of the thorns stuck into my palms. With a bewitching stare, Hon took the branches from me and began to intertwine them together to make a switch. She worked meticulously on the branches, as if this was an arts and craft project. I felt chill bumps forming on my arms. My heart began to beat faster and faster, as I waited for this beating that had my name on it. I thought that my heart was going to rupture inside of me because it was beating so fast.

I was nervous and terrified at the same time of what this whipping was going to feel and sound like. "Get naked, take off all of your clothes!" were the next words that I heard from Hon. "Undress down to your fucking bare feet, go to the basement and wait for me down there!" she screeched so loud that it hurt my eardrums. I opened the door and made my way down those creepy stairs to the basement. I felt like a murderer on death row walking towards the gas chamber. I began to take the rest of my remaining clothing off—a skirt, socks and shoes. Everything else had been torn off by Hon. There I stood alone in a cold, damp, basement waiting to be punished. "Oh help me dear God, let this be over soon, "I prayed to myself. The silence in the air was unbearable for me, and I began to shake and tremble anticipating her descent down those steep narrow wooden stairs to the basement.

I felt as though I was the most hated child in the world. I had never got a whipping or beating before; this was the first time that this had ever happened to me. My mind and body were in pure shock when this happened.

Our basement was made of solid rock and concrete, and in happier times in the summer, Hon used the two burner cast iron stove that was located in the far back of the basement to cook hot dogs and hamburgers when it was too hot to cook in the kitchen. We used to have what I called our private picnics—but this was no picnic for sure! The moment finally arrived, when I heard Hon's heavy footsteps coming from the kitchen and then down the stairs. The closer she got, the more scared I became. When Hon approached me, I saw that not only did she have the switches in one hand, but she also had a bottle of rubbing alcohol in the other hand. "Let the ass whipping begin!" she snarled. "Don't you dare try to run away from me," she commanded. "Don't even think about moving a muscle … just stand still!" she snapped with a broad smile on her face. So, I closed my eyes trying to brace myself for the pain that was coming, but there was nothing that was going to stop me from feeling that excruciating, stinging, pain of that switch hitting my naked body. Swoosh was the sound the switches made as the pain intensified with each lashing that she gave. I cried like a slave as she kept hitting me over and over again on my arms, legs, back, chest and butt. Hon held me up by my arm, and she continued to beat me for what seemed like hours to me. Interestingly, the more I yelled and screamed for mercy, the more she enjoyed the show.

Finally, the whipping had stopped, or so I thought. Hon grabbed my arm again "Come here you little Bitch!" Hon said angrily as she began to pour the rubbing alcohol on my sore bloody welts. I let out a blood curdling scream that I just knew was heard throughout the neighborhood, but no one came to my beck and call. Then all of a sudden, Hon sat down in her favorite mahogany rocking chair with a fiendish smile on her face. She began to rock back and forth slowly for minutes, as if she was studying the severity of my pain. Then without warning, Hon let out a deep bellowing laugh that sounded like it came from her gut. I couldn't believe that she was actually laughing at me! You evil woman, I thought to myself. "You were jumping around so much that you made me laugh, looking like a monkey performing in a circus!" she said joyful and light-hearted. Now I was in enormous pain, and I was trying to catch my breath and recoup from the trauma that my body had just experienced. My cries turned into sobs as the burning sensation from the rubbing alcohol began to wear off. At that instance, Hon got angry again, for no apparent reason, then she hit me in the face with her fist, and my mouth started to bleed, then she punched, and kicked me while pulling my hair. And without speaking a word, she picked up the switch again, and she aimed at my open welts. She made them bigger and bloodier with every lashing. She had my whole body swollen with blistering, bloody welts except for my hands and face.

She pulled me towards her with a smirk on her face as she poured more alcohol on my freshly opened welts. The pain was so unbearable that I literally thought I would faint. I cried from the suffering. "Shut the hell up before I pour alcohol into your eyes and blind you, Bitch!"

"No, please don't, I don't want to be blind Hon!" I cried back with sincerity.

"Shut up!" she screamed. "After all … a bitch like you don't deserve to see."

The pain had me doubled over, and I fell onto the cold concrete floor in a fetal position. "Get up you little coward," Hon demanded. I guess that I took too long to stand up, so Hon got impatient and yanked me up by my hair from the floor and stood me up. "You do what I tell you to do, when I tell you. Do you understand?"

"Yes Hon," I mumbled. She reached down beside the rocking chair and retrieved the rubbing alcohol and she began to pour it on my wounds again. "Please stop Hon! You're hurting me!" I shouted. But she ignored my pleas and continued pouring. "God, make her stop please!" I begged.

"God don't help ungrateful bitches like yourself, who deserves to die!" Hon replied back at me. Soon Hon grew tired of beating me. "All of this ass whipping has made me hungry. I am going upstairs to the kitchen and make me some dinner," she spitefully said. I stumbled up the stairs to follow her. "Where in the hell do you think that you are going?" She asked, as she turned and gave me a surprised look.

"Upstairs with you so I can eat" I said in a tearful, crackling voice.

"What? I know that you really don't think that you are having dinner tonight do you?" Hon snickered. "You are on punishment, and you are staying down here in the basement until you have learned your lesson." She said.

As I turned back to go down the stairs I started thinking that I was glad the whipping was over. And when I reached the bottom of the stairs, I looked up and as I watched her slowly, climbing up the stairs towards the kitchen, I thought she finally is leaving and now my poor body has time to heal.

Chapter 3

"Why Me?"

Alone and confined to the basement, I finally had a chance to ask God, *"Where were you? And why didn't you help me?"* I asked myself was I really all of those bad names that she called me. And most importantly did I deserve this? After the sun had gone down, I had grown weary and tired. I went and knocked on the basement door; and if only she had opened it, I would have told her that I loved her and that I had learned my lesson. But she never came as the minutes turned to hours, and I started feeling sleepy waiting for Hon to come back and unlock the basement door. I was too afraid of her wrath to put my clothes back on, even though they were sitting on the floor right next to me. So, I just stared at my shoes, my socks, and skirt as if they were some other child's clothing that had been left in the basement. I climbed into Hon's rocking chair and fell asleep. I was cold, hungry, naked, and in pain from the severe beating I took.

Hon did not return for me until the next morning, when it was time to get me ready for school. I woke up from the rocking chair by the sound of the skeleton key rattling against the lock. I bolted up the stairs as fast as I could, wanting a hug from Hon, wanting to be reassured that she still loved me and that last night she had forgiven me, because I had forgiven her. That confirmation never came.

With an expressionless look on her face, Hon took me by my hand, and we raced up the stairs through the kitchen to the bathroom. "Get into the tub so I can give you a bath," She said with a grin. Hon proceeded to give me a bath, she took my washcloth and she rubbed my body so hard that my welts began to re-open and bleed. Interestingly, Hon never acknowledged the beating and the welts that she had made last night, instead she started brushing my teeth, then combing my hair, and then dressing me. She acted as though nothing had happened, nothing at all. And I definitely wasn't going to remind her that was for sure!

Hon made sure that she had disguised my wounds by dressing me in a long sleeved sweater and a pair of pants for school. When I arrived at school, I was still shaken up by last night's whipping. I was terrified about anyone finding out about it. I still loved Hon, and I didn't want her to get into any trouble. I didn't understand why she did it, but I couldn't stay mad at her because as a child, I had unconditional love for Hon; and besides I still loved her. I tried to make myself believe that last night was a dream, but the sore welts on my body convinced me that it was indeed reality.

I knew I dare not tell a soul as to what had happened last night, especially not my teacher, because Hon would have a fit. I could hear her voice in my head saying "Now remember, you never tell anyone about what goes on in my house." So I tried not to show any discomfort, and I acted as though everything was fine, so my friends would not know my secret. But it was definitely hard not to do.

I just wanted to be left alone this morning. "Good Morning Mary, is everything ok with you?" Ms. Williams asked in a kind warm voice. "Oh yes ma'am … I am just fine Ms. Williams," I quickly replied as to not pique her curiosity. I was proud of myself because I didn't wince from my sweater sticking to my welts, when she placed her hand on my arm. Ms. Williams looked at me in silence, as if she already knew about last night. I knew I couldn't tell her, even though I really wanted to. So I silently stared back at her with respect in my eyes, until she decided to return to her desk. I was hoping that my answer was enough not to make Ms. Williams call my home.

As soon as school was over, Hon arrived on schedule to pick me up in what I used to call the bat mobile. Hon was quiet on the drive home.

But when she pulled into the driveway, she asked "How was school today?" "Oh it was good," I said. Hon nodded and opened the front door. When we got inside of the house, Hon either felt guilty or suspicious, maybe a little bit of both. She asked "Did you say anything to Ms. Williams?" "Nothing Hon … nothing at all!" I replied. "You are a damn liar!" Hon shouted. Hon went to our bedroom and when she returned she was holding her wooden cane in her hand. I quickly thought to myself, *not again*! "Get on your Goddamn knees, and put your hands together like you are praying!" she screamed at me at the top of her lungs. "Pray to God, ask God to not make me hit you with this cane!" Hon leaned her head back and brought the cane down on my back. I looked and saw the cane hitting my legs and my arms, the same arms and legs that received welts from the night before.

I felt trapped, so I tried to run to the bedroom, but Hon caught up with me. She took my head and slammed it against the bedroom door as she shouted. "You fucking idiot! I told you to keep quiet about what goes on in my house that I pay the bills at!" I didn't know what was going on because I didn't open my mouth to her about what happened last night. I was innocent.

I remember sitting on the end of my bed, feeling worthless, and crying, wondering why me? Why was I always getting into trouble?

Soon Hon shouted in a cheerful voice "Come to the kitchen I have a surprise for you!" I was afraid of what the surprise might be, but I hobbled on into the kitchen. And there sitting on the yellow foldable kitchen table in a nice shiny saucer was the biggest piece of chocolate cake I'd ever seen." I made it for you this morning," she giggled. I was scared to eat it at first. What if she poisoned it? Hon also had a big piece of cake sitting in a saucer in front of her. "You want a glass of milk to wash it down?" she asked. "Yes please" I said with a distrusting voice. We both sat down and ate cake, laughed and talked as though we were the best of friends. Go figure! Well, all I can say is on that evening I got to eat dessert, then dinner and I went to bed. According to Hon all was well that night.

Chapter 4

Bye-bye Pretty Hair

All through second grade Hon used to drive and pick me up from school. That all stopped when the bat mobile finally broke down, and Hon refused to have it fixed. Hon started walking me to and from school, which was a little embarrassing for me.

Throughout second grade I continued to be beaten by Hon. There were days when I could arrive home and be in peace and not receive a whipping, but those days were far and few in between. It usually didn't matter what the reason Hon gave me to explain why I was receiving these whipping, because at one point I just accepted what she told me, that I was a bad child.

I got so tired of getting whippings because of my hair that I started praying to God to change me into a boy. But that never happened.

Hon would threaten to me with anything and everything from an extension cord, an iron, a bat, her cane and her fists. All in the name of love and discipline.

When I was eight and in the third grade, I still had problems with friends playing in my hair. On this particular day, I guess Hon got tired too of beating me about my hair. Because when I came home Hon was sitting at the dining room table with a pair of scissors in her hand. "Hello Hon" I said as I entered the house.

"Don't give me that shit you dirty, filthy little bitch" she snapped at me.

"What's wrong?" I asked her.

"Look at your hair, you look like a hoe!" she said. There was nothing wrong with my hair.

My hair was still in the same two braids that she had sent me off to school in. I had no idea what she was rambling about. "You just can't keep those bitches out of your hair, huh?" she yelled.

"No one has been playing in my hair today," I explained.

Hon jumped out of the chair and lunged at me, she held the edge of the scissors to my throat. "Don't you know that I could kill you right now?" she proclaimed. "I hate you!" she kept shouting at me. She grabbed me by my hair, and she sat me down in front of her on the carpet, while she sat back down on the dining room chair and she began to cut my hair off. "You don't appreciate having this shit on your head! You won't just let me take care of it! Every kid has to re-braid your hair ... well, I'm tired of your selfish shit! I am going to fix your ass!"

When she finally let me up and I went to the bathroom to look in the mirror, I saw that most of my long wavy locks were gone! I had about three short patches of hair at the top of my head towards the front and one patch of hair left near my neck. The rest of my head was bald including both sides of my head. I screamed in fury about her cutting my pretty hair. I ran to my room where I prayed to God to kill her. I wanted her dead. She had caused me so much heartache that I wanted it all to end. I then asked God to please kill me, so I would not have to receive any more beatings from this woman. "Go on and cry bitch … your tears won't bring your hair back!" she said.

I didn't want to return to school the next day because I knew the kids would laugh at me. When I woke up the next morning, I still hated her and I hated myself. I had wished that morning would not come for me, but it did. The morning came and it was time to get ready for school. I needed an excuse not to go. "I don't feel good today … can I stay home? I asked Hon. "The hell if you stay here today!" she shouted back. "You are just afraid of the class seeing your new hairstyle!" she said jokingly.

It was cold on that school morning because it had snowed earlier that evening, so after Hon had finished dressing me, I grabbed a winter skull cap to put over my head as left out for school. Class had gone on as usual and I only had a couple of hours before school was out and the teacher had not said anything to me about removing my cap, so I was content. But that would soon change. When I looked up from the book that I was reading, I saw my mother opening the classroom door and she greeted my teacher, Ms. Holly. I could have slid beneath a rock at that very moment. Uncertain as to why she was there, I just knew it meant trouble for me.

My Mother asked Ms. Holly if she could speak with me. Then my Mom said in a loud, but kind voice, "Why are you wearing a cap in the classroom dear?" Then I heard a boy ask the same question. "Are you cold?" my Mother asked. Hon then started to walk over to my desk: And when she approached me she snatched off my skull cap, to reveal my badly cut head.

The next thing I heard were all of the kids laughing at me, including Hon. When I looked up at my teacher she looked at me in shock and horror as she covered her mouth with her hand. I was so humiliated that I began to cry. My Mother walked back over to Ms. Holly's desk and explained. "She was asking to play with the scissors last night, and I told her no ... I thought that I had put the scissors up where she could not find them, I guess I didn't do a good job because she found them anyway," she lied. "When I went to check in on her I found her crying in the bathroom in front of the mirror looking like this," Hon told Ms. Holly.

I knew that she was lying, but I could not say anything. I was paralyzed with hurt and anger over Hon's lies and atrocious behavior. After Hon had finished telling her lies to my teacher, she proudly left the classroom with my cap in her hand. It took Ms. Holly some time to settle the children down after Hon disrupted the classroom. When school let out, I was teased mercilessly by my classmates. And for the next seven months, I attended school with my head in patches with bald spots, until it finally grew back. It was still thick, wavy and long, but it never grew as long as it used to be.

Chapter 5

My Best Friend "Sparky"

Sparky was Hon's black female cocker spaniel. She was somewhere between four or five years old when Hon got her from the pound. I fondly remember going outside in the backyard playing fetch with her, while Hon sat on the top stairs at the back kitchen door watching and laughing at us play. I stole every opportunity to roll around in the fresh green grass with Sparky, but of course this only happened with Hon's permission. Remember, nothing in my house could be done without permission.

I was around the age of nine and it seemed that at that time in my life, Hon's patience was growing thinner by the day. The older I got, the meaner she became. Hon's temper was short and her punishments were ruthless. On my loneliest of days, which was consistently every day, the only comfort I could seek out was my best friend, Spark, and I grew to love her immensely. The back yard was a picture of perfection. On the right side there were beautiful rosebushes (red, white and yellow) that Mom had planted. Next to the roses were the sweet-smelling Honeysuckles and Lilacs that the bees just loved. Next to the flowers was Mom's vegetable garden, which she was so dedicated and proud of. It seemed to me that Mom had loved her garden more than she had loved me. Mom and I planted the seeds of red cherry tomatoes, green beans, onions, turnips, collard greens, and cucumbers; and hanging across the garden on a wire were Mom's red chili peppers that Mom used to love to eat with her food. In fact, most of the vegetables that were served at dinner came from Hon's garden.

As the turmoil of my home life increased; the name calling, violent threats of bodily harm and the daily beatings all began to escalate. On her best day, I was just a punching bag and a doormat that she walked on every day with verbal and physical threats of abuse.

Sometimes after a whipping, I would call Sparky over to me and she became my confidant. "I hate her so much Sparky," I'd whisper into her ear. "One day she won't be able to hit me." After I was done ranting and raving, Sparky would lick my face as if to say: *I understand, Mary, but I love you anyway.* This would make me laugh, and I would soon forget how bad I really felt. Sparky always sat and listened to me intently until she was called away to eat and then my therapy session with Sparky was over. During the time Sparky spent living with us, she had developed arthritis. When the disease would flare up, she wouldn't eat, nor could she run and play fetch with me anymore.

"Hon, something is wrong with Sparky!" I said begging for her attention. "All she wants to do is lay on the rug in our bedroom."

"Leave the fucking dog alone! Did you ever think that she has gotten tired of playing with your ass?" Hon snapped.

Could this be possible? I asked myself. *Does my best friend and confidant, Sparky, hate me too?*

Eventually, Hon tired of looking at Sparky lying in the bedroom, so she carried Sparky down to the basement and let her lay on the cold hard floor. In that moment, I knew something bad was going to happen to Sparky because of my many bad memories of being locked down there myself. The basement became known as the place where Hon would put you when she didn't want you anymore. I felt such deep sorrow for Sparky as all she did was yelp in pain.

I would go down to the basement every day to check on Sparky. Hon became irritated with my concern over the dog.

"You can't go to the basement anymore!" she yelled. "No more!!!"

I was so distraught by the ban on my basement visits that I could barely concentrate in school. One day when I could no longer take the restriction, I hurried home from school and changed into my play clothes hoping to see Sparky. As I rushed toward the basement door, I was met with the brutal image of Hon standing in front of the door as she blocked it from entry.

"Where are you going Bitch?" Hon asked.

"I want to see Sparky ..." I asked sheepishly. "I just want to know if she is okay."

"And who are you to be running downstairs ever day to see a damn dog? Can you heal her Bitch? Well ... can you?" she asked with disgust in her voice and an iron in her hand.

"No I can't," I had to reply, "But I can let Sparky know that I love her and that she is not alone," I said with sincerity.

"Well she belongs to me and she is my damn dog!" shouted Hon. "And I'm telling you now! If I catch you going downstairs to check on that dog, I will burn you with this iron! Do you hear me you stupid asshole?"

"Yes Ma'am I heard you" I said softly. And with that—I retreated from the door.

About a week had passed, and my heart ached because I missed Sparky, I prayed to God, "Please God, I know you hear from me a lot, but I am willing to accept Hon's beatings without complaining if you could just help Sparky.." I was hoping that God had heard my humble pleas to help Sparky to stop being in pain. I guess in his own way he did.

Because one day while I was in the kitchen with Hon watching her make a homemade peach cobbler she turned to me and said, "Run down to the basement and get me a jar of canned peaches so I can put in this pie."

"Yes!!" I replied so quickly I almost choked on the words. *Yes! Yes! Yes!* Her request meant I could finally check on Sparky without Hon even knowing. And with that, I bolted down the stairs like a track star. I quickly grabbed a jar of peaches from the cabinet that also held Hon's canned strawberry and peach preserves, and I promised myself I would take a quick look at Sparky before I ran back upstairs. To my absolute shock, Sparky was dead and stiff as petrified wood lying there lifeless. I screamed in shock, and I dropped Hon's jar of peaches right onto the floor.

"What the hell is going on down there?" Hon shouted.

"Hon! Come down here! Quick! It's Sparky! I couldn't imagine the pain that this dog must have gone through before she took her last breath of life.

"What the fuck did you say?" Hon snapped back.

"Just come downstairs!" I pleaded.

"Fuck! Shit!" she shouted from the top of the stairs. "This means that I'm going to have to stop what I'm doing right now! What have you done now, you stupid bitch!"

Hon got up from the kitchen table and came downstairs. At first sight of her broken peaches, she almost had a fit. "Are those my canned jar of peaches on the Goddamn floor? I swear that you can't do nothing right!" Hon shouted with disappointment. "Get your fucking ass over here and clean up this mess! And you better get every single piece of glass up off of this floor!" she demanded.

I turned to head upstairs to get a broom and the dustpan to sweep up the glass, but before I could get upstairs, Hon grabbed the back of my shirt. "Where the fuck are going imbecile?"

"Upstairs to get a broom and dustpan," I replied sarcastically.

"The hell if you are! You get your stupid ass on your hands and knees and you pick up this glass with your fingers, before I take a piece of glass and cut you with it!" Hon said with anger in her voice.

"Okay, okay …" I answered back.

Hon then looked over at Sparky and said. "You see … if you had done what I had told you to do and not been nosy, you wouldn't have even noticed the dog!" Hon shouted as she slapped me on top of my head.

"Ouch!!" I squealed.

"You are so damn hard headed!" she shouted.

In that moment, I wondered to myself if she knew that Sparky was already dead. And had sent me to the basement to discover Sparky's awful sight. My thoughts were soon interrupted by the sound of Hon's voice.

"After you pick up all of that glass, I want you to get a shovel and come out to the back yard. Can you do that? Or is that simple instruction too complicated for you to follow?" Hon asked with a scowl on her face.

"No … I can do that," I said under a resentful tone.

"For all that I know you might have killed Sparky yourself," she accused me.

"No Hon! Why would you say that?" I asked. "I couldn't do anything like that to Sparky!" I defended with conviction in my voice.

"I don't know what you can do, bitch … I don't put anything past your evil, sneaky ass." Those words hurt me so much. It was unbelievable for her to think that I would hurt Sparky in any kind of way. It deeply saddened me to think that she thought of me in that way.

When I had finally finished picking up all the glass that I could with my bare fingers, I retrieved the shovel from the basement. I saw Hon bend down and pick up Sparky, with absolutely no emotion on her face. She held Sparky in her arms like she was discarding a piece of trash. I, followed Hon out to the backyard where Hon stopped near her beloved garden and dropped Sparky down like a lump of dead coal, head first onto the ground. I watched the whole thing in complete horror as Hon handled Sparky's remains with no consideration whatsoever. In my mind, on that Hon confirmed that she was a cold and heartless woman.

"What the hell are you staring at?" she exclaimed. "You look like a stuck deer in head lights! The damn dog is dead. She ain't no use to anybody now!" In that moment the pain was unbearable, and I began to weep. I had lost my best friend, and she was gone forever. I was heartbroken as I looked at Sparky laying so lifeless and still on the ground.

"Are you going to start digging or do you need me to tell you to start digging?" Hon asked. "Stop all of that fucking crying! You're acting like a retarded baby, you dumb fuck!" Hon shouted. "All dogs die … just like you will if you don't start digging her grave."

Shaken and disturbed, I grabbed the shovel and started digging the grave, Sparky's new home. With each motion of the shovel I shed a tear for Sparky. For the first time in my life I felt truly abandoned. The thought itself was unbearable.

After the grave was dug and Hon had placed Sparky in it, I covered her body with dirt and said a prayer. As I prayed, I could hear Hon talking in the background, "I think that Sparky will make good fertilizer in my garden so I can grow squash."

Oh my God!

Was she serious?

I was appalled by her senseless comment. Hon took the shovel and she announced with a wide grin. "Just because Sparky died doesn't mean that you have escaped an ass whipping for breaking my jar of peaches and for checking on Sparky when I told you not to!"

Ugggh …

As if my day couldn't possibly get any worse.

Back in the basement Hon dictated that I "assume the position!" The position was on my knees in a praying position. She had requested that I take off all my clothes and wait for her. Again I did as I was told. When Hon returned from upstairs, she had in her hands Dad's Kansas

City Royals baseball bat that he had bought as a souvenir. My eyes bulged upon seeing the bat.

"What's the matter? You look scared to see me? Put your eyes back in your head because your eyes look like two fried sunny-side up eggs cooking in a cast iron skillet, you fool!" she scoffed.

After she stopped laughing at me, she began to get angry again. Her moods turned on and off like a light switch. "Let's see if you cry as loud now as you did for Sparky, Bitch!" she hollered. "My jar of peaches were more important than that stupid ass dog. And besides I didn't get a chance to make my peach cobbler because of you. You're going to learn the meaning of importance." In that instant, Hon began swinging the bat at me—hitting raw bone with every swing. I cried out in pain. I thought that she had broken my legs and my arms, because I began to swell up like a hot air balloon. The beating lasted several minutes, but it felt like hours, even days. By the time she was done, I could hardly move. To even breathe hurt my ribs.

"Get up bitch and go upstairs," she demanded. "The next whipping will take place in the bedroom. Guess what you will be whipped with next?"

"I don't know Hon" I could barely speak. Minutes later, mom called me to come upstairs.

My legs were so swollen at the time that they felt like a sack of bricks. Each step that I took I was in agony. I had knots that began to form both on my arms and legs. I had little use of my arms. They felt so heavy. I could barely lift them up to hold onto the guard rail. I had to take breaks in between climbing to the top of the stairs. I ached so much. When I finally reached the top of the stairs and entered the kitchen,

I did not see Mom. "Hon I am upstairs in the kitchen," I announced. "Come to the bedroom; that is where I'm at," she replied. I came around the corner and slithered like a snake to the closest chair at the breakfast table and I sat down. By the time I reached the bedroom, Hon was standing in the middle of the room holding a long yellow extension cord. I was so tired from walking up all those stairs from the basement that I just collapsed right in front of Hon's feet.

"Get up bitch! You're not hurt!" she screamed at me. The sound startled me. "I can't get up," I whimpered. "Okay, then take your punishment lying on the floor." I braced myself and just as I was expecting to receive that first hit from the extension cord, Hon promptly left the room.

"Where is she going?" I wondered. Hon had gone to the bathroom where she filled a small bucket with water.

Splash!

Water poured all over my face and body but luckily, it wasn't hot water.

"Why did you do that?" I asked.

"So the extension cord can sting more when I hit you," she declared with authority.

No sooner than I got caught up thinking about the water did Hon began pummeling me with the extension cord. I soon forgot about my swollen legs, and tried to crawl away from her. She followed behind me like a train following its tracks. The water made the whipping from the cord feel much more intense. This time she hit me in the head and the extension cord caught the top of my ear. "I'm sorry Hon! I'm sorry Hon!" I cried out. When Hon finished whipping me, I had thick welts in the back of my head, on my arms and my legs. My body was cold from the water, and was burning from the blows from the extension cord. I could barely move. So that night I didn't have dinner, nor did I sleep in my bed because I couldn't use my legs to walk. So I had to sleep on the floor on the rug in our bedroom until morning came.

The next morning was a school day. It took Hon longer to dress me because of my swollen legs and arms. It was hard for Hon to find a blouse that would fit over my over-sized arms, but she did. That day Hon paid for a cab to send me to school. I remember being at school focused on not moving. I couldn't go to recess even though my teacher inquired as to why I wasn't going outside to play.

"Mary it's time for recess," Ms. Powell said with enthusiasm.

"Already?" I replied as though I had lost track of time.

"Yes … you should go and catch up with the rest of the children," Ms. Powell insisted

"No … that's okay Ms. Powell, I'd rather stay inside the classroom. I have some homework that needs to be done."

"Ok then" Ms. Powell said politely.

As soon as the door closed behind Ms. Powell, I laid my head on my desk, exhaled and cried. Just before school let out, I asked a couple of my classmates to help me put on my coat. My arms were too sore to lift. When I got out of school there was a cab waiting to pick me up to take me home. When I finally made it home, I guess that Hon did have some empathy for me that night, because I was able to lay my sore swollen body down to rest for an uneventful night.

Chapter 6

Big Head, Little Faith

Days later, when the swelling in both my arms and legs had gone back down to normal, I started thinking about how much I missed Sparky. I didn't want another dog ever. No dog could ever replace my dear old Sparky. But one day while sitting on the steps in the back yard, I happened to look over at my neighbor's yard when I saw Mildred and her husband walking down the stairs and beside him was a Dalmatian dog.

I immediately ran over to the fence and Mildred's husband brought the dog to fence so I could pet it. I instantly fell in love with him. There goes my loyalty to Sparky out the window. "What is the dog's name? Is it a girl or a boy? I asked.

"Spot, and he's a boy," Mildred replied with a smile on her face. "We got him because of all the break-ins that started happening in our neighborhood. We needed protection you know " Mildred said with concern. I had heard about the burglaries while watching the news with Hon. Mom was so concerned with the reports of the break-ins that she bought a 22 caliber revolver for our protection. I didn't pay any attention to all the "adult talk" about the neighborhood break-ins all I was concerned about was playing with Spot.

I knew that I had to ask permission from Hon to even go over to the neighbor's house. So, I ran up the back door kitchen stairs to find Hon so I could ask her. "Hon where are you? I need to ask you something very important …" I said anxiously.

"What is all the ruckus about?" Hon questioned. "What are you rambling about child?"

"The neighbors got a dog. It's a Dalmatian and his name is Spot. I want to have permission to go over to their house to play with him in their backyard," I panted almost out of breath with the excitement of it all.

"Oh really? We'll see. I know that you don't expect to go over there now, do you?"

"Yes, please Mom … can I?" I begged. "Hell no!"

"Now go to your room and play with your dolls, until I decide if and when you have permission to go and play with their dog." She instructed. Devastated, I went to my room and I fell onto my bed and cried. "She doesn't let me do nothing that I want to do," I mumbled to one of my dolls. So the evening became another boring day, grieving over Sparky and feeling alone. Waiting for Mom to give me permission had me in agony, knowing that she had the upper hand left me feeling great resentment towards her.

One week passed, then two, and Hon never mentioned about playing with Spot. I wanted to bring it up and remind her, but I didn't. So I waited patiently. In the meantime, I was determined to wait this waiting game out. On the third week, Mom called me into the living room.

"Hey Asshole come here!" Hon shouted.

"Yes Hon … what is it?" I responded.

"I guess that you can go and play with the puppy," she said.

"All right!" I shouted with joy. "But we have to go over to the neighbors together."

"Okay," I responded eagerly. I didn't care how I was able to go, all that I cared about was being able to go. So, after my Mom and the neighbors sat down and got acquainted, it was time for me to go outside and play with Spot. I was so excited and happy to find another friend. Spot stopped me from thinking about Sparky's death, which was a good thing. We would roll around in the grass and play fetch, just like Sparky and I used to do.

I began to tell Spot all of my secrets, dreams and wishes. He became my sole confidant besides my dolls now. I used to tell them everything after Sparky died and before Spot came along.

On a day when I had grown the fondest of Spot, Mom called me to come to the living room. "I want you to stop playing with Spot, because the neighbors are trying to teach Spot to become a guard dog, okay?"

"Sure mom," I replied hastily.

"Can I go outside and play Hon?" I asked. "Yes, but don't play with that damn dog," Hon said as a reminder.

I didn't want to play with Spot that day, I just wanted to say goodbye to my friend. It seemed to me that everything that I loved always got taken away from me like Ed, Sparky and now Spot.

I didn't want Spot's feelings to be hurt. I didn't want him to think that I was mad at him. What can I say? I cared about the dog maybe a little too much? So I went outside to the back yard and called Spot over to the fence. I sat down beside him and began to explain why I couldn't play with him anymore. Spot looked at me with sad eyes and then licked my face as if he was saying goodbye to me to.

I left the backyard and went up the stairs to the kitchen where I was met by Hon.

"Were you playing with the neighbor's dog?" she asked as if she already knew the answer.

"No Hon … I was saying goodbye to Spot."

"You dirty, filthy ass lying Bitch!" Hon exclaimed. "I saw you playing with the G

Goddamn dog from my bedroom window, so don't you dare lie to me, you conniving whore!"

I stood there in silence in fear of what was going to come next. Mom had disappeared from the kitchen, which meant she was going retrieve something to beat me with. I didn't know whether to try and run and hide or just stand there. Soon Mom came back and she had the 22 revolver in her hand. "I hate liars!" Mom screamed at me. I really wasn't expecting Mom to have a gun in her hand.

"Uh Hon," I replied trying to explain myself. Without warning, Hon had grabbed the revolver by the barrel and then she gave me a swift, but forceful, blow to the forehead with the butt end of the gun. "I ought to kill you now where you stand Bitch!" she shouted.

I grabbed my head and fell to the floor. I remember hearing a ringing in my ears that would not go away as blood started running down my face. With my hand, I touched my forehead and to my horror felt that it had been split wide open! "Help me Mommy!" I pleaded, "My head is open!"

"Shut the fuck up! It's your fault that your head is split open! If you had left the fucking dog alone, your head would still be in one piece!" she yelled. Then she took both of her hands, put them around my neck and began choking me. "You selfish ass Bitch! You need to die!" For whatever reason that I still don't know to this day, but Hon suddenly stopped choking me and took her hands from around my neck. "Get your grown ass up!" she yelled as she kicked me in my side. "Go get a towel … you're bleeding all over my just cleaned floor!"

I was sobbing bitterly.

"Oh you're not hurt, cut out all of that drama!"

I had never been so scared in my life. I thought that this time she had killed me slowly. I thought that I was going to bleed to death. "Hon, are you going to take me to the hospital to see a doctor?" I asked in pure fright. "Hell no, there will be no doctors for you, just pray and have faith. Either God will let you die or he will spare your life," she said with a mild grin on her face. I returned with the towel and I felt Hon pushing my forehead in—trying to push the leaking cartilage back into my head. "Be still so I can get the cartilage back in your forehead," she demanded.

"Damn! I got you good, that gun went deep, didn't it?" She laughed. The towel was soaked with my blood. I began to feel lightheaded and dizzy. I did not know where Hon had run off too, all I know is that she left me alone for about ten minutes. When Hon returned back she had a fresh white towel and the bottle of rubbing alcohol and peroxide. Hon soaked the towel with the alcohol then she pressed it against my head.

"Mom, I can't take the pain!" I cried out desperately.

"Who the fuck is you? Who gives a fuck what you can take or not!" Mom shouted in my ear. "I am a nurse I know what the fuck I am doing cunt, so be quiet!" Hon snapped.

As I screamed from the intense pain, Mom placed her hand over my mouth to muffle my screams. She then took me into the bathroom, and she pushed my head down until I was on my knees, and then she stuck my forehead beneath the bathroom faucet and turned on the cold water. I jumped from the sensation of the cold water hitting my head. That is when Hon slapped me in the face and the bottom of the faucet hit my opened wound. And again, I yelled out in pain. "Shut up before I drown your burdensome ass!" she barked. After about a minute had passed, mom raised me up from the water, then she poured the peroxide onto my head. She lifted me up off my knees and wrapped a towel around my head. Mom then told me to go to bed and take a nap. I was feeling sleepy so I went to bed where I slept through the night.

The next morning I awoke up with a terrible headache and my head was swollen twice its regular size. Aside from that, this was a routine morning, but then Mom slapped on two Band-Aids across my forehead, thumped me on my head and said. "There! You're good to go." Mom called for a cab to come pick me up and take me to school. When the cab arrived, I shamefully entered. I tried to hold my head down as I handed the driver his fare. Once at school I hurried to my desk hoping that no one would notice my swollen head and bandaged forehead. But how in the world could they not notice? "Hey there Pumpkin head!" I heard one kid say.

I felt like a deformed child, and I guess in a way, I was. "Stop all the insults children and settle down. Class is about to start!" Ms. Powell instructed. "Come here Mary …" Ms. Powell said in a tranquil voice. "Yes Ma'am Ms. Powell," I answered. "Are you all right dear? What happened to you over the weekend?" she asked. "Oh my forehead, I just fell and hit my head on a rock," I lied without blinking an eye. "Did your Mother take you to see a doctor?" "Yes she did, and the doctor said that I will be just fine," I lied again.

By days' end, I was so glad for that day to be over with. I was teased and laughed at until the cab came to take me home. I went to school and back home for nearly three months with my head swollen and two Band-Aids. I thought that head would never look right again! After two months, I went down to one bandage and eventually none. Well, needless to say that I never talked nor played with Spot ever again.

Hon left me with a mark on my forehead for the rest of my life, and a hole in my heart. I knew that I had come close to death. Many days I couldn't help but ask myself, "What if she actually kills me the next time?" I knew that I had to find a way out of this hell hole. But how? I didn't have the answer and I didn't know who did. I recall on one occasion while walking home from school, I saw this policeman giving this man a traffic ticket. I had made up my mind to seek help. And who better than a Kansas City police officer. So, I waited until he was done writing the ticket and I walked over to him. "Excuse me officer. My name is Mary Ross, and I want to report a crime in regards to my mother," I said firmly as if I knew that he was going to solve my problem with Hon."

"Why do you want to report on your mother?"

"Because look at all of the marks that she has placed on my arms and my legs."

My swollen head had returned back to normal before my encounter with the officer, I said as I bent down to show the officer bruises on my body. "Ok ... little girl where do you live?" The officer asked with concern and a smile. The smile should have been a warning but it wasn't.

I told the officer my address and then we both got into the squad car. I just knew that Hon was going to pay for the way she had treated me. I thought for sure that relief was on its way. When the officer and I arrived out my house, I saw Hon pulled the curtains back so she could peep out the window to see who was approaching the house. I guess that this had given her enough time to prepare her lie. And indeed it did because that's just what she did was lie.

In fact she lied and played the role of an elderly helpless woman trying to raise a spoiled, hard-headed little girl. We walked up to the steps and the officer knocked on the door with his baton. Hon answered the door while leaning on her wooden cane. "Why hello there officer, is there a problem with Mary?" She asked in a soft voice. "No not really ma'am she just complained to me that she thought that you had committed a crime by disciplining her," the office explained. "Oh well as you see officer I can hardly get around, and I have arthritis in both of my legs and arms. I don't have the strength to do any harm to that child," she lied and said. "Ok then ... I just thought that I would bring her back home so you could talk to her. You have a nice day ma'am" The officer said as he turned to leave.

"Wait a minute" I shouted out to the officer. "Is that it? "You can't leave me here now, she will beat me!" I yelled out to the officer. But he didn't acknowledge my pleas of desperation and he entered into his car and drove off. Before I could put my foot inside of the door and the police car was out of sight, Hon had yanked me into the house, where she whipped me for talking to the police officer. Hon kept me hidden and secluded.

Even when I was at school away from Hon, her mental control over me was undeniably strong. I was too afraid to talk to anyone. I knew then that I felt that everybody was a betrayal of trust when it came to talking about Hon's secrets. I just knew that I had to do something, and do it fast.

Chapter 7

Furious & Tinker: A New Love Story

As the months passed, I went through this passionate yearning for another canine friend. Also during this time, I began to notice a different change in Hon lately. She was forgetting a lot of things that she normally always remembered. I found myself reminding her of important dates, such as the deadline for the bills to be paid and school events. The wheels in my head started to turn, and I wondered if I could start using her handicap as an advantage for me. Given that, I don't know what possessed me to come home from school one day and tell Hon this elaborate lie. But I guess that I was determined to have another pet in my house even though Hon vehemently said, "No!"

Guess what Hon" I said happily.

"What?" Hon replied.

"A policeman by the name of Officer Johnson was at our school talking to the class about us adopting a former police trained dog," I said without batting an eye.

"Oh really?" she asked with curiosity. "A police dog would provide some good protection," she insisted.

"I know … it sure would!" I replied with excitement in my voice.

"How much will it cost?" Hon inquired.

Now I hadn't even thought about any cost for the dog. But I thought if she is offering, then I sure will play my hand. "Oh just twenty dollars Mom" I said with sweat rolling off of my brow. She thought for a moment before answering. "Okay, who do I give the money to?"

"Oh just give it to me, the officer will come to our class tomorrow and collect the money."

"Okay, here is twenty dollars. When can I expect the dog?" she asked.

"Oh, in about a week or so," I said with a smile on my face. When Mom handed me that twenty dollars I could have fainted. That was the first time real money was in my little hands. Mom didn't believe in giving a child money for doing chores. After Hon placed the money in my hand, it felt good to have some money in my pocket. The next day I went to school and I bought my lunch like all the other kids. I finally felt as though I belonged. Hon never gave me money to buy lunch at school before. Hon believed why should you spend money at school for lunch, when you can prepare it at home and take it to school the next day? In fact I gave away my lunch that Mom had made for me to a kid in the lunch room, while I ate a hot lunch and snacks. I even had money to buy after school snacks from the store; even though I had to hide them when I got home. Hon could never find out that I had used her to get money. That whole day I was in seventh heaven and I was having fun.

After three days of being a big spender, the fun was over because my money ran out. But it finally hit me that I had to find a dog within a week, or Hon might call my teacher and inquire about my lie of adopting a police dog. Yikes! If I didn't bring a dog or have her twenty dollars my life was over for sure! As I was walking back home pondering on where I was going to find a dog, there across the street was this beautiful yellow and black German Sheppard dog that looked like it was lost. I ran as fast as I could to get closer to the dog. I got the dog's attention and began petting it and feeding it my snacks until he began to follow me home. "Thank you God! Good looking out! I love you!" I said repeatedly.

I arrived home and knocked on my door.

"Hon the dog arrived today!" I said proudly. Immediately, Hon rushed to the door and in a rare moment of affection she greeted me with a smile and a hug. She was so excited to have the dog that she quickly let the dog and me inside, and she began petting and hugging the dog. She ran into the kitchen to find some food for him to eat.

"What's his name?" Hon asked curiously.

Yikes again!

I hadn't the slightest idea what the dog's real name was. "Furious!" I quickly replied. I came up with name because the dog looked kind of mean. "Oh yeah" said Hon. "I can tell that an officer named this dog. That was a good name that they gave him," she declared. That day was priceless, no whippings, no beatings, just joy and laughter rang throughout the house. And best of all I had another friend and confidant to play with.

I began to have fun with Furious. I played with him every day after school and used him to put "fear" into the neighborhood bullies who used to pick on me and tease me at school from time to time. Furious became my great protector. When Hon would fly off the handle, he would start barking and step in between Hon and I, and her beatings got shorter, but the severity remained the same.

About a week after Furious arrived, I was walking home from school when I saw a dog that was not quite a puppy, but lingered somewhere between a puppy and adult. It was this cute gray and black female German shepherd who wanted to play with me. I laughed and giggled as she nipped at my hands and licked my face like she was happy to see me. I wondered to myself. "Hmmmm, can I convince Hon to accept another dog?" Could I?

"Yes I can," I told myself. "Because I want this dog too!"

I didn't have any food to feed her, and I didn't know if she would follow me all the way home without any. My worries were soon taken care of, because she followed me anyway just out of love. I felt so special. There is a special kind of love that a dog shows you. It's so pure and unconditional. On the walk home I was trying to get my lie together while thinking up a name for her, when it hit me like a lightning bolt. "Tinker is what I will call you, girl!" I exclaimed. I practiced calling her by Tinker so she could get used to hearing the name. By the time we had reached the house, I had my lie ready and the dog ready. Here we go again, Act I, Scene II:

Hon answered the door with a look of despair on her face, "What the fuck is this that you have brought to my fucking house? Did you pick this dog up from the nasty streets of this neighborhood?" I began to get nervous. Will this lie work this time? I wondered. But as a brave little liar, I carried on with my story, I was determined to convince her to let me have this dog too.

"No Mom, the Officer Johnson came back to our school today ..."

Hon abruptly interrupted me, "Again?" she questioned sarcastically.

"Yes ... he wanted me to tell you that since you were the first parent who adopted a former police dog, he wanted you to have Tinker too, at half the price of Furious."

"Tinker?" she questioned. "That doesn't sound like a good name for a police dog, and besides, she's too young to have been a police dog!"

"She was in training but she got depressed because she missed her brother, Furious ..." I said.

"Furious is her brother?" Hon asked with passionate interest. "Wow! Now I guess they shouldn't be split up now should they?" Mom said.

"No ... not at all!" I quickly inserted.

"Now how much do I need to send with you tomorrow for the dog?"

Yes!!!

The lie worked and I'm getting paid again!

"Oh ten dollars" I mumbled.

"Okay," she said. "I will give it to you tomorrow before you leave for school."

When Hon brought Tinker into the living room Furious jumped up and he began to growl. I thought, No! My lie is going to backfire! But instead the two dogs began to play and romp around the room as though they had known each other before. My heart had stopped pounding. I went to bed that night thinking of all the snacks that I would buy tomorrow at the store after school. So when the next morning came and Hon got me ready for school, she said, "Oh! Here is the twenty dollars for you to give the police officer for Tinker!"

"Okay," I said slowly. I remembered that I said ten dollars yesterday, but that was quite all right. More money meant more snacks and more hot lunches. With this comment that Hon made not remembering that I had quoted ten dollars I knew that Hon's mind was slipping at a questionable rate. *Hmmmm maybe this could turn out to be more ammunition for me to use against her at a later time.*

I was having a ball playing with Furious and Tinker. They were my two best friends. I felt that I had two protectors against Hon's harsh beatings. They would begin to bark loudly and get in between us when Mom started cursing and hitting me. But Mom got both tired and smart, just before she was about to kick my ass she would lure the dogs down to the basement with a bowl of food and then lock them down there. Then she would commence to beating my ass. On one particular day on a weekend, Mom was cleaning the house. "As soon as I am finishing vacuuming I will feed the dogs" Mom stated. Seeing Mom work so hard around the house made me feel sympathy for her, and I wanted to help her out. I thought that if I fed the dogs that would be one thing less on her to do list. So I went and got the big bag of Gravy Train dog food from underneath the cabinet sink, and I started pouring the food into the both of the dog's bowl. I had remembered that on the TV commercials the announcer has said that if you add water to it the gravy will appear. I didn't believe that Gravy was really going to appear, but I had to see if it did. And when I poured the water the Gravy appeared like magic. "What do you know, the commercials were right!" I said to myself.

I had both of the bowls on the counter waiting for Mom to see what I had done. "Okay the bedrooms, and the living room has been vacuumed" "Now I am going to take a break, but I will feed the dogs first" Mom said.

"Mom," I so joyfully called. "You don't have to worry about feeding the dogs" I fixed their food for you" "Aren't you proud of me? I asked. "You did what?" Mom asked. "I fed the dogs, so you wouldn't have to, and did you know that if you add water to the Gravy Train that it actually will make gravy?"

"Am I supposed to be proud of you fucking up that expensive ass dog food? Mom replied in disgust. "Why you stupid ass! You little wannabe grown Bitch. I am going to show you what I am going to do next!" she yelled at me.

Hon grabbed both of the dog's bowls and she placed them on the kitchen table in front of me. She bent down and she put her forehead onto mine and she stared me down in my eyes and she said. "You are going to eat both bowls of this fucking dog food until it is gone! Do you understand what I am telling you, you bubbled-eyed heifer?"

"Mom please don't make me eat this I was only trying to help you out," I mumbled with tears streaming down my face. "What the fuck are you crying for bitch? No one asked you to feed the dogs!" Mom said hastily. The dogs then began to bark. "Now see what you have done, you have upset the dogs!" Mom screamed. Mom grabbed some hotdogs and she threw them down the stairs, both dogs ran to retrieve them as if they were running at the dog tracks, and when they did Mom took the opportunity to lock them downstairs. My protectors were gone, and it was just Hon and I who were left upstairs to face one another. "I don't want to eat the dog food Mom!" I sobbed. "Well hell, I don't want you in my house either but your black ass is still here, so we don't always get to choose what we want, now do we bitch! Now eat the Goddamn Dog food before I kill you!" Mom said angrily. Hon began to shake as I kept refusing to eat the dog food.

Eventually, I thought that Mom had given up on me eating the dog food, because she left out of the kitchen. Any time Hon left the room she was picking her choice of weapons to use from her artillery. A few minutes later Mom returned. She had the 22 caliber revolver in her hand. My heart raced with fear, because the last time she got the gun my head was split in two. "Please don't hit me with the gun, Mother!" I begged.

"Then eat the fucking food!" she demanded.

"Okay I will," I said, trying to convince her to put the gun away. I put the spoon into the bowl and put some of this awful smelling, soggy dog food in my mouth. "Yuk! It tastes horrible Mom! Please don't make me eat it … I won't do it again. I promise."

"You don't want to eat the dog food?" Mom grimaced.

"No Ma'am!" I cried.

I watched as Mom took the 22 revolver and she loaded one bullet into the chamber and then she spun the chamber around and then she closed it. She then pointed the gun at my temple, and then she pressed the gun to my temple where I could see the barrel and the nozzle. She then did the unthinkable, she pulled the trigger.

Click!

Initially, I thought that I had been shot, but I found that I wasn't. "You better eat that food because the next time that I pull this trigger you might not be so lucky!" she said. Mom then reached for the spoon and she put a mouthful of the dog food on it and she told me. "Now open your mouth, bitch!"

I chewed it and then I swallowed the big chunks of morsels. I began to gag. "You better not vomit it up or you will be eating that too!!!" she warned. "Open your mouth and let me see if you really swallowed it down," she insisted.

I opened my mouth, and then Mom placed the barrel of the gun in my mouth and again she did the unthinkable. She pulled the trigger!

Click!!!

I almost passed out from the fright, but again my life was spared.

Dear God I can't live like this!

As the evening wore on I ate enough dog food that Mom was satisfied; which was about ten tablespoons. She then took the dog's bowls and placed them in the refrigerator. "They will be here for you for breakfast!" Mom smirked. And for sure all weekend long Mom sat next to me at the kitchen table with her 22 revolver aimed at my head forcing me to eat the dog food or die. That was my meal morning, noon, and night, while Mom fixed herself steak and eggs, sandwiches, and soup, and Gumbo for dinner. I watched in horror and pure hatred as she fed herself people food and I was made to eat this dog food. My stomach would sometimes start to hurt after I ate it. If I complained about my stomach, Mom would lock me downstairs with the bowl of dog food and a glass of water until morning.

The weekend was over and it was a school day. Mom got me up and she gave me a huge hug. She followed her usual routine and then she packed me a lunch. I noticed that it was lighter than usual. So I looked in side of my lunch box to see only a cool whip container inside. Curiously, I opened up the container and there it was staring back at me was that damn dog food. When I turned around Mom had the pistol aimed at my face. "You better eat it all or else! Now have a nice day at school, dear" Mom said.

"Damn!" I thought to myself, if there was any day that I needed to have money it was today. I had spent the twenty dollars that she gave me for Tinker last week. I was flat broke. I couldn't even buy snacks to replace my new cuisine. I went to school dreading for the lunch period to come. When it did I didn't even open my lunch pail. I just went hungry. I didn't want the other kids to see what I had for lunch in my lunch box. Usually my lunches would consist of two sandwiches, milk, juice, or soup, some fruit, a small bag of chips, candy, and a piece of cake. Kids loved to see what I had for lunch, because it was always enough to share … but not today.

"What did your mom pack in your lunch today, Mary?" my friend asked.

"Oh, I got hungry before lunch so I already ate it" I replied.

Day in and day out I had nothing else to eat but that dog food. And repeatedly Mom held the gun to head, each time spinning the chamber around after she had loaded a single bullet in it. And she was constantly pulling the trigger. I know now that it was by the grace of God that the gun never went off and blew my brains out. With the passing of each day, my self-esteem was getting lower and lower. I felt much less than a person. I felt as though I was the animal. Anxiety had set in, and I would bite my nails down to the nub and they would begin bleeding. I hated my own existence.

I began to zone out and gave up on being a child. I gave up on people. I was just an object in Hon's way. I figured that the less Hon saw of me the less she would get mad at me. I stayed in my room daydreaming about living somewhere else. I was frightened most of the time because I just knew that one day Hon was going to kill me. By the age of nine, I knew that I would never live to see eighteen at least that is what I thought back then. My grades took a dive and nobody bothered to ask why.

I always felt stupid and my desire to engage people was non-existence. I loved no one because no one loved me. Ultimately, my confidence was shattered just like the jar of Hon's canned peaches that I had dropped and busted open on the basement floor. I hated Hon. I hated people. And my trust in mankind was nothing.

And to top it off, for the next three solid weeks of my life it was nothing but dog food for me. That's how long it took me to eat it until it was gone. Maybe it was Karma coming back at me for lying to Mom in the first place about the dogs, or maybe this was the "straw that finally broke the camel's back," as the old folks used to say. After this incident, I knew that it was either me or her who was going to survive, and I was going to find a way to get this bitch back!!

Chapter 8

High on Cigarettes Low on Self Esteem

By the time I was a pre-teen, my attitude had darkened, and I spent most of my time wallowing in self-pity and discouragement. For the most part, I felt numb inside, but I wore a game face to the outside world. I felt condemned to a certain hell with Hon. Throughout my days, I was a nervous wreck, paranoid, and even nauseated at the sound of Hon's footsteps. I walked on eggshells every day when I entered the house and felt as though the whole world, including Hon, hated me. I was so desperate for love and guidance, and since I received neither, I became an introvert who would sometimes act out. I became dependent on the company of my dolls and my dogs. In acting out, I began to play violent with my dolls and would fuss mercilessly at them for not cleaning the floor, or leaving dust behind on the living room cabinet. To my horror, I echoed the sound of anger and began to sound more and more like "Hon."

Weekends were an especially lonely time for me. Mom's violence escalated, every day, she reminded me of just how much she hated me. She shouted out the answers as to why she hated me as if she was trying to win a washer and dryer on the Wheel of Fortune.

And then there were the times that Hon would actually spit on me as she called me her favorite words, "Trashy-ass whore."

The hatred she felt for me when she looked at me, dwelled deep down in her soul like a tar pit of sludge from an old oil field. She would say things like, "I hate you because your eyes are so damn big" and other times she would ask, "Why is your nose so flat?" Incessantly, she swore that I was not as smart as the kids in my class, "because they're getting to skip grades and advance their studies. You being the dumb-ass that you are, have to stay back with the retarded section of the class. "That is why I hate you so much!" I listened on and on, until my little ears and heart couldn't take it anymore, and I could no longer hold back my tears. My self-esteem seemed as though it had rotted inside of me, and that it was soon about to dissolve away like rain on the pavement.

When Mom did have friends over to the house, which was rarely, I was always sent to my room. Back in those day, kids were not allowed to sit in or listen to grown folks conversations. The old folks used to say that a child is supposed to be seen and not heard. I kept that same theory in mind when dealing with Hon. At the age of twelve, I still had my mother bathing and dressing me. I was so irritated with Hon for treating me as though I were a child. But at least one good thing had happened for me. Mom had stopped walking me to and from school. I had some freedom in the world, and I didn't care if it was only for thirty minutes, I simply loved it. On my short walks from school to my house, I made some new friends or should I say friends with ulterior motives.

One day after school I met Vera. She was a teenager from the neighborhood who had a rep of being "cool." In the afternoons, she would sit on her front porch drinking beer and smoking Kool cigarettes. She would always speak to me when I passed her house. She invited me over one day after school to have a beer and cigarette with her. I politely declined the invitation. Neither Hon nor Ed ever had liquor in the house nor did either one of them ever drink. After a few weeks of trying to avoid Vera, I finally gave in and visited her at her place. "I can't stay long," I warned. "What do you want Vera?"

"I just want to know your name," she said real cool-like.

"Mary," I replied.

"Where do you stay, Mary?" she wanted to know. I didn't feel comfortable giving her my real address, so I made one up. "Two blocks over on Fortieth Street."

"Cool," was her reply.

"Hey you want to smoke a cigarette with me?" Vera asked.

"No, I don't smoke, besides I heard smoking is bad for you."

"I'll give you one of mine" she insisted. "Just take a puff, that's all I'm asking you. If you don't like it, I won't ask you to smoke with me again. Fair enough?" she asked.

"Well okay, just one puff," I confirmed. I took a small puff of the lit cigarette, and held the smoke in my mouth. Nothing happened, so I thought that smoking cigarettes were a cool thing.

"No you need to take a strong puff, and inhale it until you feel it hitting your lungs!" Vera instructed. So, I took another puff, and this time a much bigger one.

I inhaled the smoke until it had reached deep into my lungs. Immediately, I felt my lungs began to burn, and I simultaneously began to cough and choke both at the same time. I thought I was going to cough up my lungs.

"Here take this thing!" I insisted. "I don't want anymore," I said when I finally caught my breath. Vera just laughed at me and said. "Ok, well if you should decide that you want to buy a pack you know where I stay."

Fat chance at that happening, I said to myself. But believe it or not, the very next day I was back at Vera's house for round two; trying to learn how to smoke cigarettes. I guess I went back to Vera's house because I wanted to learn how to smoke cigarettes. I found out that when I smoked a cigarette that it helped calm my nerves. It was a coping mechanism that eased me in dealing with Hon. So, I mastered the concept of inhaling within the first week, and soon thereafter, I talked Mom into giving me some money to buy a pack of cigarettes. At that time a pack only costs fifty cents, but you had to have a note from your parents. I convinced Hon to write a note for me so I could go to the store and buy and by them. I then became a cigarette smoker.

Damn. In the beginning, I was a random smoker and a pack of cigarettes would last me a whole month. Early on I noticed the cigarettes calmed my nerves. In between puffs, I always hurried to get home so I wouldn't be late. Hon always timed my walks home from school, and if I was late that was a guaranteed ass whipping. On this one particular day, the jig was just about up. I arrived home and the moment I entered the door I was met with a "Bitch have you been smoking cigarettes?"

"No Mom, of course not," I lied.

"Don't lie to me damn it," scolded Hon. "I will put you in your grave without a plot!"

"I wasn't smoking," went the lie. "But on my way home, I passed by a bus stop where a lady was smoking a cigarettes. I guess the smoke must have gotten on my clothes."

"Well bitch, if that's the case then here is what I suggest to you, then you need to start taking another route home and not pass that Bitch smoking at the bus stop!" Hon chastised me.

"Okay Mom," I said thinking that was the end of it. "Wait a minute you stupid whore, do you think that I was born yesterday?"

I thought to myself, "*No … but maybe the day before!*"

"You are ten minutes late coming home from school. I guess that you were too busy smoking your damn cigarettes to notice the time!" Mom barked.

"No Mom," I said.

"Fuck that shit, bitch! You think I'm crazy. I'm about to fuck your ass up!" she hollered. "Go change your fucking school clothes now!" The dogs began to bark. Mom said. "And you two son of a bitches need to shut the fuck up too, before I kill you both and feed you to this lying ass bitch!" Mom hurried into the kitchen, her fat thighs rubbing together sounded like a bundle of rubber bands being snapped. Mom got some meat from the refrigerator and she threw it downstairs to the basement. And my dogs once again stopped barking and went to fetch their meal. "Why are you in the kitchen, you nosy ass bitch? "Didn't I tell you to go and take off your damn school clothes" "For Christ Sakes! Listen to me you fucking water on the brain, bitch" Mom screamed. "Yes Ma'am," I replied.

I really wanted to watch and see what weapon she was going to use on me this time, but she had caught me trying to peek. I went into my room and took my clothes off and placed them on my bed. A few minutes later, Mom entered with a knife. I gasped, "Mom please don't hurt me!"

"Put your arm on the bed!" she demanded.

"Why Mom?" I sobbed.

"Don't question me you little piece of shit … I'm not going to tell you again."

I placed my arm on the bed, and Mom proceeded to slowly slice a small piece of the skin off from my elbow. I screamed from the pain of the knife cutting my skin. And again, there was blood. "Please Mom, let my arm go," I pleaded. "You want me to let your arm go? Fine, I'll let it go" Mom agreed. She left and returned a few minutes later with her favorite bottle of rubbing alcohol and a bottle of iodine.

"Put your Goddamn arm on the bed again, you imbecile!" Mom ordered.

I did as she asked and when I did, Mom poured the rubbing alcohol and Iodine all over my elbow and my favorite turquoise bedspread. I yelled with a deep gut wrenching scream. "Shut up Bitch, I don't want to hear all of that noise!"

In that moment, I noticed the bedspread was stained with blood. Minutes later, Mom left again and returned with a Band-Aid, which she placed over my cut elbow; but only after she snatched the loose skin that was hanging from the back of my arm from the cut she had made with the knife.

"Ouch!"

"Clean up this damn mess, and change the bedspread when you're through" "Oh by the way, do want Jell-O or pudding for dessert after dinner?" Mom asked with a smile on her face. I cried "Jell-O."

"Okay, dinner will be in a couple of hours. She said sarcastically I just stood there in the middle of my bedroom, staring into the space of nothingness, filled with pain on the outside, numb on the inside, high on cigarettes and low on self-esteem.

Chapter 9

Cancer vs. Puberty

While attending school one day, I saw that a few of my friends were talking to each other in a circle on the playground. I went over to be nosy and find out what they were talking about.

"Look! I'm starting to fill out my shirt," said one girl.

"So did I!" replied another.

"I'm still flat-chested," commented a third grader.

"Mary have you gotten breasts yet?" The first girl asked me. I was around twelve years old, and I didn't even get a good chance to answer before one of the girls cut me off. "No! She's still bare!" she said with a cackle.

"Not yet," I replied, even though I didn't really have a clue about what having breasts or "filling out a shirt," really meant. Both of them sounded bad, but I didn't want to look dumb in front of my friends. But eventually, I ended up finding out what they were talking about when a couple of weeks later I started having growing pains, especially in my chest area. I would complain to Mom, but she would just ignore both my complaints and questions.

"What's happening to me, Hon?" I'd ask repeatedly. "What's going on?"

It seemed that one day I went to sleep flat-chested and bare, only to wake up and discover "lumps" forming in my chest. I soon became worried. Something weird and potentially dangerous was happening. As much as I typically tried to avoid Hon, I desperately needed some answers. So I approached Mom at her desk, reading the bible. I approached cautiously, "Mom can I ask you a question? Something is wrong with my chest Mom," I said.

Mom slammed the Bible closed and mumbled, "Let me take a look." I came closer to her. I had on an undershirt and pants at the time. "Well you need to lift up your undershirt, you fucking retard, so I can see what the hell you're talking about. I lifted up my shirt and Mom started to laugh at me. "What's so funny Mom?" "What is it?"

Mom looked at me and politely said "You have Cancer."

"What is cancer Mom?"

"Fuck! It's a disease that God gives girls … all right?"

Mom opened her Bible back up and began reading again. "But Mom, why did God give it to me?" I asked with a sincere heart.

"Fuck! How would I know? I ain't God. Why don't you ask him and leave me the fuck alone. Maybe he gave it to you because he wants you to die Bitch. Now get the fuck out of my face!"

I ran to my room, climbed onto my bed and I asked God why did he want to kill me? I thought that my Mother was going to kill me; not God. After Hon told me I had cancer, I cried for days upon days about my pitiful situation. I went to school with a heavy heart knowing that I was going to die, "but when Lord?" I asked. Maybe Hon had the answer since she used to be a nurse. I went home and I asked Hon. "Hon, since you used to be a nurse do you know how long it will take me to die from this Cancer?"

Hon smiled and with a straight face said, "Oh about three months give or take. I can't wait for it to happen. If your death was up to me, I would kill you before you had time to eat dinner!" Mom said as she laughed and walked away to the kitchen. I became more saddened by Hon's reply and I began to cry.

I soon started begging Hon to please take me to see a doctor regarding this thing called cancer. But mom continued to refuse my requests. I was so upset one day at school that my teacher had noticed that my behavior had changed. Nothing was important or fun to me anymore since I was going die within three months. "What's wrong Mary? Ms. Nolan asked. "I just wanted to let you know that I will miss you very much, Ms. Nolan," I said. "I will miss you and all of my friends here at school."

"Why? "Where are you going Mary?" Ms. Nolan asked.

"Well I am going to die in three months," I said.

"Die?" she gasped. "What on earth is making you think that you are going to die within three months, Mary?"

"Well, Ms. Nolan, I hesitated "I have cancer!" I blurted out.

"Oh my God! Ms. Nolan screamed. "When did the Doctor tell your Mom this?"

"I haven't seen a doctor yet," I confirmed. I didn't want to tell Ms. Nolan that my Mother had refused me from seeing a doctor.

"Excuse me class I'll be right back," said Ms. Nolan grabbing my hand and pulling me towards the Principal's office. "You all finish working on your projects until I return from the office."

Ms. Nolan took me by my hand and we went to the principal's office. "May I use your phone Mr. Nash to call Mary's mother at home?" Ms. Nolan asked.

"No, Ms. Nolan … you don't have to do that!" I replied in desperation.

"It's ok Mary," Mr. Nash reassured me. I'm thinking to myself "No its not."

I was asked by the principal to sit and wait in the lobby while Ms. Nolan spoke to my mother. When Ms. Nolan got off the phone she said. "I have good news for you, Mary, I've spoken to your mother regarding your statements of having cancer and not seeing the doctor yet, so she is on her way to come to the school to take you to the doctor. Okay Mary?"

"Okay," I replied back with worry and grief twisted up inside my vocal chords.

Twenty minutes later, Mom comes walking through the principal's door. Mr. Nash, Ms. Nolan, and my mother began "chatting it up" like they were lifelong friends, but I knew that this phone call would cost me an ass whipping, but at least it would be worth it. I get to see and talk to a real doctor.

We made the bus trip across town and finally arrived at the doctor's office mom checked us in at the receptionist's desk. We waited in the lobby for a short while before the doctor came out to see us.

"What's going on with you today?" the doctor asked me.

"I have cancer, sir," I replied.

"Oh my," he said, "That's a very big problem for a small girl to have. Why don't you come back with me to my office and let's talk."

I went back to the doctor's office where he took his stethoscope and listened to my heart and lungs. "Breathe in for me Mary ... that's good ... now breathe out. Great!" he said.

He took my pulse and checked my blood pressure. Within minutes of my examination he exclaimed, "Mary I have some good news for you!"

"Really?" I asked. "What is it? What? What?"

"Well, you don't have cancer," he assured me. "What you do have is a case of growing up or becoming mature ... it's called puberty."

"What's puberty?" I asked.

"It's when a young girl such as yourself begins to grow what we call breasts all women have gone through this stage, Mary. You will be all right. If you have any more problems have your mother call me, okay?"

"Yes Sir!" I replied as I smiled back. I was so relieved to hear the doctor tell me that I didn't have cancer. I didn't think that I was capable of smiling at anything while under Hon's rules, but I was smiling now. And now in regards to Hon, I was hotter than fish grease at her for lying to me about having cancer.

"Why would she tell a child that they have cancer and were going to die?" I wondered. I left the doctor's office with a wide grin on my face. I went back out in the lobby to rejoin Hon. Hon and the Doctor talked briefly, Hon paid the Receptionist and we were on our way home on the bus. No sooner than we entered the house, Mom slapped me into the wall of the living room. Here we go! The dogs started barking, I started crying, and mom started cursing and yelling at me. She took off one of her orthopedic shoes and threw it at me. She then picked up a heavy glass snowball and she threw it at me; just missing my head if I hadn't ducked and got out of the way. I ran and hid under the bed. "Come here you big-mouth bitch!" Hon squealed. The dogs ran and went beneath the bed with me, barking like crazy. Mom came into the bedroom and coaxed both dogs out from under the bed with some bologna. Once she got the dogs out, took them to the basement. Mom returned to the bedroom with a broom swinging it from side to side until I came out. She slapped me across my face and I landed on my bed. Once I was on my back, she started wailing on me with the broom, all the while screaming like a maniac, "If I wanted your teacher and the principal to know that you were dying of cancer, I would have placed an ad in the local newspaper.

Mom went to the bathroom and when she came back she placed a wet bar of soap in my mouth and pinched my nose close. Then she hit me in my mouth with her fist. She left again and this time when she returned she started beating me with a pot that she had retrieved from the kitchen. That ass whipping lasted on and off for an hour. Every part of me was hurting and throbbing with pain. I had no dinner, no dessert, and no feeling in my body that night. Damn, puberty sure does hurt.

Chapter 10

Spilled Blood Twice a Month

It was a nice, sunny crisp day in Kansas City. The morning was uneventful and Mom seemed to be in a good mood. She was in the living room sitting on the vintage green couch enjoying her cup of coffee and reading the *Kansas City Star Newspaper*. After breakfast, I asked Mom if I could go to my room and play with my dolls and she gave me the okay. While I was playing, my stomach began to hurt badly. At first I thought it was hurting because I had ate too much, but this was a very different kind of pain I was feeling. It felt as if my whole stomach was in knots and the cramping was so intense that I knew that I had to talk to Mom about it.

I walked into the living room, holding my stomach while bent over. "Mom my stomach is killing me!" I said in anguish. Mom slowly put down her newspaper and looked over it with her eyes peering into my soul like a broken mirror. I stared back waiting for a reply, but all she did was put the newspaper back up to her face and continue reading. "Mom, I'm sorry to interrupt you from reading the paper, but my stomach is hurting so bad" I repeated.

"There's nothing wrong with you," she insisted. "It's all made up in your imaginary mind. Now please go back to your room, play with your dolls and quit disturbing me. I'm trying to say it nicely before you piss me off," she said calmly. And with that I did as I was told and went back to my bedroom and crawled in the bed. But I couldn't get comfortable, and no matter how I positioned myself in the bed, my stomach just kept cramping. I began to feel nauseated, and suddenly felt a urge to go to the bathroom.

"Mom please May I go to the bathroom?" I asked.

"Dammit child! I can't read my newspaper in peace without you needing to ask me something. Go ahead, you look like you about to piss on yourself anyway."

I scurried to the bathroom, and sat on the seat. To my amazement when I pulled down my underwear, there was a big puddle of dark red blood. I rushed out of the bathroom with my underwear down to my ankles to show Mom what I had discovered. "Mom! Look! I'm bleeding in my private area!" I said anxiously.

"Oh really?" she said. "Let me see what you're talking about." After viewing my underwear, "Yeah bitch, that's blood!" she spat without a hint of emotion.

"Mom why am I bleeding like this?" I asked. "Is this why my stomach is hurting?"

"You are bleeding from your cunt because God is punishing you for being a bad girl!" Mom replied back.

"What did I do to God?" I asked. "How long will it last Mom?

"Oh, for about seven days straight until your body bleeds out," Mom explained.

"What happens after I bleed out?" I asked.

"Why do you have so many fucking questions, you little scoundrel of a bitch?" Mom hollered back.

"I just want to know Mom that's all. I said. "You are going to bleed to death at the end of the seventh day, and then you'll die. So, go pray for your good for nothing little life and who knows maybe God will save you, Mom yelled. "Go get a fucking towel out of the cabinet!" Mom ordered me. I went and retrieved the towel out of the cabinet and Mom started ripping an old T-shirt of mine. Then Mom opened up the Black Singer Sewing machine table and she commenced to sewing. "Put the damn towel between your legs whore, and hold it in place until I finish sewing this garter belt." She insisted.

I stood there in the dining room holding a big white towel in between my legs like a dunce sitting in the corner at school. I waited about thirty minutes before Mom said, "its finish! Now let me get a few safety pins and make this thing work."

Mom brought me in close to her as she rolled the towel up three times, then started pinning the towel to the front and the back of the garter belt. After she was through she said. "Now go get your fucking draws and put them back on! And let me go and find you something to wear." After Mom had found me a pair of pants and a shirt, I looked in the mirror at myself, and when I looked down, I saw was this bulky towel bulging from between my legs as if I had male implants. I felt so embarrassed, but at least I was at home where no one could see me.

"Can I read your Bible?" I asked.

"Now you want to read my Bible!" she exclaimed. "Why? Because you know that you're dying soon? Hell the fuck no!" Mom shouted. "In fact … I can't wait to watch you take your last gasp of air and die. Now get the fuck out of my sight and die quietly like Sparky did."

I ran to my room once again with my eyes filled with big crocodile tears flowing down my cheeks. I couldn't wipe them away fast enough before new ones formed. I couldn't understand what was happening to me, first it was chest and now I'm bleeding from my private. I wondered if the two were connected.

The same old routine happened with Mom except for giving me a bath. Mom said "You can't get your feet wet nor could any water touch your body, because if it does, you will catch pneumonia and die." So I did not get to take a bath when that time of the month came around. "But what if it's raining and it's a school day Mom? I asked. "Bitch what did I say? Your black ass will die, and if that happens all I'm going to do is bury your dumb-ass in the backyard with Sparky."

Mother then proceeded to make me breakfast and then sent me off to school. Mom sent me to school with a big old towel to absorb the blood. She might as well have placed a blanket down there because the towel felt like a blanket. I went to school trying my best not to stand or walk around much in class, and I definitely wasn't going outside for recess, on Mondays we always played kick ball.

Not interested in kicking a ball today!

I was one happy camper when school let out that day. I hurried in the direction of home and happened to pass Vera, who was sitting on her porch smoking a cigarette and having a beer.

"Hey Mary, do you want to have a beer with me?" she asked.

"No that's okay, I have go home," I said.

"Okay maybe another time," she said.

When I arrived home, I walked up the steps and knocked on the door.

"Hello Hon," I said when Hon opened the door.

"Hello, get out of those school clothes," Mom grunted. The moment I changed into my play clothes, Mom started checking my school clothes. *What's she doing now?* I wondered.

"Come the hell in this room now … you bleeding ass cow!"

"What Mom?" I answered.

"Don't ask me what, you already know what" Mom said. "You little, nasty, filthy ass whore! You have soiled your fucking school clothes with your whore blood. Do you know how expensive clothes are today? You haven't bought a damn thing in this house Bitch, especially not any clothes. Now I have to throw this bloody shit away."

"I'm sorry Hon" I said in remorse, "I didn't mean to soil my clothes."

"Don't say another fucking word to me, bitch, or I will take my hammer and nail your head to the fucking wall!" Mom shouted.

"But Mom can I ask you something?" I asked.

"Damn! You want my foot in your ass is that what you are going to ask me?" she blurted.

"No Mom, all I want to know if this ever happened to you before?"

"Goddammit! Has what ever happened to me before?" Mom asked.

"You know bleeding?"

I was knocked backwards off of my feet by Hon's swift back-handed slap to my face. "Don't you ever ask me no kind of shit like that again, bitch! You are a fucking child! You have no right to ask an adult anything. Now get hell out of this room before I claw your eyes out with a hammer and roast them on a stick like fucking marshmallows." She demanded.

Defeated and distraught, I immediately ran to my room so I wasn't about to lose my eyes to the crazy woman.

That night, I went to bed scared of dying, and I woke up knowing that each day was getting closer to my demise. Sometimes, I was scared just to wake up because I knew that I was really going to die this time. I didn't believe that Mom would have lied to me again about dying. *Or could she?* I asked myself. Obviously, the answer to that question would be revealed in due time.

On the third or fourth day of bleeding, I came home after school without stopping at Vera's house. Upon entry, I saw Hon sitting on the living room couch awaiting my arrival. She grabbed me by my hair and she pulled me into the living room. "Why am I getting a phone call from Ms. Lee, telling me that the children in your class are complaining that you have a foul odor? That fucking bitch is Asian and can't even speak English correctly; and you're having this foreigner call my house about your black ass. Bitch! Go get me the broom!" Mom yelled.

"Please Mom, I didn't know that she was going to call you!" I cried out. I went and retrieved the broom and Mom had me strip down to my bare body in the kitchen and she began to hit me with the broom. "You let those fucking Asians make soup and rice, and not call me on my fucking telephone bothering me about your stank ass. You ungrateful little whore! I wish your ass would get hit by the school bus and die as road kill!" Mom shouted.

After the beating was done, Hon sent me down to the basement and locked me downstairs. It was just me, my garter belt and a bloody ass towel in the cold, damp basement. There was no dinner, TV or dogs to entertain me.

I was locked in the basement till morning.

Mom unlocked the basement door the following morning. I could hear her in the background calling my teacher. "Hello Ms. Lee, I am so glad that you contacted me regarding Mary's issue. I'll be taking her to see the doctor so she will not be attending school today. "Thank you Ms. Lee" Goodbye," Mom said.

"When are we leaving to see the doctor Mom?" I asked.

"Shut the fuck up and suck my ass! We ain't going to see nobody!" Hon barked. "You are staying home for the next three days until you stop bleeding, Slut."

I went in the room to play with my dolls since Mom had not mentioned anything about breakfast this morning. When lunch time rolled around I asked Mom. "Mom what are we having for lunch?"

"Well … I had a club sandwich, tomatoes soup and I am on my third cup of coffee," Mom replied joyfully.

"Am I going to eat anything?" I asked with concern in my voice.

"What are you eating now, Bitch?" Mom asked.

"Nothing" I replied.

"Well that's your fucking menu Bitch, now enjoy it, and act like you are Helen Keller and shut the fuck up."

Mom let me go hungry for two days straight, until she decided that I could have my daily three meals. The seventh day arrived, and I opened my eyes and I was alive and well. I had stopped bleeding. God had spared my life. He let me live. I also woke up to Hon standing over my bed just staring at me. The whole room was silent until Mom said with disappointment in her voice. "Damn! You didn't die yet? Fuck! That means another day that I got to feed you breakfast, Bitch."

On the seventh day, I was furious that Hon had lied to me about dying *again*. This time I was going to ask her why she had not told me the truth. But I wasn't going to do a damn thing till I got fed first, so after breakfast, I asked Hon. "Hon, did you know that God was going to save me?"

"I swear you are the most dumb-ass child that I ever dealt with!" Mom said. "Sometimes, I think that there is a cement block lodged between your big-ass head inside of your brain. Do you have Down's Syndrome, Bitch? Mom asked.

"No … I don't think so," I replied.

"What the fuck do you know? Talking to you is like talking to the back of this dog's ass!" Mom said.

I left the room sobbing and wishing that she would be the one to drop dead.

When I was on my period, she insisted I read the Bible to admit my sins of being a Whore. And although the cramps were bad for me—I still had to scrub the kitchen and bathroom floors on my hands and knees with bleach and ammonia. Mom didn't appear to care about me or my well- being at all. All that she was really concerned with was that there was food in the refrigerator to eat and a TV to watch. Damn me. Interestingly, I always bled twice a month. Once with my menstrual cycle and again from Hon. I had begun to wonder if every child's household was like mine. And if not, then *why* was I chosen to endure all of this turmoil? I began to question everything about my body and my entire existence?

Did anyone love me at all?

Chapter 11

Obituaries, Dead People & Me

It was the summer of my twelfth year of life, and the school semester was finally over. Everyone was on summer break and enjoying being out of school, myself included. The only thing I regretted about being on vacation was I had to give up my vice of smoking, since I was home with Hon every day. Of course I had to do the annual spring cleaning of our house, which was boring and mundane to me. Everything else remained status quo. Frequent beatings and name calling were as routine as getting out of bed and walking to the bathroom.

There were certain chores in place that were non-negotiable: accompanying Hon to the market or going fishing early in the morning, which I despised. Sometimes Hon would take me over to her friend's house so she could socialize. The adults would talk in code as if they were in a James Bond Movie, or like I was retarded, and couldn't connect what they were talking about to each other.

In between boring house visits, chores and beatings, there were rare and fleeting happy moments with Hon; and these, I took full advantage of. For example, moments like reading to Hon from the newspaper. She loved it when I read to her because she felt like someone was "telling her a story." I liked it, too, because it helped me to read better. But on one particular calm Sunday morning, I read something to Hon that I shall never forget.

I remember the day well. It was hot that day and the sun was beaming down on the neighborhood like a heat laser. I was in the dining room and I started reading an article from Hon's favorite newspaper, *The Kansas City Star.* Hon was sitting in a chair at the dinner table, After I had finished reading her the article, I decided to take a look at the obituaries; pretty weird for a twelve year old kid to do. I thought, but I just wanted to see if there was anyone that I recognized. At first glance, I saw something that captured my undivided attention.

Holy Hell!

I did see someone that I recognized. She was a very tall and pretty fair-skinned black woman that I remembered seeing when I was around the age of two. Don't ask me how I remembered, I just knew that I had seen her before. She and her mother used to babysit me when I was a toddler from time to time. And I hadn't seen her in a long, long, time.

"Hon did you see this?" I asked in awe.

"Have I seen what? Hon asked with an inquisitive tone.

"This lady in the obituary, I've seen her before!" I said with astonishment. "Look Hon her name is the same as mine. Her name is Mary Ross too." I kept reading with passionate interest, until I saw something that almost made me gasp. "Wait! My name is here too," I said with an inquiring mind.

The smile that Hon once had on her face, grinning from ear to ear where you could see every man-made denture in her mouth, soon turned into a fiendish frown as she jumped from her chair and walked towards me. I knew then and there that the fun was over and the devil was back knocking at the door! She snatched the newspaper out of my hand with such force that it startled me. Maybe I shouldn't have asked Hon who the lady was in the picture, I thought. Perhaps the bonding time might have lasted longer, but the curiosity that I felt was so strong that I couldn't pass up this opportunity to find out who she really was.

"Give me the Goddamn paper, and let me see who the fuck you are talking about, bitch!" Mom said angrily.

"Who is that, Mom? I asked anxiously waiting for Hon's answer.

"Oh, that is your bitch-ass, whore of a mother. That's who that Bitch is!" Hon spat callously.

"What? I replied in pure shock.

"Must I repeat myself, bitch?" Hon asked. "I said that is your motherfucking, biological tramp-ass mother. Did you read the entire article? Her bitch-ass died from a gunshot wound to her head. And that funky-ass whore was only twenty-five years old when her Bitch-ass died!" Mom said with emphasis, as if she was enjoying each uttered word of horror. In that moment, I knew she was trying to break my spirits, and she came pretty damn close. I wanted to see her dead, if not only for this act alone, but for all of other careless acts of mistreatment and abuse that I had to endure from her. I was in a rage, but the devastating storm brewing within was being completely ignored by Hon as she continued to rant and rave, and spit insults at me like a venomous snake. "And I believed that the whore deserved what she got! I'm glad that her boyfriend killed her!" Mom exclaimed. "She was nothing but a whore, just like you."

"You mean that you lied to me, about being my mother? I asked, my voice cracking with grief.

"Bitch, who the fuck are you anyway?" Hon asked. "You're just a fucking child! Who do you think you are? You think that an adult must never lie to your black-ass!" Mom complained.

"So that is really my name in the obituary, too?" I had to ask for clarification. "I am her surviving daughter?" I asked with tears forming in my eyes from a broken heart.

"Hell yes bitch, that is your name in the fucking obituary," Mom confirmed in disgust. Now angry because she had lied to me, I asked Hon. "So who are the other people listed under her picture?"

"Fuck, the questions just won't stop with, will they?" She shouted.

My voice began to get louder as the pain began to grow inside of me. "Who are they? "Please tell me, I have to know, for God's sake tell me!"

Wham!

That was the sound effect made by Hon's forceful, closed-fist backhand as it pounded my face and knocked me clean out of the chair I was sitting in. I fell onto the carpet sobbing, and reflecting upon all of the time I lost being with my real mother because I had been living with this evil, sadistic witch. My thoughts were interrupted by Hon's bellowing voice.

"Get up off the floor bitch!" Hon ordered. "You will not be under this roof in my house talking to me in that tone of voice."

Mom went to the white cabinet and she opened it with such force that when it slammed back against the wall, I thought the glass was going to shatter. Mom reached into the cabinet like a stark raving maniac and retrieved her favorite weapon of fear, her revolver. She placed one bullet in the chamber as she often did to intimidate me, as she spun the chamber around, then she closed it like she had a "bit part" on a Dirty Harry movie with Clint Eastwood. Slowly, she approached and pointed the gun in my face. "I guess that you are going to die today, like your good for nothing, whore-ass mother!" Mom said harshly. "Let's see bitch, what's on the menu for today?" she cruelly joked. "I know a bullet to the head bitch, with a side order of your dead momma."

Interestingly, fear was not my enemy today; not at this moment. All that I could feel was betrayal. Hon was a gigantic imposter, perpetrator and liar. My heart felt as though a bus had ran over it several times without let up. I ached so badly with the knowledge I just received. I had held so much pain inside of me that I just wanted to explode with raw emotion to learn that my *real* mother had been alive all of this time, and I didn't even know it.

I was never told!

"Why? "Why didn't you tell me, Hon?" I asked with self-pity lingering in my voice.

"Bitch, it was on a need to know basis, and I decided that you didn't need to know!" Mom said without showing emotion.

"Who are the other people listed in the article, Hon?" I asked with a grief-stricken heart.

"Well first of all that's your mama, then this is your father, and these three names here are your fucking brothers, and your asshole grandmother, along with your two slut sisters!" Hon said as if she was reading off of a menu at The Sizzler.

Anger was building up by the minute, the more Hon spoke. I wanted her to somehow start feeling my pain. And even though Hon pointed the gun at me this time, but negated to pull the trigger, I still felt as though I were already dead. I felt like I had a real beat down this morning—but this time it was all mental and emotional, which is the worst kind of whopping a human being can withstand. But I had no recourse for these blows. Usually, my body would swell up, bleed, or my skin would come off and then grow back after Mom's violent rages and temperamental beatings; but this beating here left me breathless and distraught from all the confusion and drama.

Now I knew the truth, the real honest to God truth. Hon didn't love me at all. She hated me because I was never *hers* to love in the first place. Now that her secret was out and I knew about it, I was left to hold and unravel this puzzle of baggage that Hon had held in her consciousness for many years. "This was too big of a burden for a twelve year old to bare!" I thought to myself. And when Hon saw that I wasn't about to flinch from her threatening me with the gun, she began to pummel my soul away with her bare hands. I cried not because of her punishments, but because I had a mother that I never knew of, until she had died. Now that I finally knew the truth, I was determined to release myself from the *need* to have a mother ever again!

But how?

Chapter 12

My Family Tree

As the days passed, I just couldn't shake the truth about my real mother. I walked around the house like a zombie at a graveyard. I felt as though I'd been mummified. The joy of playing with my dolls and the dogs had all but deteriorated. I hated Mom's guts now. I began to play back memories of my early childhood; and I remembered how she always made me look like a fool, whether it would be at school or at home. She did things like send me to school on "show and tell" day with a Ziploc bag of Swiss cheese; telling me that the cheese had come "from the moon," and that "Ed had brought it back down with him when he was an astronaut."

What the hell?

At the age of twelve, I knew this was a bald-faced lie, but in my seven-year-old mind (which is how old I was when this happened), it made perfect sense.

But only until I arrived at school and presented my ridiculous scenario to the class. The whole class laughed at me that day, including the teacher. And how could I forget the time (again at the age of seven) that I had lost my teeth.

My classmates had been telling me that they had found quarters and money beneath their pillows when they loss their teeth, because the tooth fairy came to their house. So, one day I asked Hon about this.

"Hon ... why didn't I get money under my pillow when I lost a tooth?"

Her reply was simple and straight to the point. "I'll give you a hundred dollars in monopoly money for knocking out every damn tooth in your fucking head, whore. Would you like that?"

"No Hon," I replied.

"But why Hon? Why didn't the tooth fairy never came to my house?"

"Oh ... the Tooth Fairy got hit by a car on his way over to the house, and while he was lying in the street some hoodlums robbed him of all of his money."

That' s a sad story but you know what's sadder? I actually believed Hon. Like a fool, I went back to school and repeated Hon's wacky story to my friends. Well, needless to say that I was friendless after that ridiculous story! The kids just laughed, pointed and thought I was a weirdo. And just when I didn't think it could get any worse, Hon made a surprise appearance in my classroom and announced to the class that I was a "bed wetter."

Unfortunately, it was true.

More ammunition for the kids and less friends for me.

Interestingly, I noticed that Hon always left out pertinent details in the re-telling of her tales. The memories kept coming into my mind, and I would replay them over and over again in my head, like a film projector. The flashbacks were so vivid that I could almost reach out and touch them.

I relived every minute, second, and hour of horror that Mom had made me endure. I had to sacrifice my happiness and childhood for her scornful mind. I still was depressed about not having my mother around, and not getting a chance to even know who she was, or what her favorite color was. I had so many questions about her such as, "When was her birthday?" "Why didn't she come and visit me?" And the most important question of all, "Why did she leave me here with Hon?" Did she love me, or was I hated by her too? All I knew were that there were too many unanswered questions, and too many unresolved feelings surrounding these issues. My heart and mind felt like the fourth of July. My memories were attacking my head like fireworks.

I couldn't help but replay Hon's negative comments about my real mother. And how dare she talk about my mother as though she were a two-bit criminal? This day was no different than any other, except Hon wanted to talk about my mother.

Throughout the rest of the summer, I listened to Hon tell me about my dysfunctional kin folks. She spoke as though she were the only sane one in the whole bunch of all of us. Hon started on me as soon as I woke up. "Good Morning, you trifling whore! Get your bubbled-eyed black-ass out of bed, before I throw you out by your teeth!" she ordered.

"Yes Ma'am," I said still half asleep.

"Let's have some breakfast together and talk," Hon said with authority in her voice. "What do you want for breakfast?" she asked.

"Well," I thought for a second, "I want " Soon Hon interrupted me

"Do you really think that I truly give a fuck about what you want for breakfast, Bitch? Well the fucking answer is no! I'm going to fix what the fuck I want to eat. The hell if I'm going to fix the request of a non-working ass imbecile Bitch like you. You can put your head between your knees and kiss your ass good-bye, Bitch, if you're waiting for me to care about your fucking wants or damn desires." She said with a cold-hearted voice.

As I mumbled beneath my breath, I followed Hon to the kitchen. I then sat down at the yellow folding kitchen table, with the yellow tablecloth, that had floral designs and trimmed in green lace. Hon got the skillet from under the stove and she slammed it onto the top burner. "Did you know that your Mom was shot in the head like a deer at Christmas?"

"No Hon," I replied.

"Yes the whore was" Hon said as she laughed. "Your Mother fucked men like a cat breeding a litter of kittens. She was a slut, "She shared her body like someone passing a tray of potatoes at dinner," Hon said with ease.

I didn't want to believe her after she had lied on so many prior occasions. I wondered why she would be telling me the truth now. "I knew that fucking Bitch," Hon said.

"Who?" I asked. In that moment, I was thumped on the forehead by Hon.

"Your Mama bitch. Are you listening to me at all?"

"Yes I am" I said. "Why must you talk so bad of my mother?" I asked Hon.

"Don't you question me about your fucking family, bitch!" Hon stated. "You have one more time to interrupt me, and you will be shitting your tongue out in the toilet, because I will knock you so hard in your mouth that your tongue will be lodged in your asshole. Do you hear what I'm saying to you?" Hon asked in the heat of the moment.

"Yes Hon, I hear you."

"Now going back to what I was saying …" she cleared her throat and continued. "Your Albino ass looking Grandmother … she said that she was full Cherokee Indian. Personally, I think that she was full of shit. That fat bitch isn't any Indian. The closest that bitch has been to a Teepee is at the fucking museum. Your Grandmother looked like a bad bowl of oatmeal!" Hon howled. "She always was stone faced. She never laughed. Your Grandmother looked like a goat in heat," Hon squealed. "Fuck that bitch! If Cancer had a face, your Grandmother would be it!" Hon ranted.

"Your whole family is a bunch of liars, that's how I know that you were born to be a liar!" Hon said.

Your grandfather was as black as the bottom of this cast iron skillet that I'm cooking with," Hon said. "In fact, he was so black that he looked like midnight. I heard that he walked with a wooden leg. If he had been my husband, Hell I would have took his fucking leg off and threw it in the fire place to build a fire with!!" Mom cackled.

"Hon that's not nice to say!" I said.

"Shut the hell up you stupid bitch before I head butt your ass into the kitchen wall!" Mom screamed at me. I exhaled and just kept quiet from then on.

Before I could sit back down in the chair Hon slapped me across my face. I started to cry. "Get your ass up and go to the living room so I can finish telling you about your dope fiend family!" Hon yelled. As I walked toward the living room, Hon threw a pot and it hit me on my head. I ran into the living room holding my head and wanting to express my anger towards her, but I knew better.

So I sat on the dark green couch that had a sheet over it waiting for Hon's arrival. Hon soon came into the living room. "Get your nasty filthy ass off of my couch and sit your rusty ass on the floor Bitch. Who do you think you are?"

"Nobody Hon," I replied.

"I know that already bitch!" Hon laughed before continuing on with her story. "Now, your bitch ass daddy is a fucking pervert. He would fuck the Devil in the ass if he had the chance.

"What Hon?" I asked

"You heard me, he has fucked your grandmother, his mother, He would beat her ass until her hearing aid came out of her ear," Hon boasted with a sick joy in her voice.

But her words were very confusing to me. I had never heard language such as this, so I was totally confused by our conversation. "Your fucking father was an alcoholic, and he would have his mother to suck his dick, without her dentures in, not that it mattered. Sucking dick is sucking dick as far as I'm concerned. It really doesn't matter how you do it whether you have teeth or you have to gum it!" Hon said. "He would go and eat his mother's gray-haired pussy like he was eating a club sandwich, he didn't care."

Hon's conversation was beginning to gross me out, but I couldn't say a word.

"Your father used to tell me how he would dry butt fuck your frail ass grandmother in her ass!" Hon said. I couldn't believe what she was telling me. I had no idea what she was talking to me about, all that I knew was that it sounded so awful to hear, especially how Hon was explaining it to me. It felt so weird. Hon kept on talking until my behind starting to hurt from sitting on the carpet for long periods of time. I was so happy when the need to use the bathroom came, I could get permission and I would get a break from hearing all of these awful things about my family. According to Hon's version everyone in my family was a liar, a slut, an alcoholic, a drug user and ugly. After a while of being in the restroom, Hon came to the bathroom. "Get your rotten stinking ass off of my toilet and come back and listen to what I have to tell you about your family!" she ordered me. I wasn't allowed to close the bathroom door whenever I used it. Hon had to see what I was doing at all times in the house. I guess it could be likened to being in prison.

On and on went this ridiculous conversation with Hon. I was getting tired of hearing her bash my family, but she continued to down my family members with the sword of her tongue. "Now, your aunt on your Mother's side was a fucking kiss ass" Hon stated. "If your Aunt Eva was standing on the edge of a cliff and your Grandmother told her to jump, that bitch would jump off of the cliff like a stampede of a herd of cattle, and fall to her fucking death, like the motherfucking air-head bitch that she is! She can't control her children and she certainly can't control her husband. Don't get me started on your dumb-ass uncle!" Hon laughed. "I hate your fucking family, just like I hate your ass." Hon said.

I was in a whirlwind of emotions as a result of Hon's comments. I wondered to myself, *when is it going to stop?* Could someone call her on the telephone or even knock on the door so I could get a break from this crazed woman's stories? Well, I had no such luck. I had to sit still and listen.

"No one wanted your black ass as a baby. Not your Mama, your Grandmothers, not your father and definitely not your bitch aunt. I am the only one who ever gave a damn about your demonic soul" She said wrapping it up, "You wanted to know who all those bitches and bastards were in that obituary, so now I told you" Hon said, quite pleased with herself as if she had just read me a night time story.

"Are you through talking about my family?" I asked Hon.

"Hell yeah, now get your ass in the fucking tub so I can bathe you bitch"

I was simply *mortified* by what I had just heard. I took my pajamas off and met Hon in the bathroom where she gave me a bath and got me dressed. For the rest of the day, I cried about the thought of not any of my family wanting me.

I could no longer form my lips to call her Mom, nor did calling her Hon seem appropriate either. I just wanted hear the truth. I just wanted to be loved; truly loved. And most of all I wanted to hear my name, Mary, instead of hearing the word Bitch, all day, every day and not to have the word bitch echoing in my head at night.

Mary.

Mary.

Mary.

My name is really Mary.

After all I was still a child with feelings. How could she not care? How could she be so selfish and cruel? And how could no one love me at all?

Chapter 13

Independence Day

Once it was all said and done, and all ugly truths or bitter lies were told, Hon decided to take me on a road trip. Not the kind filled with scenery, detours and vacation activities, but the kind where you meet the family so you can "see for yourself," what's real and what's not. The family lived in Missouri where we lived, but they lived several cities over, so it was a journey of sorts. I looked forward to meeting my family so I could see whether Hon's lies were going to be thrown in her face.

The first stop that Hon and I made was to see Grandma Francis on my Dad's side. Hon had made up her mind to finally have the Bat Mobile repaired, so off we went bright and early in the morning, speeding down the highway to Independence, Missouri, where my father's mother lived. I always sat in the back seat of the Bat Mobile, behind Hon on the driver's side. I don't recall if there were any seatbelts back then or not. I know that I never wore any such thing. When we finally arrived at Grandma Francis' house, I noticed that her house was much smaller than ours. In fact, our house looked like a palace compared to hers. She lived in a heavily wooded area in Independence and there were no other neighbors in sight for miles.

"Francis!" howled Hon. "Bring your ass to the fucking door! I have your granddaughter here to meet you!" Soon Grandmother came and answered the door.

"Well hello there dear," Grandmother said. I stood in silence from the sight of her. I looked her up and down from her head to her toes. She was a very thin, dark woman who was wearing a dress that sagged on her frail body. She had on a wig that looked like it hadn't been combed in a while. The woman had wrinkles on both her hands and face. She had not one tooth in her whole mouth. "Hon, she don't have any teeth," I said out loud. Then I felt a slap across the back of my head, that came from Hon. "Shut the fuck up before you end up swallowing every Goddamn tooth in your fucking head, after I kick you in your face, Bitch," Hon snarled back.

I just stared at Grandma Francis for a brief moment, but it must have seemed too long for Hon. "Say hello you rude Bitch!" Hon yelled at me.

"Oh hello Ma'am," I said. I thought to myself, now I'm a Bitch in public. What's going on? Hon had never called me a bitch outside of our house before. "Don't speak to the child like that Gussie," Francis told Hon.

Yes! I thought.

Someone is taking up for me.

"Get her Grandma Francis," I said quietly in my head.

"Fuck you!" said Hon, "Oh excuse me … I guess your son has already done that to you," Hon replied back.

Oh well, Francis got shot down real quick by Hon. My cheering section for Francis had stopped and came to a screeching halt! "Your black, frail black-eyed ass can't tell me shit," Hon said. "Why don't you tell your granddaughter how you got that black eye?" Hon suggested.

"I will," Francis said with no protest. "Let's have a seat on the couch."

Francis sat next to me and she said. "I have a terrible story to tell you, dear, about your father, my son. I received this black eye two days ago from your father. He had got mad at me for not giving him any money to buy alcohol," Francis said. "Tell her how her Father, your damn son, fucks you in your ass," Hon said.

"Oh Gussie, why must you interrupt me? Francis asked. "Because I want you to tell the bitch what happened to you so she can know," Hon said, exasperated with boredom. "I could be at my funeral, die and then be placed in a grave by the time you explain your story" Hon said.

I was in the middle of two adults talking about subjects that I didn't know the meaning of, and I was expected to know what they were trying to tell me. "Well you see dear" Granny began telling her story, "Your Father came over to my house, then sodomized and raped me," she said. "He took what little money I had, sat down and told me to fix him some breakfast when he had finished," Francis said with sadden eyes. "Baby girl," she said. "I'm eighty years old and I can't defend myself against my son's violent rages towards me."

At that time I couldn't process what she was saying to me. How would a child wrap its mind around something so horrific? All that I could think was, "Yikes! Eighty years old! She is ancient!" The woman did not even weigh a hundred pounds wet. She looked like the skeleton figure that you see in the doctor's office, only she was wearing clothes. She wore ugly black orthopedic shoes and walked with a cane. And honestly, I didn't know if I believed her story either, just because it matched Hon's story didn't mean it was true, I thought. But yet, I could not overlook granny's swollen black eye, it was shut closed. "May I use the bathroom, Grandma? I asked. "Of course child, yes you may. You are such a polite child," Granny politely said.

It was nice to hear a kind word coming from somebody. "Bitch, the bathroom is in the back yard. It's called an outhouse!" Hon hollered out to me. I didn't believe her at first, but as I went further into Granny's old shack, I couldn't find it. I saw two small bedrooms and the tiny kitchen that had an old Westinghouse refrigerator in it. Where is it at?" I asked.

"Damn it to hell you deaf and dumb bitch, I said that it was outside!" Hon yelled. "If you had of listened to me the first time you would have heard me. Fuck! I'll take you back there!" Hon said. And for sure it was in the back in a wooded area. I saw this dollhouse looking building with a raggedy old brown wooden door hanging off one hinge. Immediately I became frightened and figured I could wait until I got home. When all of a sudden Hon grabbed me by my hair and then she opened the door and shoved me inside.

"Yuk!" I said. It smelled so awful in there. "Do I have to shit for you Bitch, or do I need to find a shovel and dig the shit up out of your asshole?"

"No Ma'am," I said "I only have to do number one." But before I could get my pants down, I heard Hon yell through the door. "Hurry the hell up and get your monkey ass out of there! And you better wipe your ass real good, because I don't want you to get in my car smelling like shit, bitch!"

"Okay Hon," I said. "I don't want to be riding with a shitty bitch!" Hon said. When I had finished, I wiped myself and opened the door to come out. Hon wouldn't move out of my way so I could come all the way out. I didn't know why she was blocking my path, and dare not ask her to move, so I waited for her to move. We were standing face to face with one another like two chess pieces. Finally, Hon moved out of my way and grabbed my pony tail as she swung my head around. Hell, I thought I had whiplash. "Don't waste my time, Bitch, over here with your lame brain Granny. You heard what she had to say about your diarrhea fed Father so let's go! I want to go home. When we go back to that land field that she calls a living room, I want you to ask me if we can leave."

"Okay," Hon said. "Yes Hon I will," I said quickly so she could turn my hair loose. When Hon and I returned to Granny Francis's living room, we both sat down at the same time as though we had choreographed our movements to be in sync with each other. "Hon I'm getting hungry, can we go home now?" I asked.

"Yes of course we can," Hon said. "Well Francis it's been nice visiting you but we got to go.

You have had a chance to sit and meet with your Grandchild so the show is over." Granny Francis gave me a hug and a wet sloppy kiss on my cheek. We both said good bye, hopped into the Bat Mobile and Hon sped home. As we drove down the highway, I was sitting back reflecting on everything that had just happened. It suddenly dawned on me that Hon had known all of this time how to get in touch with my relatives, and she never even told me. The only lessons that Hon taught me that day was 1) how to keep a secret and 2) how to have deceitful behavior. I guess to "Gussie," a lie was only a lie, if someone else knew the truth.

Chapter 14

Flossie

Summer was hanging on by a thread and threatening to end, but there was still a sliver of it hanging around; and I was still taking intermittent road trips with Hon. On this particular day, we were on our way to see a woman named Flossie. As we drove to her house, I had no explanation as to who she was, so I waited patiently while riding in the back seat of the car biting my nails wondering what was waiting for me at Flossie's House. And though I didn't know much, I knew I was fed up with all of this "family truth." I wanted to do kid things like play or watch TV. But that wasn't going to happen. According to Hon, it was time to meet the family.

When Hon and I arrived at Flossie's we were greeted by Grandpa Walter at least that's what Gussie told me his name was.

"Hello there," Grandpa Walter said.

"Hello there Sir," I replied back.

Soon I heard Hon bark. "Get your black-ass out of the doorway and go get your fucking wife." I then heard another woman's voice say, "Who's at the door, Walter?

"Trouble," he replied sharply.

"I would not speak about trouble, if I were you," said Hon. "That takes a lot of nerves to say to me, especially coming from your rotten legged ass. Every time you sit your black ass inside of your truck, the oil light comes on! Check engine! Check the fucking Goddamn engine, bitch!

"Is that you Gussie? Haven't I asked you not to use profanity in my house?" Flossie roared.

"Fuck you bitch, this is a free motherfucking country, and I can go any motherfucking place that I want to go and say whatever the fuck I want to say!" Hon yelled back. I kind of got the feeling that these two ladies didn't like each other, but at least Hon was cursing at someone else other than me for a change.

Finally this tall, statuesque, overweight, almost pale white complexion woman with hazel eyes arrives at the front door. Her hair is wrapped up into a bun and she wears a long floor length white dress. She looked like a giant Casper the friendly ghost, only with a frown though. Now this was my grandmother on my mother's side; and she was a woman who was straight forward and blunt with her words. She always had a stone-faced expression. She didn't laugh, cry or hold long conversations with you. Most of the time she would answer you back with just a single word. *Yes, why, what* and *really* seemed to be her favorites.

"What are you doing at my house, Gussie?" Flossie asked.

"I stopped by so this bitch could meet her fucking Grandmother, that's why I'm here." Hon snapped back.

"Gussie I am not going to warn you again about cussing in my house!" Flossie scolded.

"Fuck you then, you pasty-faced bitch. You can bite my left ass cheek and choke on it. That's what I think of your fucking warnings, with your fake Indian ass. What are you going to do go get your Tomahawk and scalp my hairy fat ass?"

What a circus, I thought.

I laughed out loud at one of Hon's insults. "Bitch what's so fucking funny?"

"Nothing Hon, nothing at all," I said. Hon stated that if she heard me laugh out loud again that I could join Flossie and eat the right side of her ass cheek out and suffocate. I stayed quiet for the rest of the verbal bouts between Flossie and Hon.

"You know Gussie, I want you the hell out of my house now. If you are not going to abide by my rules then you need to leave!" Flossie demanded.

"I just thought that you might want to spend some time with your bubble-eyed granddaughter. Maybe the two of you can have a pow wow, and you can teach her how to do the rain dance while having a feather crammed up in your asses. Wouldn't that be fun, Flossie?" Hon asked.

"I don't like your attitude Gussie, and I never did!" Flossie yelled at Hon.

"Well I never liked the smell of your cement breath either," said Hon. "It's like talking to a cement mixer."

While the two of them argued, I noticed that Grandpa Walter had slipped into the background into another room where he politely shut the door. As for myself, I was enjoying the back and forth put downs—or more like Hon putting Flossie in her place. The both of them were at each other's throat. Flossie didn't curse, so many of her insults were more scolding than actual insults. "I want some fucking water, Flossie!" Hon ordered.

"Okay ... I go get you a glass, Gussie," Flossie answered back.

"The fuck if you will, Pocahontas! I know where the damn kitchen is; I don't want your gorilla hands touching nothing that I'm about to fucking drink."

When Hon left the living room to go into the kitchen this gave Flossie and me a chance to sit down and introduce ourselves to each other. "Hello Grandmother, I'm Mary," I said with enthusiasm.

"I already know that," Flossie replied.

"I'm so glad to finally meet you," I said.

"Okay," Flossie said. I thought to myself this conversation is awkward.

"How old are you now?" Flossie asked me.

"I'm twelve years old."

"Good," Flossie answered. Then Flossie just stared at me as if I was a mid-term quiz that she had no idea what the answers were. We just sat there, like two bumps on a log, wondering what to say to each other next. Flossie broke the silence when she said. "Would you like to see a picture of your mother?"

"Yes!" I said with joy.

Flossie jumped up from the couch to get the family album. When she returned, in her hand was a big thick photo album book, which reminded me of an Atlas. "See, here is a picture of your mother" Flossie said.

"Oh wow! She was so beautiful" I remarked.

In the picture Mom was sitting on the couch and looking into the camera. She had a big, broad smile which showed all of her pearly white teeth. She wore a dress and her long pretty brown hair was wrapped up in a bun. She had big beautiful brown eyes just like me. And all of the family members said that I looked just like her. I fantasized about having a real mother, but no sooner than my happy thoughts appeared, they disappeared on the heels of Hon's booming voice. "That bitch wasn't beautiful, that bitch was a whore!" Hon shouted out from the kitchen. "Gussie, you better stop telling this child lies about my daughter!" Flossie shouted back to Hon.

"Shut the fuck up, Flossie, before I snatch your husband's wooden leg off of him and start beating your motherfucking ass with it!" Hon bellowed.

"You're crazy, Gussie! I'm not listening to another word that comes out of your mouth! I'm trying to talk to this child for God's Sakes!" Flossie said. "Oh and look here," Flossie continued. "These are your three brothers and your sister. And here is a picture of your aunt, her son and daughter and your cousins," Flossie said.

"I have sisters, brothers and even cousins," I said.

I was impressed to see that I had other family members and that I really wasn't the only child.

"Grandmother, may I have this picture?" I asked.

"Of course you can," Flossie said.

"Oh hell the fuck no!" said Hon. "You're not bringing that wide mouth bitch's picture into my house! That will be the day Flossie's Blue-black husband grows a natural leg," Hon said.

"What's wrong with the child having a picture of her mother, Gussie?" Flossie asked.

"I wasn't talking to you Flossie, sitting on that raggedy ass Goodwill couch, looking like an old, out dated bag of cheap-ass flour," Hon said. "If you bring that picture into my house, Bitch, you will lay beside your dead ass mother!" Hon warned.

"That's it!" Flossie shouted. "I have heard enough of your crazy insults. You can talk about me ... but not about my daughter." And seconds later, Flossie returned her attention to me, "As I was saying Mary, your cousin is in the military and your Aunt Eva wants to meet you as well."

"Really?" I was ecstatic to learn that someone in my family was eager to meet me. I was hoping that maybe Aunt Eva could rescue me from Hon. "Maybe when you come over again Eva will be here," Flossie said.

"I sure hope that she will," I said.

"Fuck your motherfucking hopes!" Hon said as she entered the room. "I'll give you some history about your mother" Hon said. "That bitch, your mother, fucked like a damn jack rabbit!" Hon said.

"Gussie, I'm about tired of you talking about my daughter," Flossie said.

"Well Flossie if you are so damn tired ... then take your fat fucking ass to sleep!" Hon shouted. "Let me tell you, your mother went through men like diarrhea running out of your asshole," Hon said.

"Get out of my house now Gussie before you make me say something that I will regret," Flossie yelled.

"Fine Flossie, but I did want to hear you say something that you would regret ... like the birth of your whorish daughter," Hon said as she giggled.

"Leave Gussie!" Flossie said again with more anger in her voice this time.

Well that was my cue that visitation time with Grandma Flossie was over. And besides, I guess that Hon got tired of listening to Flossie talk about my mother and my siblings, so she wanted to leave anyway. I didn't get to spend much quality time with my Grandmothers, mainly because of all of the interruptions from Hon; but I did get the feeling that I was both missed and wanted by my new found family. I got up from the couch and told Flossie goodbye. I went to give my Grandmother a hug and that is when Hon grabbed the back of my neck like she was grabbing a chicken to be slaughtered.

"Come on Bitch, it's time to go home. I've had enough of this Quaker Oats bitch," Hon said, as she grabbed my arm and whisked me away to the door. On the ride back home, all I could think about were those pictures of my family where everyone was smiling. Hon never took any pictures of me. In fact, there were no pictures of anyone hanging on our walls at home. I even asked Hon if at all I would ever meet my father. Hon never uttered a word. So as I sat back in the car I realized that I was glad to have met and talked with both of my grandmothers even though Dad's mom conversation was way over my head. I still loved the fact that she knew who I was and that I existed. I didn't feel so alone now. I thanked God for the moment I shared with them, and I couldn't wait to meet my Aunt Eva. It was a special day for me. I had learned that I had an aunt, sister, brothers and two grandmothers. I had family that Hon always knew about, but told me that I had none. My resentment, anger and distrust for Hon grew stronger. I had wondered what other lies I would have to face as a result of Hon's hidden secrets.

Chapter 15

Heads or a Tailspin?

I woke this morning and everything seemed to go wrong for me. This was like a "bad luck" kind of day all-the-way around. I got out of bed with welts and sore arms and legs, wishing that I hadn't woke up because the night before Hon beat me mercilessly with a wire coat hanger because I had asked a question about my father. "Hon, do you think that I will get a chance to meet my Father soon?" I had inquired the night before.

I didn't mean any harm. I just thought that since she was taking me over to meet my real family, that she might also let me meet my Dad. I guess talking about my Father to Hon was a bad idea. She was pissed and when she re-entered the dining room—she had three wire coat hangers in her hands. And she intertwined them so they would be "thick" for the beating.

Let the ass whooping begin.

She hit me in the head, my arms, legs and butt. "Bitch, your Father ain't shit and you want to see him?" Hon snapped. "Your father is a fucking, begging ass tramp who never liked to work a day in his rotten life!" Hon shouted at the top of her lungs. "He don't love you, bitch!" Hon said. "He loves a bottle of cheap ass liquor. Hon added. "He didn't marry your dead ass mother, and he never sent me a dime for taking care of you. He never bought you a gift for your birthday or Christmas, and you want to see him!" Hon said. "I will beat your ass so bad that it will fall off of your body bitch, so don't ask me again about seeing that low-down dirty, wanna-be-a-pimp-so-called daddy of yours.

I went to bed with Hon angry.

I woke up the next morning to Hon holding a rolling pin shouting over my bed. "You are an ungrateful little Bitch!" Hon shouted as she thrashed the rolling pin alongside my head. I screamed and I tried to run away from her, but the basement didn't have any hiding places for me. Hon grabbed my arm as if she knew that I was thinking of running. The blows from the rolling pin kept coming and my terrified screams sounding. Hon just kept on swinging the pin. I gave up trying to block the blows, and surrendered to the beating like a prisoner of war. She soon returned with more ammunition. This time she had her cane. I begged her to please not hit me anymore, but Hon ignored my pleas. She also had her handy bottle of rubbing alcohol. But instead of her pouring it on my open welts from the wire coat hangers, she sat down in her rocking chair with a bucket down at her feet.

"Bitch put your arm over the bucket and pour the alcohol on every welt," Hon ordered.

"Please Hon, No!" I pleaded. Hon grabbed me by my hair and said, "I ought to pour bleach in it just to see what will happen!"

"No Hon, please don't!" I begged.

"Then you better start pouring this alcohol on those open wounds, or I will get the bleach and whip you again. But this time I will go get my gun!" she promised. And with that, I slowly began to pour the alcohol on my welts.

I screamed my heart out and cried my soul out. Hon took my arms, one at a time, and held them down in the bucket of rubbing alcohol for several minutes. With blurred vision, I looked up to see Hon laughing at me once again. "I won't ever ask about my Father again … okay Hon?" I proposed. Hon then lifted my arm out of the bucket, and she grabbed the bottle of rubbing alcohol and she told me to follow her upstairs. Once in the kitchen Hon said, "Sit your crying ass in the chair until I come back."

I sat in the chair looking at my wounds and crying, wishing that someone in my family would save me from this living hell. Hon returned to the kitchen. "Are you hungry?" Hon asked. "Yes Ma'am" I said. Hon reached into her apron pocket and pulled out what looked to be a Hersey Chocolate candy bar. I really didn't want candy for breakfast, but at least it was something. I tore off the aluminum wrapper and commenced to eating it. "You can have the whole candy bar if you want to," Hon laughed and said. "Thank you" I said while still sobbing. After about thirty minutes of eating the candy, my stomach started rumbling and it started to cramp up. "Hon, may I use the bathroom? My stomach is hurting," I asked with urgency in my voice.

"Why?" Hon asked.

"Please Hon," I begged. "I feel like I will have an accident if I don't go to the bathroom now!" I cried out.

"Okay Bitch you can go to the restroom," Hon said.

When I was finally done using the restroom, I asked Hon. "What kind of candy was that Hon?"

"Oh, it's call Ex-Lax," she laughed.

"I don't like that kind of candy," I complained bitterly.

"Don't nobody give a rat's nut what you like and don't like, Bitch!" Hon barked. Seconds later, Hon got up from the kitchen table, snatched me by my arm and led me back downstairs where she told me to stay until she called me back upstairs.

"But what about my stomach?" I asked with great anxiety. "I might have to use the bathroom again." Hon looked at me and said, "bitch, you better use that damn bucket to piss and shit in."

Oh hell.

I was down in the basement *again* with nobody but myself. It was pitch black in the basement, but this time I refused to cry. I was tired of crying over Hon's punishments, and I just didn't want to have another "*why me*" pity party. I sat back down in the rocking chair, sulked a bit, said my prayer and thought about life without Hon as I fell asleep. The next morning I was set free and life went on with a painful echo of all that it had been in days prior to all that it had been before.

A week passed and Hon never mentioned my father to me again, and given her last beating, I dared not bring it up. She went about the house cleaning up, and giving me my daily hygiene ritual. There were some days that I was able to just play around in the house or outside, and not get socked around like a rubber punching clown. On this particular day I was trying to stay out of Hon's eyesight and way, because it had seemed that just my presence in the house could provoke her into a tyrant rage. I just wanted to enjoy a day without bruises and bumps. Suddenly, the telephone rang and Hon answered it. I raced out of my room into the dining room where the phone was located. I thought that maybe it was dad calling to speak with me. It was Flossie. "Get your ass into the other room while I talk to this bitch!" Hon shouted at me. I hurried off into my room and jumped onto my bed. No sooner that I had laid my head down on the pillow, Hon was in the doorway. "Jump on that bed again and I'll make your ass jump out of that window!" Hon yelled. I lay quietly on the bed as Hon left the room.

She returned to her conversation with Flossie. I couldn't hear the conversation, so I did what I do best, looked out of the window and fantasized what my life would be living with dad. Soon the conversation was over, and I was hoping that Hon had some good news for me, but instead, she told me to go clean-up for lunch. So I did. When I came into the kitchen Hon had fixed club sandwiches for the both of us. I sat down at the kitchen table, said a prayer and we both began to eat.

"You know what I have been thinking?" Hon asked.

"What? I asked.

"Whether or not you could meet your father," Hon said.

"Really?" I replied.

"Fuck! Get your milk back in your titties, bitch" Hon said. "And don't you think that for one minute, that I started thinking about a visit from your dad just because you had asked me."

"Well are you going to let him come over to the house to see me, Hon?" I asked.

"I might, but don't want you to badger me about it!" she demanded.

"Okay Hon, I won't," I replied.

I was hoping, praying, and wishing that Hon would let my father come over to the house, so I could meet and see him for myself. I had a strong burning desire to have a family member in my life. There was a hole in my heart that needed to be filled and it could only be filled by daddy, I thought. I didn't know how much more my body would hold up to Hon's whippings; or how long my mind could stay normal with all of the mental abuse. I needed someone who would give me a chance to be a child and who would love me unconditionally because I was their child and not the product of an evil old woman who hated my guts.

Of course Hon kept me waiting on her decision. She didn't discuss it nor did I bring it up. I just waited around in silence, always under Hon's control. I wondered why she couldn't understand how I felt. I soon came to the conclusion that Hon had no feelings about anything, or anyone. Time and again Hon would ask, "Would you like to see your father?"

"Of course I would Hon," I replied. And then she would not utter another word about it. She dangled the idea of meeting with my father over my head like someone holding mistletoe at Christmas. I hated the fact that she was doing that to me. She would get my hopes up high and then she would shoot them down as if she was playing with a yo-yo. She had my emotions in a knot, and I didn't know whether I was coming or going. This was a demented game of "Heads or Tails," and all that I knew for sure was that I was in a tailspin by the very fact that I played it. She knew how bad

I wanted to see my dad, but she really didn't care about what I felt. All she wanted to do is to see the anxious look upon my face turn into a saddened heartfelt moment. I was Hon's soap opera, and I had long grown tired of playing the starring role.

Chapter 16

The Visitor

One month had passed and there was no word from Hon on a visit from my father. The conversation had fallen "silent" and we were back to business as usual. But on a day when I least expected, an ordinary day became quite extraordinary indeed. Hon made breakfast that morning, and I helped her clean the kitchen afterwards as customary. Afterwards, I ventured to my room to play with my dolls. While playing in my room I heard the doorbell ring. I didn't get up to see who it was, because I knew that whoever was at Hon's door—they weren't here to see me, so I continued to play uninterrupted. Seconds later, I heard Hon open the door and begin a conversation with a man in the living room. The sound of faint whispers echoed throughout my bedroom. Shortly thereafter, Hon entered the bedroom and stood in the doorway with her hands on her hips.

"Hey bitch you have a visitor."

"I have a visitor!" I said in shock. I wondered who it could be, so I dropped my dolls down on the floor in a hurry and I rushed out of the room to see who could possibly be visiting me. When I arrived in the living room there he was, sitting on the green couch, my father. I instinctively knew who he was. I remembered his face from back in the day when Hon took me over for routine babysitting at what I know now was Flossie's house. I had gone a couple of times as a child. I rushed over to him and threw my arms around him, "Hi Daddy!" I said with excitement.

"Hello darling," Daddy said as he gave me a bear hug. "I have missed you baby. But daddy is here now," he said with a wide grin.

"Thank you Hon for letting Daddy come over!" I said.

"Don't thank me, bitch. I never wanted his black ass here in my house," Hon bellowed. I ignored her response, and I continued to have a conversation with dad. "Where have you been daddy? What took you so long to see me?" I asked.

"Well dear, daddy has been trying to find you for the longest of time," he explained. "And I've been traveling back and forth from Colorado to Missouri."

"That's bullshit and you know it Homer," Hon rudely interrupted. "You have been traveling back and forth to the doctors to get rid of that Gonorrhea that you caught, you lying-ass bastard!"

"How dare you disrespect me in front of my child, you fat bitch!" my father shouted.

"Your child?" Hon barked. "I've taken care of her since she was two. "And as far as me disrespecting you, that's a fucking joke," Hon laughed. "You can't respect an alcoholic, pervert like yourself!"

"You can't talk that way in front of her!" dad said.

"You stupid ass," Hon snapped. "It doesn't matter what I say in front of her or in back of her, you're still the fucking low life of the earth, and I hate the air that you breathe, motherfucker!" Hon said.

Oh boy.

The visitation had definitely taken a turn for the left.

Dad was furious with Hon, and Hon wanted him out of her sight *and* house as soon as possible.

Now where was this going to leave me?

"Daddy I want you to know that I love you dearly," I said.

"Oh ain't that sweet, Daddy loves you too baby girl," my father said.

"With all of this fucking love going around, I need to take a shit!" Hon barked. "You two are a pair of pathetic, worthless pieces of dog shit!" were her final words on the matter.

"Just ignore that jealous, fat old bitch," daddy said. "How old are you now, Mary?" Daddy asked.

"I'm twelve-and-a-half Daddy," I said.

"There's nothing about either one of you motherfuckers that I'm jealous about!" Hon shouted. "You two need each other like flies need shit," Hon said.

"I'm getting tired of all your fucking insults, Gussie. You've never liked me and I don't understand why!" Daddy exclaimed.

"Well it could be because you treat your mama like she is a two bit whore, working a trick on a water-logged mattress at a cheap motel!" Hon said.

"Bitch, you have no idea what you are talking about!" daddy defended. "This is my little girl here! Do you realize that you're putting lies about me into her head?" Daddy asked.

"Well at least I'm not giving her head like you have your broomstick mother do to you ..." Hon chuckled.

"Fuck you Gussie, you just wished that I would fuck you, that's what your problem is," dad said.

"Yeah right! The only way that you could fuck me if I was flat on the floor, dead as a doorknob" Hon said with authority in her voice.

I just sat on the sofa watching these two tear into each other like two starving tigers on a National Geographic documentary. I felt so upset with this visitation, all of this animosity was taking away from my time visiting with Daddy. Hon always messed up my visits with family members. She was one of the most inconsiderate people on the planet. Hon and Daddy's bickering was getting out of hand, and I wanted my time with him so I could talk. I had so many unanswered questions that I was desperate for him to resolve. And I couldn't do that with them at each other's throats. I had to quickly think of something to interrupt their verbal debate of hatred.

"Excuse me, may I please say something?" I asked.

"And what the fuck is on your piss filled brain, bitch?" Hon inquired.

"Daddy can we go out somewhere? I asked.

"Why sure darling," Daddy replied. "Where would you like to go?" Daddy asked.

"You are not taking that bitch anywhere but to that damn couch, you dirty son of a bitch," Hon said. "You will have that twelve-year-old turning tricks for you, so you can make some money," Hon said. "You know that your daddy can't keep a job, and do you know why? Because he is one, lazy, cocksucker who thinks the world needs to kiss his ass at all times!" Hon said.

"You are just an old miserable ass woman, who seeks attention all of the time, Bitch!" Daddy said with disgust in his voice.

"Well if I'm miserable it's because I have to look at your alcoholic, won't-get-a-job-because-I-hurt-my-back, lying through your yellow ass teeth, motherfucking, dusty ass," Hon said.

These two were throwing insults back and forth at each other like they were in a championship tennis match at Wimbledon. I felt short changed, like I got the short end of the straw and nobody cared that my visitation was being interrupted by their selfish need to bicker and argue with each other.

"Hon, may I be excused?" I asked.

"Hell no, Bitch! Your damn daddy came all the way out here to teach you how to become a hooker. You better sit your black ass back down before I knock your ass back down!" Hon instructed.

"You don't ask to be excused from visiting with your father … that is completely out of the question," Daddy said. It was a no win case for me. I sat back down on the couch and continued to listen to them call each other names for a good twenty minutes more.

"Gussie, I am not going to sit here and listen to your crazy-ass! I came over to visit my daughter," Daddy said. "Honey would you like to have some money?" Daddy asked me.

"Sure Daddy, I'd like to have some money!" I said with excitement. Daddy reached into his pocket and handed me a five dollar bill. "Thanks Daddy" I said with much appreciation. Suddenly Hon walked over to the couch and snatched the five dollar bill out of my hand. "Good! Now I can go and get some bait for my fishing trip in the morning," Hon said.

"Gussie give that girl back her money before I put my foot in your ass!" Daddy said.

"Motherfucker, I would just love to see you try and do that!" Hon said. "If you even tried to raise your foot or hand at me you would draw back two stubs, then I would shoot you in the head!"

I began to cry because Hon had taken my five dollars. She had no right to take it away from me. "What the fuck are you crying about, whore?" Hon asked. "A child is not supposed to receive money! What the fuck were you going to spend it on anyways? It's not like you have any bills in your name. You don't have to buy food, clothes or gas for the car," Hon said. "So fuck you and your dumb-ass daddy!" Hon added.

"That's it, I'm leaving before I hurt you, bitch" Daddy replied.

"I know that you meant to say that you had better leave before you get hurt," Hon said.

"As old as you are Gussie you shouldn't be acting this way," Daddy said.

"And as stupid as you are, you were still riding on the little yellow bus when you were seventeen!" Hon shot back." I began to wonder if there was anybody in my family that Hon liked. She had cussed out all of the family I met.

"Well baby girl, Daddy's going to leave now. Maybe we can schedule a date to see each other again soon," Dad said.

"Sure Daddy, that will be okay," I said. But I spoke to soon.

"Well nobody asked me a goddamn thing about another visitation!" Hon said. "And since this bitch is in my custody and she lives with me, I have the final decision as to whether she will visit with you again."

"Can he Hon?" I asked.

"Sure he can," Hon said with a chuckle, "Just as soon as I go and get my gun and shoot you both in your fucking mouths! Then you both can visit each other while you burn in hell!"

"You are such a mean, fat bitch!" Daddy said. "In fact you are so fat, that I could fit my whole body in your ass!"

"And when you did I would shit your black-ass out right at your home ... in the fucking toilet!" Hon howled. "This is my motherfucking ass house, Homer, and not you or your cunt-ass daughter runs anything around here. You better hope that I don't throw this Bitch out in the middle of the highway to get hit by a fucking semi-truck," Hon said.

"If you hurt my daughter, I will kill you bitch," daddy said.

"Oh, did I just hear a threat? Or did you just fart? Because now you are talking from your asshole!" Hon said. Seconds later, Hon then left the living room and I knew that Daddy was going to be in big trouble. "Daddy maybe you should leave ..." I warned him. "When Hon leaves the room, she is ready to battle," I warned him.

"I will leave when I am good and goddamn ready, that fat old bitch don't scare me" Daddy said. "Bye daddy" I said.

I knew that I had to leave the room. I ran to my bedroom and peeped out, like a scared mouse hiding from a hungry alley cat. And just as I predicted, Hon re-entered the living room with her trusty friend, the twenty-two revolver. She ran into the living room, her thighs slapping together like an audience applaud at a baptist church. "I will blow your damn head off Homer in this living room if you don't leave my fucking house now!"

"Why are you so upset? You didn't have to go and get your gun, Gussie" Daddy said.

"Why is your dumb ass still here? It shows me that you can't follow simple instructions," Hon said.

"Gussie you are so full of shit," Daddy said. I thought to myself right at that moment that Daddy should have been gone, as soon as he saw that Hon had a gun. Maybe he was stupid, just like Hon said. I knew better. I left the room when I saw her leave, but Daddy just stayed in the living room cussing Hon out. "Homer, I will shoot you in your ass and then take my carving knife out and slice your bullet riddled ass to my dogs, if you think that I am so full of shit."

As I stood nervously in my doorway, I wondered if Hon was really going to shoot my daddy in the head right before my eyes in the living room. I could see it now. When school starts back and the teacher ask me, "Mary, how did you spend your summer vacation?"

"Well," I would begin. "I found out that my mother was not my real mother, and that my biological mother was shot and killed, and I found out who she was by reading her obituary. And oh yeah ... my grandmother on my dad's side gets beat up and raped by my father, my grandmother on my mother's side is a fake-ass wanna-be-Indian, and my daddy was shot in the head in the living room in front of me on his first visit with me." What a hell of a story that would be!!!

I would probably get expelled from school, after telling that story to the class. My thoughts were soon interrupted by Hon throwing a glass vase at my father's head. Luckily he ducked just in time, as the vase missed his head by inches and shattered against the pale pink living room wall. "I'm leaving!" Daddy shouted. "You are one crazy bitch Gussie! I swear you are!" said Daddy as he ran out the door.

"And don't you forget it you toothless, skeleton looking bastard. Don't you ever come back to my damn house again?" Hon said.

I soon heard dad's car speed off, and then Hon shut the door and put her gun back up in the cabinet. I ran and climbed up on my bed, hoping that she would not blame me for his visit and turn her wrath onto me. The whole house was silent until it was broken by a knock at the door. I rose up out of my bed and stood in the bedroom doorway. I was hoping that it wasn't Dad again, because this time he was sure to die where he stood. It wasn't my dad, instead it was the nosy neighbor who lived next door to us.

"Ms. Gussie," are you all right?" The neighbor asked.

"Oh sure Rose, I'm fine, I just got a little upset because that man who you just seen leave out of here, was trying to rob me of what little money that I have ..." Hon lied. "Then he tried to get violent with me so I had to defend myself, that's all."

"Oh my God!" the neighbor exclaimed. "Do you want me to call the police?"

"No ... but thank you anyway. My arthritis is trying to flare up. I need to go and rest, and prop my legs up now. That man almost gave me a heart attack!" Hon exclaimed.

"Did you know him at all, Gussie?" Rose inquired.

"No," Hon continued with her lie. "He was just a homeless man who knocked on my door wanting a bite to eat, so I fed him. You know it was the least that I could do as a God fearing woman," Hon boasted. "But if you should see that man again hanging around in the neighborhood, please call the police ..." Hon insisted.

"I sure will, Ms. Gussie" Rose said.

"Goodbye" Hon said.

I couldn't believe how she had just lied on my father and how she acted as if she had done a good deed. And now she just put out an APB (All Point's Bulletin) on my dad in the neighborhood. Hon could sure play the role of an innocent old woman when she felt the need to.

I returned to my bed and turned my attention to the window. I couldn't help but wonder how Hon could get away with so much lying, dishonesty and cruelty. She should have become an actress instead of a nurse. She would have won the Oscar several times over. I could also feel a deep and profound sadness that I would probably never see my father again; but at least I was grateful to God that I had an opportunity to meet him at least once.

Geez!

What a summer it had been!

I'd learned nothing but hatred from Gussie. I knew now for sure that I was dead set on getting revenge on her. She had abused me, disrespected my family, and somehow believed that she got away with it. But I was determined to find a way to may her pay for it all. I would soon turn thirteen and I decided that I was not going to take any more of Gussie's crap when I became a teenager. I was going to make her pay for all of her evil deeds, but how?

That was a question that needed to be researched and investigated. I was going to find her weakness, battle her and win this war. "Please Dear Jesus ... help me make her pay," I prayed that night. "Please help me make her pay."

Chapter 17

My Best Friend

I returned to school in the fall of my seventh grade year. Autumn in Missouri was my absolute favorite. Mother Nature was at its finest, both colorful and busy, dropping seeds of tranquility and balance in the air. The trees lose their leaves and their colors fade like soaked, bleached jeans. The air is cool and crisp, and the wet morning dew shined like someone had sneaked onto the lawn in the midnight hour and tossed uncut diamonds on the ground just for the beauty of it all. The birds were gearing up to fly south to their respective "vacation homes," and the squirrels were gathering up walnuts for the winter.

I was especially fond of the seventh grade because academically I did well, making high marks on my report card throughout the year. Sadly, the beatings and insults were still the "*status quo*" in my home. I had no friends, no independence, and still carried a kindergarten lunch pail to school each day. I was an introvert and spoke very little to the kids around me. I worked more, socialized less. I was also an angry child, so when Hon gave me the permission to hit the kids back who liked to pick fights and antagonize, I was off and running out the gates like a Greyhound chasing the rabbit at the dog track. I fought daily. I fought because someone was jealous of me or because they thought that I was a snob.

I also took a lot of heat for being a "four eyed" girl with glasses. Hon had taken me to see the eye doctor before school had started, and quite naturally, she picked out the ugliest frames I had *ever* seen. They were a "cat style" with a blue frame. The kids at school started calling me four-cycs, and meowing at me when I walked by them.

So of course I had to make a few kids trip and fall when I heard them make fun of me. I was soon becoming tired of school. To me it was a waste of my time. I had grown bored of getting up early, class assignments, the homework, the fights, the jokes and the damn glasses. I got insults not only at home, but also at school—just a little less harsh. I thought I could go to a place where I didn't get laughed at and picked on. School wasn't fun or exciting anymore, and it didn't matter what I did in school. All of the awards, accolades and achievements collected and received throughout elementary went unnoticed by Hon. I got tired of going to the auditorium and receiving certificates for excellent attendance or winning a spelling bee, because when I went out on the stage, all I saw were my classmates parents in those seats. Nobody ever came to the auditorium to see me. Hon always acted as though she was too sick on the day of my ceremony to attend. And of course when I would arrive home she would be all healthy and well. "Why didn't you come to my classroom ceremony at the school today, Hon?" And her answer was always the same. "I don't need to go to the damn school to see your dumb ass, I see you here every day bitch!" And sometimes, when I would show Hon my awards, she would burn them with a match right in front of me. "This is what I think of your fucking achievements, now get the fuck out of my face I'm trying watch the TV." I would run to my room and sob, wondering *why am I alive? Why don't I have twenty-twenty vision like the other kids? Why couldn't I have been living with both of my parents instead of her? Why was my life so fucked up?*

I always had a bunch of questions.

Never had any answers.

Sometimes, I still don't.

But not everything was lost to the "fire" in the seventh grade. One thing good came out of being in the seventh grade was my best friend, Patricia. Even to this day I love her to death. I never talked to her about my life living with Hon. She didn't care that I wore cat glasses, or that I brought a lunch pail to school. She looked at my heart and not my appearance. In class she always helped me with my school work if I didn't understand it. We had lunch at the same time. We laughed and talked together. She would stick up for me and verbally defend against other bullies in school. She told me that she wanted us to become friends. At that time, I didn't know what having a friend meant, because I never was allowed to have one. Sometimes we would get re-assigned desks so we could be separated because we talked so much in class. I had found out that she lived one block behind me on Park Street. All of this time she was living there, and I didn't know it because I wasn't allowed to go outside and visit. I loved Patricia. I didn't feel burdened and depressed when I was around her. All of our laughter drowned out all of my sorrow, self-hatred and self-pity.

Initially, I tried to keep my distance and push Patricia away, but still she liked me as a human being. At first I wasn't sure if I could trust her. I doubted that anyone wanted to be friends with me. I hated myself. My self-esteem was shattered. I just existed with the other people in life. I was a loner in school. I didn't respect myself, and I didn't expect for anyone else too. Patricia and I were like long lost sisters who had just found one another. I knew that she would be my friend for life. We were partners in crime, and each other's confidant; or at least I was hers. I didn't talk too much about my life because it was way too depressing and it would have taken all of the joy out of our friendship. She taught me what a friend really was.

I couldn't wait to come home and tell Hon that I had met a girl in my class and that we became quick friends. I wanted to tell her that Patricia lived in the same neighborhood as we did.

"Hello Hon" I said joyfully.

"What the fuck are you so happy for?" Hon asked.

"I have found me a friend at school, and I was just wondering if you would let me go over to her house, or maybe she could come over here?" I asked.

"Come over here right now, bitch" Hon replied.

"Are you going to hit me?" I asked in fear.

"No I'm not going to hit you," Hon said in a calm voice. So like a trusting fool, I walked towards her.

"Yes Hon," I said.

Hon placed her hand on my forehead. "You don't seem to have a fever." Hon retorted.

"No, Mom I feel just fine," I said.

"bitch, I thought that you had a fever and was coming down with pneumonia" Hon said.

"Why would you think that, Hon?" I asked.

"Because you have to have some kind of Dementia, to even form your motherfucking mouth to ask me such a dumb-ass question. Well guess what, bitch? Now I'm going to hit you!" Hon yelled. And then it came, a fist to my mouth.

Again I hit the floor. I was getting fed up with getting knocked down all of the time. She would land blows to my head, mouth and body like she was in a fighting ring and she was fighting for the heavy weight championship belt. And I was the outweighed contender who no one had heard of. And of course, when I got my balance again and I stood up, I had another question for Hon. "Well, Hon if she can't come over can I call her on the telephone?" I asked.

"Why you ignorant ass whore!" Hon then took off her orthopedic shoe and she began to beat me with it. "I pay the fucking bill for that damn phone!" she yelled at me while beating my leg with the shoe. "I will kick you in your fucking eardrum, bitch. I will put my foot so far up in your ass that you will be reading my shoe size." Then she started kicking me as though I was an empty soda can in the middle of the street. "Please stop Hon, I'm sorry!" I pleaded.

"I will pour lye and bleach into your fucking eyes and make you as blind as a bat!" her threats continued. "Fuck you and your new found friend! I don't give a flying fuck about you having a best friend" Hon said. "She better not show her ass up here at my house. I will play target practice with her and shoot her lungs out!" Hon said. "You need to tell that bitch tomorrow that you hate her guts and that the last thing on earth that you want to be is her fucking friend." Hon said.

Well of course Hon was never happy to see me happy. She always had to have the last fucked up word. That night I wasn't fed any dinner, nor did she let me have any water. "Take your 'I have a best friend' ass down to the fucking basement bitch." Hon ordered. I walked slowly down the stairs to the basement. This time Hon did not follow me. Instead she left the basement door cracked as she fixed smothered pork chops with mash potatoes. I smelled the aroma of the pork chops that made my poor little stomach growl even louder with hunger. "Come upstairs dinner is ready!" Hon said. I rushed up the stairs, ran to the bathroom and washed my hands. Then I returned to the kitchen table and took a seat.

I saw Hon with the huge plate of three pork chops and a big scoop of mashed potatoes dripping in brown gravy. I began to salivate at the sight. "bitch, what are you staring at? This is my plate!" Hon declared.

"The food looks delicious that's all …" I replied back. "You said that dinner was ready," I stated.

"Yes I did say that, *my* dinner was ready," Hon laughed. And she made me sit there at the table while she ate every bit. "Can I have some water? I asked. "Hell no you bitch. But I would be glad to give you a glass of dog piss to wash down your empty belly."

She laughed and chuckled as she gobbled down her dinner.

"Well that was a damn good meal," Hon said. "Now take your horse fucked ass back down to the basement."

"Why did you ask me to come upstairs?" I asked Hon, with tears streaming from my eyes.

"So you could watch me eat, bitch! Any more questions?" Hon asked.

"No ma'am," I said.

"Well then get before I slam your big ass head into the concrete floor. "Good night, bitch" Hon added. Then she slammed the basement door and locked it. I sat in the rocker calling Hon every bad name that I could think of. I loathed every breath that she took. I had wished that my friend Patricia was here so we could have jumped on Hon together. But as usual I had no one to defend me. My reality was that I was alone when it came to Hon, but I was determined not to let Hon take my best friend away from me.

Chapter 18

A Girl, A Boy, A Man, A Rape

It was spring 1974 and the sounds of nature were synched like a Philharmonic Orchestra. The birds were chirping in harmony like a church choir, and the aroma of the freshly bloomed flowers filled the air like a Botanical Garden. The trees were coming back to life again and everything was reborn. The colors of spring were so vivid and vibrant that it always took my breath away.

This was going to be my year. I was thirteen years old and entering the eighth grade. I had already made up my mind that this was going to be my year. I would no longer be Hon's doormat. I was going to stand up for myself and not be shy and compliant with things I didn't like. Well, at least that's what I told myself. Daily, I tried to convince myself to be strong instead of weak. Once I reached junior high school, I was mandated to attend a new school, which was located across town. My previous school only went up to the seventh grade, and Hon had received a letter in the mail about the transfer to a new school because the city wanted more black students to become diversified and attend school

124

with whites and other ethnicities. I was so excited about attending this school. The campus was huge and there were no elementary school age kids there. The new school had its own school bus, which was "hella good news" for me, and I no longer had to worry about driving to and from with the Wicked Witch of the Midwest. This gave me a much coveted sense of new-found freedom and independence from hanging off Hon's right hip all of the time. The bus stop was only two blocks away from my house, and the icing on the cake was my best friend, Patricia, had been transferred to the same school so we could walk and ride together.

For the most part, everything was status quo. Life appeared to be "normal" or as normal as it had always been. Somehow I always believed our normal was a little different than most as far as normal goes. But within the usual and customary events of the day, for about a good month, I had begun to notice that Hon's memory was failing like a frazzled piece of torn cloth. I observed that her "gap in memory" was putting her in a vulnerable, borderline helpless position. For example, she would forget to do the dishes, and as a result, they stayed in the sink until the next morning. This was unheard of, Hon *always* did the dishes. And there was a cardinal rule in the house—I was not allowed to touch the dishes, otherwise, I would have just washed them myself. I also began to observe that she began misplacing her money. "Interesting," I would say to myself. She would forget which purse her wallet was in and spent hours searching for it, looking through the same purse over and over again.

In observation of this absurdity, I pounced at the opportunity to take advantage of the situation, almost like a kitten playing with a ball of yarn. Daily, I built courage to take advantage of the newly discovered weakness. As I contemplated and with the growing challenges of each new day, my nerves became raw and unstable, therefore, I returned to my vice of cigarettes. By now, I was up to two packs a day, so I began asking Hon for twenty dollars a week so I could afford my habits of cigarettes and store bought snacks. But the trick was, she didn't know she was supporting my habit. I had it down to a science and each week I would begin my morning with the same old hustling story, "Good morning, Hon."

"What the fuck is so good about it, bitch?" Hon asked.

"I have to pay my membership fees for the junior cadet training," I informed her. *Now, of course there was no junior cadet training!* You and I know that, dear reader, but Hon didn't know that!

"Oh yes, I remember," Hon said enthusiastically. "Let me get you the twenty dollars, so you can pay Officer Johnson," Hon said. Hon had this bizarre reverence and affection for the Kansas City Police Department; therefore, I had an easy time convincing Hon to give money whenever the police were involved. I would take my twenty and be set for the week. But within a short amount of time at my new school, I grew bored and restless attending my classes, especially when I learned that I had to take Algebra. I hated math. I had a terrible block with numbers, remembering that some of my worst beatings came as a result of my failure with timetables and the struggle to learn the State Capitols. Given that, they could keep geography too, I wasn't interested in either.

My favorite class was gym. In gym class I could relax for forty-five minutes, and the bonus: no homework! My other favorite was our weekly assemblies, where the band would get on stage and play. We all cheered, yelled and caught the vibe of team-spirit. I loved that! However, aside from gym and the assemblies, my boredom with school was growing thicker than meringue on lemon pie. So one day, I got a bright idea. I would get up as usual, let Hon dress me for school, meet my friend Patricia, catch the bus to school, then slip out of the building and ditch. There was a small park at the side of the junior high school, and a post office in a woody hillside across the street. So, I just relaxed outside smoking cigarettes and just chilling until school was over. It was sort of a mini-vacation. But I always made sure that I attended gym and English class. Those were my best classes, I liked them both and besides, I was very good in English.

At day's end, I would then catch the school bus back home and everything was sweet. I began this ritual three times a week; and I was surprised to discover no one said anything to me nor did Hon receive any calls.

Sweet!

One clear, sunny day, while I was sitting on a park bench, smoking my cigarette, I happened to look up and sitting across from me about two park benches away, was this older young man looking back at me with a wide alligator smile, showing all of his pearly whites. I shyly smiled back at him and then I got up from the bench and went back to school to attend my English class. Soon, I began to notice this boy was out in the park on every day that I ditched—three times a week. I never approached him, nor did he approach me. We just sat on our benches making eye contact with each other and throwing a wave of our hands at each other every now and then. Then one day I didn't see him sitting at his usual spot in the park. For some sort of reason I began to miss the fact that he wasn't there. *Did I have a crush on this boy?* I wondered. Hmmm … after all he was a tall boy with a sleek muscular body, a nice chiseled dark face with a short afro, and a slight mustache. Yes, he had caught my eye. I caught myself ditching class in hopes of seeing him out there. Then out of nowhere I happened to look behind me and there was my school girl crush. He placed his hands on my shoulder, bent down and whispered into my ear.

"Hello there beautiful!" he crooned into my ear.

I was instantly caught off guard. I had a brain freeze for a moment and could not speak. No one had ever called me *beautiful* before. I wasn't sure if he was speaking about me. "Hello" I replied back. My heart was racing like it had done many times before with Hon, but this time it didn't race out of fear, it raced because I liked this boy. So he sat down on the bench next to me and cut right to the chase. "Do you have a boyfriend? He asked. "No, I am way too young to have a boyfriend," I blushingly replied back. "No, you're not," he replied. "I would like to be your boyfriend. In fact I would like to kiss you," he said with a lot of charisma and charm. My heart was melting faster than butter on hot toast. "I would sure like to be alone with you so we could talk and kiss without everybody watching us," he suggested. "I guess I could take a walk with you," I said in a girly voice.

As I got up off the bench and followed him, I remember that there was a steady breeze in the air. Hon had dressed me in a burgundy skirt and a white blouse with burgundy strapped leather shoes. I remembered this because I was wondering how I looked to *him*. And of course Hon had made me wear this fake, white rabbit waist length jacket with a brown furry collar. I looked and felt like Pam Grier in the movie Foxy Brown, or even Get Christie Love in the TV series. So, here I was walking from the park hand in hand with the strange boy who had exchanged smiles back and forth for weeks. He decided to take me to the wooded area of the post office. As we walked, all of a sudden a bad vibe rushed through my body like a possessed kindred spirit. Immediately, I let go of his hand and hurried back down the hill until I reached the sidewalk. I looked back and saw that he was running behind me. When I stood on the sidewalk, I noticed the bad feeling I had felt in my gut was gone, and I was relieved. When the young man caught up with me he said. "What's wrong? "What's the matter? Why did you leave me back there?" He asked with concern in his voice.

"I got really scared about being in that area with you alone" I replied. "You don't have to be afraid of me, it's not like I'm going to hurt you," he said in a reassuring voice. I guess that I was waiting for him to disarm the bad vibe that I was feeling about him and he did. I felt that the threat was gone. So again he grabbed my hand and gave me a soft kiss on my forehead. And we walked hand in hand back to the wooded area of the post office. We found a big rock to sit on alongside a dirt pathway; and again he kissed me, but only this time it was on my lips. He then took his hand and reached over to take my glasses off of my face. He then placed them down on the dirt beside me. "It's better to kiss you without your glasses on," he said. I enjoyed kissing him that day, but as we kissed on the rock, I began to hear footsteps in front of me in the grassy knolls of the wooded area. At that moment I had stopped kissing him, "What is that?" I asked. "Somebody is coming … I hope that it's not the police coming to talk to me about ditching class," I said. "Oh girl you worry too much," he said. "I don't hear a thing. Let's get back to kissing." So again I did as I was told, and shortly after we began to kiss again, I heard the footsteps louder and closer; and when I turned my head and opened my eyes, I saw him there … another man. But this man was even older than the boy that I was kissing. I rose up and looked over my friend's should to see this older man running towards us. "Who are you? I asked. "Just shut up!" the older guy ordered.

"What's going on here? I asked. I began to get scared and I could feel my chest closing up and I began to hyperventilate. I felt threatened, and then I blacked out. When I came to, I was alone again and my glasses were on the ground beside me. When I found them I wiped the dirt off of them and put them back on. I knew that I had to leave that area soon, just in case if the two guys returned. My blouse, coat and skirt now had dirt all over it. That day I was wearing my Mickey Mouse watch and when I looked down at it, I saw that it was nearly the time for the school bus to arrive to take us home. I knew that I had to pull myself together before I reached that bus. I had to put my game face on and act as though I was all right, but I wasn't.

But on this day and by the time I reached the bottom of the hill, I looked across the street and I saw the students and the school buses lined up to take us home. I ran across the street, and as I approached the bus I heard a voice in the background say. "Hey Mary! I was looking all over the school for you." It was my friend Patricia.

"Oh I guessed that, I beat you out here," I replied.

"What happened to you? Why is your hair all messed up and your coat so dirty?" Patricia asked me.

"Oh, I was in a fight with another girl" I lied. Patricia began wiping off the dirt from my skirt and coat. "Really? Did you win?" Patricia asked.

"Of course I did," I said playing it off. "It must have been a big fight because you have a bruise on the side of your face," Patricia pointed out to me.

"Oh really I didn't even realize that she had hit me in the face," I said trying not to get to close to Patricia when I talked. The other students were staring at me because of the way that I was looking, but I couldn't really blame them. My hair was all over my head, my clothes were dirty and I just looked like a complete mess. But it didn't bother Patricia, she never judged me. And we laughed and talked as usual on our bus ride home. In fact she made me forget how painful I felt inside. But don't get it twisted, throughout the entire bus ride home and between every beat of laughter and line, I had one thing and one thing only my mind: *how in the hell was I going to explain this to Hon?*

Chapter 19

A Bizarre Omen

The day was wet and damp, and the sun was nowhere to be found. The shine was hiding from the world as if it was taking a break from Kansas City. The air was fresh, but the clouds hovered over our neighborhood like a magical mist of fog sent by a leprechaun. I had put the rape behind me as best I could. No truer words were ever spoken than those that remind us, "Life goes on." I still didn't have a *real* social life, and was in no position to nurture a budding friendship with anyone. While at school and on the bus, I would overhear the conversation of fellow students sharing stories about shopping trips with their parents and the privilege of picking out their own clothes.

"I wish I could do that," I would say to myself.

I entertained the idea long enough until I had the notion to make it a part of my reality. So, one afternoon, I ditched school with a girl I knew from class (not Patricia), and we caught the bus downtown so she could go shopping. I was deeply intrigued about our outing. I watched in a strange and bizarre fascination as she hand-picked personal items and then plopped down *real* money on the counter to pay for them. I was riveted by the simple transaction. I felt like I was taking a tour of a "futuristic museum" and much less like I was in the midst of normal activities that regular folks do every day. I had never had such an experience in my life and couldn't help but ponder, "What does it feel like to buy your own clothing?"

"How did you get the money to go shopping" I finally had to ask.

"Oh, I saved up three weeks of my allowance," she said without skipping a beat

"What's an allowance?" I asked with a glaze in my eye as though I'd grown up in the back woods and out of civilization.

"Oh it's the money that my mom and dad pay me to do chores around the house," she said.

"Cool" I said. "How much did you save up?"

"A hundred dollars," she said again without batting an eye.

A hundred dollars!

Holy hell!

Now that was some money!

My friend was nice enough to by me an outfit and she treated me to a restaurant called McDonald's. I had seen the "golden arches" many times in my life as I rode in the back of Hon's Bat Mobile, but I had never eaten there. Hon didn't believe in "fast" food. She said if food wasn't cooked "long" then it just wasn't right. So fast food was out of the question. Again, I felt like I was new to civilization as I took my first bite of a fast food hamburger. The taste was distinct, delicious and instantly addictive. I enjoyed it immensely. In fact, I cherished the entire afternoon with my friend. I felt so much freedom and an independence which surrounded me like a waffle cone surrounds ice cream. I was out and about in the world eating fast food and living it up. No one even asked us if we had parents. They just let us shop and shop till the money was gone.

"Thanks for inviting me to go shopping with you, and for the new outfit," I said smiling proudly. "Next time I will treat you!" I promised with confidence in my voice. During our outing, I had caught snatches of authentic happiness. At least this was the closest to "happy" that I had ever felt. I had almost forgotten that Hon even existed. She was the *last* thing on my mind that afternoon.

After we finished shopping, my friend and I caught the bus back to school, so we could catch the school bus and return home. I was lost in a daydream of how much fun the day had been. Now all I had to do was explain this new outfit in the shiny bag to the old battle axe.

Big sigh.

On the school bus I saw my best friend Patricia, and I eagerly shared with her my adventures of the day. Of course, Pat scolded me, but her scolding didn't matter. Nothing could bring me down. When the bus arrived and I headed home, I contemplated what elaborate tale I could share with Hon about how I acquired these new clothes.

Hmmmm.

The police department worked for everything else, so I decided to give that another go. As I approached the steps to my house, I practiced repeating my lie over and over, as if I was at play rehearsal. I took a deep breath, knocked on the door and waited for Hon to answer it. Hon finally showed up at the door. "Hello Hon, guess what happened to me today?"

"What? Hon shot back. I took another deep breath and side-stepped her low blows and insensitive comments. "No Hon," I said. "Look what the policeman gave me as a gift …" I said displaying the bag proudly. "It's a new outfit. He said that I will have to wear it sometimes when I go on stakeouts after school."

"Oh okay," Hon slowly responded. "I don't want to see the damn outfit," she scolded as I tried to pull it from my bag. "I'm sure that if the police bought it for you then you must have needed it."

I just stood there with a noticeable look of disbelief on my face.

Oh my God! Was she really that gullible? Hmmmm. was it that easy to fool her?

The more I observed, the more I saw her mind weakening. This was another case and point, and on this day I made a very strong mental note that Hon's mind was in fact, deteriorating. With each passing day, Hon became more forgetful and was also complaining of being a lot more tired than usual. Although I didn't know exactly what was happening to her, I could see that her health was failing. My day of reckoning would soon arrive.

Given that Hon fell for that story with such ease, I contemplated another story so that I could get my own money to go shopping. All I needed was a good lie. In that moment, I remember that one night I was watching TV with Hon when I saw my idea right in front of me on the screen. This show was having a fundraiser, and that's what caught my eye. I knew that Hon would support a fundraiser, especially if it involved her favorite people: The Kansas City Police Department. *Yes, of course that would work.* I had it all planned inside of my little head, all three steps. All I have to do is 1. Put the lie in motion; 2. Put a price on it; and 3. Let Hon provide the outcome.

I waited until the next day after school and upon entering the house it was show time. "Hey Hon I saw the policeman today at school," I said enthusiastically.

"Oh really?" she inquired curiously. "What was he doing at the school?"

"Oh, he wanted me to ask you if you would participate in a police fundraiser event. He said that the event will cost a hundred dollars."

"Sure" she said without hesitation. "I'll give you the money in the morning. Just remind me okay?"

"Yes," I quickly responded.

"Where will the fundraiser be held at?" Hon asked.

I thought that Hon was asking for more details than usual, but of course I thought up another lie real quick so she would not get suspicious of me. "Oh, it will be held at Swope Park!" I answered. I knew that Hon was really familiar with Swope Park, because she had taken me there on various occasions to fish and have picnics at Wyandotte Lake.

"Okay," she said without further inquiry.

I could hardly believe and was thrilled that I had just convinced Hon to give me a hundred dollars! That was the most money that I'd ever swindled out of Hon. Throughout dinner, I was just imagining all of the clothes and records that I would buy tomorrow. That means another "ditch day" from school. I had to make sure that I explained that to

Hon, too, just in case the school called about my absences. Now, they had never called before, but I didn't want to take any chances and mess this good thing up!

"Oh Hon, I meant to tell you earlier that Officer Johnson wants me to get fitted for some clothes tomorrow morning, so I can do undercover surveillance with him soon," I mentioned casually over dinner. "He said to tell you that I will have to miss a day of school," I said proudly.

"Okay," she said without a problem. "Just as long as you are with the police, helping to end crime I don't mind."

"And if the school should call just tell them that I'm sick, because this is top secret work I'm doing for the police," I said. "Only me, you and the police are aware of my work with them," I explained to Hon.

"Oh okay ..." Hon agreed. "I'll tell the school that you're sick," Hon repeated back.

Holy Moly!

It couldn't get any better than this!

Soon I will be riding the bus downtown to Montgomery Ward's to shop for clothes that I like. Yippee, let the shopping spree begin. I could barely contain my excitement and couldn't wait for morning to come. I went to sleep that night dreaming about my financial up-rise. The morning came and the sun seemed to be more radiant and bright than other days. I felt good this morning. Hon's daily protective custody issues didn't bother me today. She bathed me, dressed me and fed me. "Oh Hon I'm about to leave, can I get that hundred dollars?" I asked.

"Sure, just let me get my purse," she said. Hon disappeared into the bedroom and came back with her large black pocketbook. She then retrieved her matching black wallet and handed me a crisp one hundred dollar bill without hesitation. That was the first time that I had seen a hundred dollar bill. I went out the door and on my way to a shopping adventure.

When I arrived downtown, I hurried inside to Montgomery Ward's. I bought a few outfits, shirts, blouses, skirts and pants. And then I headed out to checkout JC Penny's. I shopped there for a little while. I got socks, shoes and more pants and blouses. I bought underwear and some sweat suits. I was balling. When I was finished shopping, I got hungry so I went to McDonald's to grab a bite to eat. I ordered a Big Mac, large fries and a strawberry shake, things that Hon would never allow me to have. I was full as a pig eating slop. I had a lot of bags and they were getting heavy to carry, so I decided that it would be best if I started to head back home. I was very proud of myself. I had all of the latest fashions. I went home and I unloaded all of my bags onto my bed. I told Hon that I had to put on one of my new outfits. Hon didn't even turn around to look at me. I hurriedly changed my clothes and showed them off to Hon like I was a runway model in Paris. Hon just shook her head and continued to go on about her business, cleaning up the house.

Meanwhile, I went to the living room and sat down in front of the TV to relax and enjoy my new clothes. I noticed that whenever I talked to Hon about doing work for the police, I never received a whipping from her. I thought that I might be onto something that could possibly make her stop the beatings. Well, at this moment everything was pleasant and calm. That night was also another uneventful, no stress night, the kind that I liked. *Thank You God,* I prayed.

The next morning arrived, and I got up early. I waited for Hon to finish running my bath water and when she did, I told her that Officer Johnson had requested that I wear one of my new outfits. Hon frowned but did not say a word nor did she try to interfere. I was so glad. After I had finished dressing myself, yes that's right! I was able to dress myself for once!!! Hon did not want to be bothered with my new clothes so she allowed me to be in charge of that. I could see that my mounting lies had given me some independence, which I enjoyed in magnitude. I completed the school week without further incident. Dare I say that I had created my own heaven, right smack dab in the middle of hell?

When the weekend rolled around, I remembered that I had promised Patricia I would call her to see how she was doing. I knew that I couldn't ask Hon to use her telephone, but thought I could "sneak a quick call" while she was in the other room changing our bed sheets. So, I walked quietly to the dining room, sat down at the sewing machine desk and I pulled out Patricia's phone number from my pocket. I dialed the number and when Patricia answered the phone, I started whispering into the receiver. Our conversation couldn't have been more than two or three minutes, but just before I could say goodbye, I heard the slapping of Hon's thighs race from the bedroom to the living room. She caught me talking on the telephone. Hell was about to be re-birthed on earth. "What the fuck are you doing talking on my goddamn telephone, bitch?" Hon screamed at me at the top of her lungs.

Then as Hon drew closer, she grabbed a hold of the phone and tried to get it out of my hands. But I wouldn't let it go and we fought a violent battle of uncivilized tug-of-war.

I wasn't about to let go and neither was she. She snatched the phone and hit me in the head with it! In that instance, I erupted into an emotional explosion of anger, fear and embarrassment. I just knew that Patricia had heard all of Hon's yelling and screaming. I jumped up from my chair and stood eye-to-eye with Hon. I completely black out for a moment and before I knew what had happened, I cold-cocked Hon dead in the mouth with the telephone receiver!

Oh shit!

Hon's eyes widened in sheer horror and disbelief. She couldn't believe that I had hit her. And truth be told, I couldn't believe it either. I watched as her bottom lip swelled and blood began to trickle down the side of her mouth. "Bitch, I know that you just didn't hit me with the telephone!" Hon screamed. "I will kill you where you stand!" Hon shouted at me. She immediately disappeared into the bedroom to retrieve some sort of weapon. I was used to that. The only difference this time was that I was *prepared* to fight back with my own choice of weaponry.

I immediately hung up the phone and ran straight to the kitchen and grabbed the broom to arm myself. I went back to the dining room where I took a stance like a Power Ranger, waiting on Hon's return. ***This time I was going to stand up for myself.*** Do or die, I was ready to battle. I felt a surge of adrenaline rush to my head and my heart. I felt as though I were about to stroke out or have a major cardiac arrest, but if I was going down, then I was going down fighting! I waited for Hon in a warrior's pose, as if I was a Roman Emperor waiting for a joust. Moments later, Hon returned from out of the bedroom. When she entered the dining room, I noticed that she had nothing in her hands.

What?

What?

No weapon?

Was this a mind game?

"What the fuck are you doing with the broom?" she asked slightly curious, but was disarmed of the anger I had witnessed just moments prior. "Are you about to sweep the dining room carpet without me having to tell you to? Well I'll be damned" she laughed. "I guess I have taught you something!" Hon declared proudly.

I stared at her with the most profound look of confusion.

"Well bitch, start sweeping!" Hon barked. "But you're still a dumb ass!" she added.

Are you kidding me? I asked myself.

This can't be happening.

Hon has short-term memory loss, Dementia for real.

"Oh yeah," I stammered in disbelief. "Sweep the carpet, that's what I was getting ready to do." Instantly, I felt the raw emotion of victory. It was a bizarre omen. My soul had been set free. And I knew in that moment that Hon would never, ever, ever beat, torment, torture or hurt me again.

Ever.

Chapter 20

Payback a Bitch for Real

My head was still swimming from the night before. I couldn't get over the fact that I had actually hit Hon in the mouth and she forgot about it within two minutes. After the incident, I began feeling myself. *I'm invincible,* I thought. *She's weak. I can do whatever the hell I want now.* I was feeling larger than life. Everything had changed overnight. One pop to Hon's mouth and you couldn't tell me anything. My confidence was raging on ten, and I started feeling like I was grown, at least half-grown anyways. So, what do all adults need? Money. More money. I had been nickel and diming Hon for a while, but now I wanted some big money. So, I began to devise more creative ways to get more dough. One lie in particular put me over the top, and when Hon was least expecting, I dropped it on her like a bomb.

"Hon!" I said enthusiastically. "Officer Johnson has chosen me to become a junior police cadet! I need five hundred dollars a month to pay for my tuition."

"Wow!" Hon exclaimed in shock. "Officer Johnson has chosen *you* to become a police cadet! I know you must be doing something right in order to be asked to join the police!" Hon agreed, co-signing my lie.

"Yes!" I quickly agreed grinning ear to ear.

"Five hundred dollars isn't bad," she said thinking it over. "I'll give you the money to give to Officer Johnson in the morning," Hon said.

Shazam!

That's how it's done ladies and gentlemen, and just like that I was $500 richer every month.

During this elaborate tale of my "secret life" as a cadet with the police, Hon never so much as made one phone call to the school to verify that he was recruiting students to become cadets. In addition, she never called the local police station to see if there was an Officer Johnson who worked there. The dynamics of our relationship were changing and changing fast. For example, one afternoon when I arrived home Hon said. "This house needs to be scrubbed the fuck down, and I suggest that you start cleaning this house up, bitch!"

"That's not my fucking problem," I countered, "and if you want the house to be cleaned up then you need to do it!" I snapped back.

None of these moments were met with violence by Hon. She surrendered her position in the wake of my rising power. There were other uniquely emerging moments such as the night she waited up late for me to come home and when I did I was met with her ugly stare. "Bitch, I'm not running no goddamn brothel! Why are you coming in so fucking late at night?"

"I was on a fucking stakeout!" I shouted back in equal volume. "I was working so just leave me the fuck alone!"

By now and at age 13, I was doing whatever the hell I wanted to do. I was buying clothes, snacks and jewelry. I was pushing the boundaries on all levels. I remember the priceless expression on Hon's face the very first time that I used her telephone to call my friend. Hon had this evil, diabolical scowl on her face. If her face was a knife, I would have gotten cut. After I finished my call, she just sat in silence and disbelief at the dining room table. I think she knew that she had been defeated. But I didn't care. I didn't care about anything. I absolutely *loved* spending Hon's money. I had no budget and no real sense of the value of money. I spent the money so carefree that it was going through my hands like water. I hid the money in a sock and I unzipped the back of my teddy bear and stuffed the cash there. I had to because if Hon had ever found her money on me—funeral arrangements would have been made because I'd be dead.

Interestingly, during this time my emotions were raw and numb from all of the years of abuse. When I did attend school I was buying my classmates lunch or giving them twenty dollars just for the hell of it. I repaid the girl who took me shopping by taking her on a shopping spree. You would have thought that I was a millionaire by the way I was spending Hon's money.

When I had money I noticed that I had more friends; and when I was broke those same friends disappeared or became distant. I wanted friends so I had to find a way to get more money from Hon. Money had become my power over Hon, and it was the key that opened many doors to friendship both good and bad. I had longed for friendship so many times in my life. Money was my driving force—it had become my crutch and my drug. I was beginning to become popular because of my connection with money, so I needed it. I was tired of being lonely and secluded in my house. I gained friends who drank alcohol and smoked marijuana. I got into *that* kind of crowd. I re-visited Vera, my old beer drinking, cigarette smoking friend, more often. I stayed out late at night playing with my friends in the neighborhood and using curse words to express myself. And all of this new found freedom and independence was done in the name of the law, yes Kansas City's finest. Officer Johnson was to thank for my new rebel attitude. I went hardcore wild.

Although I didn't attend much of my classes in the eighth grade, I was still passed onto the ninth grade. At fourteen, Patricia and I were both transferred to a new junior high school that was further away than the previous school. For some odd reason, I didn't like that school. I always would ditch and act up. I got brand new radios that I had bought with Hon's money taken away from me by some school bullies, but I didn't care, because all I would do is buy a bigger and better on the following week. I wanted to put out the message that no one could stop my flow. I had anger issues and didn't tolerate much. I was very protective of my new found freedom.

When I grew bored of drawing the five hundred dollars per month (which was a hell of a lot of money back then), I raised the stakes. I knew that eventually Hon would start asking about a "graduation date" from the Academy, so I decided to beat her to the punch. I came home one day after school and I told Hon. "Hey Hon guess what?"

"Why in the fuck are you calling out my name?" Hon inquired.

"The junior police academy cadets are having a graduation ceremony, and I'm one of the top ten cadets who will be graduating the junior academy with honors," I lied proudly.

"Well ain't that a turd going down the toilet!" Hon laughed and said. I had no idea what she meant by that statement. "Damn Bitch you accomplished something, I would have never expected that the police wanted your dumb-ass in the first place to join their cadets program," Hon said sarcastically.

"Well, I'm going to need one thousand dollars to pay for the ceremony," I informed her.

"Fuck!" she shouted. "Can't you get your diploma the next day without attending the ceremony?" Hon asked.

"No, it doesn't work that way,"

"Yeah I guess not," she reluctantly agreed. "I'll give you the money tomorrow morning," Hon said. She wasn't thrilled about the money but she was excited about the graduation. *Interesting,* I thought to myself. Hon was finally excited about something that I did—even though it was a damn lie. "Where will the ceremony be held at? And at what time?" she pressed. "I surely want to attend that!" she volunteered.

"Oh, you're not invited and you will not be attending this graduation," I said strongly.

"Why the fuck not?" Hon asked.

"You never wanted to attend any of my academic awards ceremony, so why should you attend this?" I asked.

"If I don't attend then I'll be damn if I pay for that motherfucking ceremony!" Hon snarled back.

"Well," I mulled it over. "I'll have to ask Officer Johnson first and see what his decision is " I replied.

"I don't give a fuck who you have to ask I just better be invited!" Hon said angrily.

Now I pondered on what to do about Hon's wanting to attend this fake ceremony. Hmmmm ... I definitely wanted the money without having to patronize her. "Hon, will you allow me to make an important government phone call on your phone to the KCPD so I can speak to Officer Johnson?" I asked sincerely meaning to screw with her head.

"Yeah ... I guess you can only if you're calling Officer Johnson," she replied.

"You can't be in the same room with me while I'm talking to him!" I ordered. "You will need to go in your room in order for me to make this call," I demanded.

"Fuck!" Hon shouted.

"I have to leave my living room," Hon said.

"Yes you do!" Hon bitched and moaned, but she carried her fat ass to her bedroom. I went to the telephone and I held the disconnect button down, while I pretended to be talking to Officer Johnson. I was praying and hoping that none of Hon's friends would call her at that exact moment and cause the phone to ring, and blow my lie out of the water just like a torpedo blowing up a ship. I had talked loud enough so Hon could hear what I was saying in the other room. "Okay Officer Johnson my mother can attend the ceremony, boy she will be glad to hear that" I said. "Ok well thank you so much Officer Johnson goodbye!" I played it off like I really just had a conversation with an Officer Johnson. Hon came back to the living room area and she sat down on the couch and asked naively, "Well, what did Officer Johnson say?"

as if she had not overheard a single word I'd said. I played along. "Officer Johnson decided that you can attend the ceremony."

"Great! I've never been in a room full of dedicated police officers! I'll have to buy myself a new dress for the occasion!" she squealed. Hon was excited for the rest of that evening, and all I heard her say was, "Finally the Bitch has done something that I can be proud of!"

She bragged to her friends and neighbors that she was going to be the best dressed woman at the ceremony. *Not if I can help it,* I thought to myself. "I might just splurge on myself and buy some new shoes too!!" Hon said. If only she knew that there wasn't any ceremony. After I got off the phone, Hon came rushing back into the living room and said. "Did Officer Johnson say what date it is going to be held on? And where will it be at? And what time?"

"Stop with all of the goddamn questions!" I shouted back at her. "He has my number he will let me know" I replied. Hon gave me an evil stare and then she returned to her bedroom like a scolded child, similar to the way that I used to return to my room, broken and disheartened. A week had passed and I hadn't mentioned the graduation, but I had say something soon because Hon was looking for an answer to the questions she had asked last week. Now she would forget to send a bill off, but she sure didn't forget the graduation. I came home one afternoon from school and let myself into the house; because I told her that I needed to have a key just in case I arrived home late in the wee hours from a drug bust. I called out to Hon.

"Hon, are you home? I have some good news for you!" I yelled. Soon, she came into the living room. "Now that was a retarded question to ask me, bitch" Hon replied. "Where else in the fuck would I be if I wasn't here?" Hon asked. I ignored her smart ass remarks and said.

"Officer Johnson came to the school and he said that the graduation will be held next month at the Kemper Arena," I said in one lying breath. "It will be at 8 p.m. in two weeks. Okay?"

"Fuck yeah, I'll be there!" Hon laughed.

The next evening Hon handed me one thousand dollars in my cash. Now I was the one who was jumping up and down like a caged test animal just being released. I had a thousand dollars in my hand! *It's time to go shopping with Mary.* That was the title of the imaginary game show in my head. I stayed over at friend's houses and got *wasted (official police business, of course).* I got up the next morning just in time to go back to Hon's and take a bath on my own and change my clothes. It was time to shop again. Hon never got any wiser to the scam which meant I could do as I pleased.

The day of reckoning arrived sooner than later. It was the day of my fake graduation. I sat back and watch Hon dote on herself for this occasion. She even spent money on getting her hair curled. She bought herself a new dress and a new pair of shoes. She spent hours in front of the mirror trying to doll herself up. I don't know if she was trying to look for another husband who was a policeman or what, but she made a big deal out of this graduation. It was the first time that I had even seen her have emotions of happiness without causing pain to me. That's not to say, this entire incident was completely without regret. I had weak moments in which I actually felt sorry for her and felt bad about lying to her about the graduation. But only until I shouted in my own damn ear, "Fuck that! Get this Bitch back!" And then I regained my revenge strategy. I watched as Hon pranced around the house all privy like she was a Kennedy.

I, too, had bought myself a real nice hip dress with new shoes so that the lie could appear to be authentic. I told Hon, "I need to make an official police business phone call to Officer Johnson, so you know the drill … go to your room."

Hon went off into her bedroom like a dog with his tail in between his legs. But this time, instead of a fake call to Officer Johnson, I made a real call to a taxi cab company. When the cab arrived at the house, I called out to Hon, "Are you ready? The taxi is here to take us to the ceremony," I summoned.

"Okay," she said eagerly. "Here I come." As she fussed with her last bit of make-up and perfume, I just made sure I had my money. I allowed Hon to exit the house before me and I made sure that the front door was unlocked when we left out. But since I walked faster than Hon did, I quickly scooted past her and jumped into the cab. When Hon got close enough to the taxi door, I looked into her eyes with the rage of fire and quickly locked the door and yelled at the driver, "GO! GO!" He stepped on the gas and as the cab sped away, I rolled down the window and screamed, "Fuck You! You ain't going any motherfucking where with me, bitch! How do You like being disappointed!!!!" She stood on the sidewalk with shock and horror tattooed into her expression. Utterly devastated, she faded away into non-existence the second we turned the corner.

I sat back in my seat.

Smiled.

And went to the movies instead on Hon's dime.

Payback is a bitch for real.

Chapter 21

On the Rise

Needless to say I didn't return home that night. I stayed at a friend's in order to avoid the wrath of Hon. When I did return the next day, I had already bought me a new outfit and changed clothes so Hon wouldn't be reminded of the ceremony that she didn't get to attend. Interestingly, I felt really good about what I had done to her. I wanted her to feel some of those anguish and unloved feelings that she had made me feel as a child. I enjoyed the sick pleasure of getting her hopes up high and then delivering a devastating blow like a wrestler on the WWE.

When I walked into the door the next afternoon, I found Hon crying at the dining room table. That alone reveals just how much our roles had changed. I boldly walked right past her without uttering one word. I felt nothing for her tears. My heart was cold and black, remembering all of the times she had violently abused me and made me cry. All of the cruelty she dealt was being returned in appropriate measure. An again, I felt nothing. No compassion. No mercy; nothing but a certain hatred for her. I went into the bathroom, took a bath, brushed my teeth and combed my hair. Long gone were the days of asking permission to do every little thing—from getting a glass of water or even taking a dump. It felt so good to finally be able to do those things for myself. When I had finished bathing, I was prepared to leave again. Hon finally rose up from the dining room table and asked me, "Don't you even want to know why I'm crying?"

"Not necessarily," I replied callously.

"Bitch, you didn't let me go to the graduation ceremony!" Hon yelled with a fierceness. These days, she vacillated between helpless and rage-filled, both personalities struggling for their rightful place within her.

"First of all," I said pushing out my chest, "My name is *Mary* and not Bitch. And second of all, what the hell are you talking about!!" I shouted. "You *did* go to the ceremony!" I pushed out the words with power, feeling myself to the point of almost pushing-up on her. This was about establishing dominance,. I had to be strong, in control, in command. I could never let Hon see me flinch. As a junior police cadet, I was rising in power, and I had to keep the illusion going until I reigned supreme in that house. I had to bring Hon to her knees.

"What do you mean that I went?" Hon stumbled over the question, deep confusion etched into her face.

"You really need to go see a doctor about your memory lapses!" I chastised her with pleasure, playing out my role like a mystic, voodoo witch doctor … messing with her head and taking her weaknesses and turning them against her to level her to the ground. "You sat right there next to me, and you even met and spoke with Officer Johnson!" I said without skipping a beat.

"I did?" Hon answered with astonishment in her voice.

"Yes you did!" I snapped. "Now if that is all I need to head out ... I have some police work to do today," I said void of emotion.

"Oh ok then," she replied in a fog of confusion, "Don't tell Officer Johnson that I forgot that I attended the ceremony, ok?"

"Yeah I won't," I said without emotion. I walked boldly out the door to my friend Vera's and Robin's house. It was time to celebrate the new me.

After spending half of the day partying with my two friends, I came back home to go to bed because I was wasted. I entered the house and there was Hon sitting on the sofa watching TV.

"Wait one goddamn minute," she shouted as I walked past her. "Why do you smell like alcohol?" Hon asked. Now being drunk and questioned at the same time, began to irritate me, so I gave Hon a smart ass answer back. "Because I have been drinking, you fat ass Bitch!!" I said. "I was undercover so I had to act like a drunk!" I added.

"So where are you going?" Hon said. "To bed if you would fucking let me!" I shouted. And with that Hon retreated and went back to watching TV. I was in awe of the changing tide and was loving my new role of power and her new role of weakness. That evening, I was dead to the world and was out like a light.

The next morning I did have a humongous hangover. My head, stomach and eyes were hurting ... all at the same time. I really didn't feel up to leaving the house and pretending to go to school. The first thing on my agenda that morning was to get reacquainted with the toilet, as I hurled up my intestines. That is what it felt like. The room was spinning and I was on my hands and knees clutching onto the seat of the toilet as though it was a life jacket, and I was at sea hanging onto it for dear life. In between my chucks and moans, I could hear Hon's voice from afar. "What the fuck? You ain't throwing up all over my clean bathroom floor! Who's going to clean up this shit?"

"You are bitch!" I shouted back. "Can you just wait until I'm through and just leave me the fuck alone? Please!" I ordered.

"Fine," she said submissively. "That's why I don't drink in the first place." And again, she retreated and surrendered her position. Every time she gave in to me, the stronger I became and the more power I took. After thirty minutes of bonding time with the bathroom, I got up and went back to bed. Hon followed me back to the bedroom and asked. "What about school? And what about the academy? I'm not paying all of that damn money for you not to attend!"

"Why don't you take your nagging ass in there in the bathroom and start cleaning it!" I shouted. "I have the day off from school and the academy."

"I'll clean up the bathroom this time, but you better not come in here drunk again."

"Get the fuck out of my bedroom and go clean the bathroom and quit talking to me!" I yelled. Hon then left my bedroom and started to clean the bathroom up. I slept the whole day, and by the time I woke up it was 3 a.m. the next day. Alas, I felt like a human again. Like most people who had drank too much, I prayed and made a promise to God that if he would let me feel better that I would never drink alcohol again. Well, that promise was good for about a month. And after that, I was back to partying again but the only difference this time was that I knew my limits.

The following day I got up and pretended that I was on my way to attend school, but I was really on my way to ditch school and go back to my old junior high school to see my old gym teacher, Ms. Simmons. I ate breakfast at home that morning, and I still had a thousand dollars burning a hole in my pocket waiting to be spent, since it was a new month and the academy tuition had to be paid. So, off I went to visit Ms. Simmons. I had arrived at my old school a little early. It wasn't time for Ms. Simmons first gym class which started at 9:00 a.m., so I waited at the small park located across the school. I took a seat on one of the park benches, and I lit up a cigarette. As I was smoking my cigarette I noticed a fair complexion black man circling around the park in a sky blue, four door, Cadillac convertible. I thought to myself that I better get the heck out of the park before I get into trouble. So I hurriedly entered the school, passing by the security guard and went downstairs to the gym. When I had arrived at the gym office and had a quick visit with my gym teacher. I just wanted her to know that I loved her. She was kind to me, and I never forgot that kindness. I wasn't as cold and heartless as I seemed.

"I love you, Ms. Simmons" I told her before leaving.

"I love you too Mary, now promise me that you won't be ditching class to visit me," she said with a smile.

"I promise," I said exiting the building. Now, it was time to go to the mall. As I was crossing the street at the stoplight, who do I see again? None other than the guy in the blue Cadillac. I played as though I didn't see him and kept walking until I had reached the bus stop bench. Of course it would be my luck that no one else was at the bus stop. I was alone with this man. I was hoping that someone, anyone would come and sit on the bench with me. But no one did. As soon as I sat down, he pulls his car right in front of me and stops his car. "Hello, my name is Ronnie," he said. My heartbeat started racing again, because here is another stranger danger situation. "Hello" I said.

"Where are you headed to?" He asked.

"Why?" I asked back.

"I thought that maybe you'd like a ride," he replied.

"No thank you, the bus will take me where I need to go," I said without hesitation.

"You know something … you are *cute*," he said. I thought to myself at that precise moment. Oh no here I go again … the opposite sex telling me that I am cute. The last guy that told me I was *cute* coaxed me into the woods and raped me with another man. I ignored his statement as I got up off of the bench to look to see if the bus was coming. All the time wishing that this man would go away and leave me alone. After a few minutes of him striking out from all of his pitches, he finally said. "Well … since you won't accept my offer to give you a ride, will you accept my phone number at least?" I stared at him for a few minutes, not knowing how to answer that question. I had just been raped last year and I wasn't sure if I could trust a boy again, but this was a full grown man. I wondered if there was a difference between the two on a mental level. "Hello there, did I lose you?" he asked. "I would like it very much if you would take my number and call me sometime," Ronnie said. He reached his arm out of the car to hand me his phone number. Just at that moment, I saw the bus is coming. I quickly grabbed the phone number and entered the bus.

I paid my fare and took a seat on the bus. I looked out of the window and watched this Ronnie fellow smile and pull off. I thought maybe giving him a phone call won't hurt. He definitely can't rape me over the phone, I reasoned. I also thought that I shouldn't punish him for what those other two did to me. But the fact that he looked much older than me made me nervous. Before I arrived at the mall, my mind was made up. He was way too old for me. I turned my attention back to toys and electronics. The subject of boys was soon erased as soon as I saw this big shiny radio. By the end of the day I had spent several hours at the mall shopping for just myself, and boy did I love it! I had so many bags that I had to call a cab to come pick me up from the mall and take me home. I made sure that before I had arrived home that I had gotten rid of all the sales receipts. Soon the cab was pulling up in the front of the house. I paid him his fare and I struggled to get all those bags of toys, clothes, radio to the front door. I got out my keys and opened the door.

"Hey, did you pay for that cab that just drove up here?" Detective on-duty, nosey Hon asked. "Hell no I didn't pay for the damn cab!" I blurted out. "The police paid for it!" I said.

"Oh" Hon answered. "What are all the bags for?" Hon asked.

"It's more equipment for me to do a stakeout from my bedroom," I quickly lied.

"Oh good … a stakeout at the house. How can I help?" Hon asked with enthusiasm.

"You can help by leaving my goddamn room, Bitch!" I shouted as I slammed my bedroom door in her face. I then placed all of the bags on my bed and began to empty my pockets. I kept all of my loose change in a big Folgers's Coffee canister on my dresser. As I was empting my pockets … there it was … Ronnie's phone number. I sat it on top of the dresser debating on whether I should call him or not. I finally decided that I definitely wasn't calling him today. I had to try out my new radio and hang my new clothes up. After listening to the radio for a while I got my new toys out to play around with them. I had bought a new movie viewer, Sorry, Candy Land and Monopoly board games. I was ecstatic. I didn't need friends over to play … I had a variety of games to play myself. While I was in my room having a ball with my games, Hon was in the kitchen making collard greens, spaghetti, and frying catfish. No McDonald's for me tonight. My grub was going to take place right here at home. Hon had finished cooking and she soon called me in to eat. I ate like a pig, and afterwards, I fell onto my bed and went to sleep.

The next day I woke up with Ronnie on my mind. I told Hon that I had to make a call to a policeman I had met on the force, so she wouldn't get nosy, and so I could have some privacy while talking to him. When I called him on the phone that day, he sounded so good. He was so smooth in his conversation with me. He made me laugh, and he made me feel like I was a grown up. After that first phone call with him, we talked on the phone every day for several hours at a time. I always prefaced it as "official police business" and excused Hon from the immediate premises so I could work.

After weeks of phone chat, I decided to go out to dinner with him. He took me to a nice restaurant where there was a waiter who served us. Ronnie pulled out my chair for me and he treated me like a princess. But my guard was still up. I remember sitting across the table from him, I couldn't help myself from staring at him. He was tall, about six-one or two and he had a protruding muscular chest. It was the kind of chest that comes from weightlifting. He always had money and drove a nice car. Back in my day you were a baller if you drove a Cadillac. We had fun together. His age difference didn't bother me at all. I truly believed that I had found my soul mate. I was mature and felt that I could learn a lot by being with him. Shortly after our first real date, he began taking me over to his house, where I met a woman he introduced as his sister. We did this routine for weeks, until I had gotten comfortable being around him. He would take me shopping, but I never would accept any clothes or jewelry that he would offer to buy me. I just couldn't understand why he wanted to spend so much money on me so soon. We had only known each other for a couple of months. On the third month, I began to notice that his demeanor began to change when he was around me. He began asking deeply personal questions such as, "What kind of work do your parents do? And how much is their income?" I also began to notice his temper flare. He would have tantrums for petty things—like me not wearing my hair down. Once again I was headed down the road of trouble, but I didn't care. I was "hooked" on this guy. He had been so nice once upon a time ago that I just couldn't let him go. I had no blinkers to turn. I had no brakes to stop myself from the soon-to-be head on collision that would leave me for dead on the highway with my emotions piled up like wreckage. The accident was called *love*. My mind and my heart were being towed away by this new man that I had called my "boyfriend." But sadly, it would be short lived. In short, he broke my heart. The full story will be revealed someday. But today is *not* the day.

Chapter 22

Extortion

I was not in the mood for Hon today, and because of my sour attitude, things escalated quickly one morning over biscuits and gravy.

"You don't need to be trying to date, Miss Fast Ass" Her words came out of nowhere. *Why did she say that?* She doesn't realize who she's fucking with. All of the anger and hatred balled up inside of me was starting to boil over. I was so done you could have put a fork in me. "What the fuck did you just say to me?" I confronted her.

"You heard what I said, bitch!" Hon exclaimed. At that moment, I went completely ballistic. I was ready to beat this old woman's ass. But instead I refrained from a physical confrontation and shouted, "Fuck you, bitch! Look! I'm getting really fucking tired of your fucked up attitude towards me!" On the heels of those words, Hon slapped me across my face. In fury, I ran to the white cabinet and retrieved her 22 Smith & Wesson revolver. I pointed the gun right in her face and gave my final warning, "If you *ever* in your life put your hands on me again, I will blow your mother fucking brains out, bitch!" Hon was frozen in motion. Silently, she stood afraid to move. She had bit her lower lip so hard she drew blood.

"Yeah …" I said, "How do you like staring down the barrel of a gun, Bitch? Now you got a feeling what I was feeling, all of those times that you had me afraid that you were going to shoot and kill me!" I said.

She was silent.

"Oh what's wrong? You ain't got nothing to say to now, you shit-talking, motherfucking fat ass bitch! Make me pull the trigger, Gussie! Come on, I know that you can make me pull the damn trigger!" I challenged. "Oh I see you're as quiet as a church mouse." I said. "And as far as you complaining about the tuition for the academy, Officer Johnson said that he's willing to provide you full police protection," I informed her with the gun still pointing at her head.

"How much will that cost me?" Hon asked under petrified eyes. This was the first time I'd ever seen her afraid. I never even knew she could feel fear.

"The initial set up the fee will be seventeen hundred dollars," I demanded. "And after that the price will be fifteen hundred dollars a month!" I quoted her.

"I don't have that kind of money!" Hon cried out.

I shook the gun in her face and said, "Then bitch you better find a way by tomorrow morning, or I will let Officer Johnson know that the prisoners that are scheduled to be released will have full reign to do what they want with you."

"Okay," she quickly responded. "I'll have it, but I have to go to the bank tomorrow," Hon said.

"I don't give a fuck what you have to do to get the money, just get it, bitch."

"Okay," she said.

"Go to the basement, Bitch!" I ordered her with the gun still pointing in her face.

"Why?" Hon asked.

"You can either die where you stand or walk to the basement your choice," I said without blinking. Seconds later, Hon slowly shuffled down the basement stairs where I locked the door behind her, and hid her gun in my room where I retreated to bed thinking, plotting and scheming how I was going torment Gussie. The tables have turned, and there was definitely a new sheriff in town. I had had enough of all the bad things happening to me over and over again. The anguish that I was feeling was now going to be unleashed on Hon. I wasn't going to tolerate anything from anyone anymore. I felt that if God was not going to help me, then I was going to have to help myself. I was ready, more than ready. Fear was no longer in my vocabulary. There was not an ounce, nor a drop of love left for her. She was my enemy. My body shook uncontrollably as I cried about my life. Through my sobs, I could hear Hon asking to please come upstairs. I got up and I went to the door but I didn't open it. "I need to come upstairs to use the bathroom," Hon said.

"bitch you better find that bucket that you used to make me use and piss and shit in that!" I said. "And if you call my name again," I shouted, "I will shoot your fucking tongue out, Bitch. Now be quiet and go to sleep!" I ordered her. When I returned back to my room, I got Hon's gun back out. I looked into the chambers and I noticed that there had not been one bullet loaded in it. I was so glad that Hon didn't remember that she had not loaded it. I went to bed with the thoughts of revenge and retaliation. As I drifted to sleep I sang myself a lullaby, *"Sweet dreams, Gussie, because your ass is mine."*

Chapter 23

Eye for an Eye: Now we Both Blind, BITCH!

A new season had arrived. It was the winter of 1975. The cold air cut through your coat like a Thanksgiving carving knife. You definitely had to bundle up if you were going to go outside. The streets were laden with fresh snow, and even though the sun was out, the temperature felt like Mt. Everest in the wintertime. The snow was ankle deep and fresh like powdered sugar on a plain doughnut. It was unbelievably beautiful.

I was still a freshmen in high school and had become the master of class ditching. I had eliminated that ex-boyfriend pimp; and in the wake of that burden gone, I had a grand 'ole time enjoying the excess of Hon's money. I bought the latest records Earth Wind and Fire, The Jackson Five, War and a special newcomer, Natalie Cole. I would sit on my bed in Ed's old bedroom, as I had demanded my own room, and I would take Hon's old portable suitcase shaped phonograph into the room and play Cole's *Inseparable* for hours on end.

I just loved her voice, style, demeanor, and her elegance when she sang.

It was a new day at school too. When I was attending the ninth grade some of my classmates were the bullies from elementary who used to play in my hair and get me into trouble with Hon. Now they were older and thought that I was that same naïve little girl. I had to prove them wrong. When one girl thought that she would have her friend double team me after school in a fight, I had a surprise for both of them in my leather pocket. I pulled out the twenty-two revolver that I always carried, and I shoved it into her face and I asked them both. "Which one of you girls would like to die first for fucking with me?" Their faces turned pale and drained of color when they met my friend, the revolver.

"Oh … we didn't mean nothing by it," one of the girls stuttered.

"We were just playing around," the other said.

"Just as I thought, two cowardly bitches," I said as I trotted off in the other direction.

That's right Bitches.

There's a new sheriff in town.

I was Betty bad ass and this was my Wild, Wild West.

I got rid of a lot of bullies, both girls and boys by showing the gun. But I was just perpetrating because the gun was empty of bullets. And I didn't have any real intention of shooting anyone. I just wanted them to believe that I would. I had just wished that I had the gun the day I got raped by those two dudes and Ronnie. People had stopped picking on me and they started giving me the kind of respect brought on only by fear. I didn't care what caused you to respect me, just as long as you did respect me.

It was not long after I demanded the funds for full KCPD protection that Hon plopped a whopping seventeen hundred dollars cash into my hand. That was the largest amount I'd ever swindled out of her! But it was only the beginning of a new kind of hustle. I had convinced Hon that the fifteen hundred dollar monthly installation was a real bargain. And blindly, she agreed. I was in seventh heaven and rich! I also began to note Hon's mind deteriorating so rapidly, she would even forget who she was talking to on the phone. I took full advantage of the situation and began to get bold in doing what the hell I pleased. I began to buy and smoke cigarettes in the house in front of Hon.

One day while I was sitting on the couch in the living room smoking a cigarette, I was getting tired of Hon staring me down as though she wanted to make her foot a permanent attachment to my ass. I decided to see how far I could go with my manipulation of Hon's weak mind. So I said to her, "You know ... Officer Johnson and I had a very serious conversation about you the other day." I just knew that this statement would pique Hon's curiosity. "Really what did Officer Johnson have to say about me?" Hon lit up to ask.

"He told me that the cigarettes that I'm smoking helps your memory and makes you stay healthy," I said in a serious voice.

"How does he know that? What makes him such a fucking expert on health, when his job is to catch fucking criminals?" Hon asked in a skeptical tone.

"His brother is a doctor and he told him to smoke these cigarettes," I said without flinching. "Maybe you should try one," I suggested.

"Okay," she said slowly, "if Officer Johnson smokes these and his brother the doctor says it's okay then I will try it," Hon said with eagerness attached to her voice. Now mind you, Hon had never smoked in her life. So when she took her first puff, she must have coughed for five minutes straight.

"Take another puff" I pressed, "You'll feel it working soon," I said sounding like an infomercial. Hon took one puff, then another as I sat back and watched her inhale like a pro. "Do you feel any better? I asked.

"Hell yeah ..." she insisted. "I feel like I'm young again. This shit really works, huh!" Hon said co-signing my mythical lie.

Oh my God!

So gullible!

Soon Hon was addicted to nicotine and every time that I came over she asked for a cigarette, or either she wanted me to buy her a pack. And I would oblige her with either request. Once again, I had conquered her and Hon was at my beck and call. I had Hon by the horns, and I wasn't letting her go. I started buying her Kool cigarettes, which were fifty cents a pack back in the day. I was buying more than just cigarettes back in those days. I spent so much money on buying weed from local dealers and paying some adult to go in the liquor store to buy me beer. There were times when I even paid the local winos to buy my friend Robin P. and I some wine. We would get messed up on Night Train or Annie Boones Farm. Those were the days. I loved it.

It was a new play at my house and I was the star this time. But I found out the hard way that when you have an entourage your money goes faster than a rollercoaster at Magic Mountain. I was spending Hon's money at school for lunches for myself and for several classmates. I was eating out instead of at home. I was buying clothes, liquor, cigarettes, records and snacks. I was giving away money because I knew that I would have more the next month. And Hon never questioned me about the stuff that I brought home. I was living high on the hog and no one could tell me shit.

On one evening while visiting a friend house, we both got wasted on weed and wine. After I was high as hell, I decided that I would call up Hon and disguise my voice to extort more money out of her.

My funds were getting low and I needed more money. "Hello may I please speak to Gussie?" I asked in a buzzed voice. "This is she speaking, who's calling? Hon responded. "This is Officer Johnson from the Kansas City Police Department," I said. I waited to see if she would bust me, but she didn't. I was shocked that Hon didn't recognized my voice; but she wasn't accustom to hearing me speak over the phone since I only called her once before when I got into trouble with Ronnie. So, on with the lie

"Your daughter is going on an overnight trip with some police officers in her squad," I said wanting to laugh but I didn't. "She will need five hundred dollars by tomorrow so she can catch a flight out of KC International Airport ... all right?" Hon paused. "Ummm ... I just gave her seventeen hundred dollars for the academy." I fell silent when she said that. "You mean that she will need an additional five hundred dollars for this overnight trip?" Hon asked reluctantly. "Yes she does," said the fake ass Officer Johnson.

"It would be a shame for her to miss out on this trip!" I said convincingly.

"All right I will give it to her in the morning …" Hon said drudgingly.

"Great! I'll let Mary know that you agreed!" I said hanging up the phone without even saying goodbye. When I disconnected the line, my friend and I fell out laughing.

Later that night, I strolled my drunk ass back down the hill to my house. As I strolled into the house, Hon stopped me in the living room. "Did you talk to Officer Johnson today? She asked. "Of course I did, do you have the money for the trip? I asked. "No, I don't keep that kind of money here for your Bitch ass to steal!" she shouted. "I have to go to the bank in the morning and get it." I had to laugh to myself because I was already stealing her money right under her pathetic little nose. Anyways, all I wanted to do was lay my ass down and go to sleep. But before I could I had to call my friend May May, to let her know that I would be spending the night over at her house to make the lie seem real.

"When does your flight leave? Hon asked.

"Now why would you ask me such a stupid ass question like that for?" I screamed at Hon. "I haven't paid for the fucking ticket yet you old senile Bitch!" I said. Hon looked at me with a constant stare as though she could have killed me with her eyes, but that was just too damn bad. Hon wasn't running nothing here but her mouth.

"Look I have to make a private, top secret police call," I informed Hon.

"So fucking what? "Why are you telling me for?" Hon asked. "What do you having to make a private call to the police have to do with me?" Hon asked. "Do I need to spell it out to your ignorant fat ass? You cannot be upstairs when I make the phone call, Bitch!" I yelled back at Hon. "Besides an officer is supposed to come over to the house and talk with you today," I informed her.

"Really? When?" Hon asked with excitement in her voice. "He is going to meet you at the basement back door any time now, so you better go downstairs and wait for him to show up," I insisted. "Okay ..." she said trying to sound tough, "Well ... you should have told me that in the first place," Hon said. Hon ran down stairs to meet the officer who wasn't coming. As soon as her feet touched the last stair, I slammed and locked the basement door behind her. I also locked all of the entry doors so she couldn't gain any access to the house from the outside. After the doors were locked, I called my friend, May May, to let her know that I would be spending the night at her house the next night.

Once I was done with my call, I could hear Hon screaming at the top of her lungs for me to let her upstairs. "Open this motherfucking door you trifling Bitch!" Hon shouted as she hit her fists against the door. Instead of going to unlock the basement door, I went to my bedroom and fell asleep. My dogs Furious and Tinker looked at me in disbelief. They looked at me as if to ask, *isn't something wrong with this picture?* They almost seemed to ask, *aren't you the one who is supposed to be locked in the basement?* My dogs went to lay down by the basement door as I slept the rest of that evening away.

The next morning I got up early and grabbed Hon's 22-revolver just in case, she was still upset with me for making her sleep down in the basement. Only when I had the weapon in hand did I dare to open the basement door. Hon had deep anger and resentment in her eyes when she looked at me. In fact, ironically, it was the exact same look I had always given her the countless nights that I slept in the basement. "You fucking little Bitch!" Hon shouted. "I ought to stab you in your fucking heart, for leaving me down in the basement to sleep! I'm going to get my gun and shoot your ass dead as a doorknob!" Hon said. "Uh I don't think so Bitch!" I said as I pointed the barrel of the gun to her head. "Now go clean your ass up and get dressed," I ordered her. "And go get the fucking money from the bank for my goddamn trip, whore!" I said with a smile on my face. She stared at me with a violent hatred. "Go ahead," I warned her. "Talk some shit so I can put this gun in your mouth and blow the back of your neck off!"

One thing that I had learned over the years of abuse from Hon was how to curse and intimidate. Hon then quietly walked to the bedroom to get her clothes and then she began to run her bath water. I started watching TV as I waited for Hon to get ready to go to the bank. When Hon had finished bathing and had gotten dressed she came out to the living room with her hand on her fat rounded hips. "What if I decide not to give you the fucking money after all? Huh Bitch?" Hon asked.

"Well," I quickly replied, "If you want to look like a liar to the whole Kansas City Police force then you should do just that! After all you did tell Officer Johnson you were going to give me the money today. I can call him up right now and tell him what you said …" I threatened. "No don't do that!" she quickly protested. "I don't want the police force to think I'm a liar," Hon said proudly as though she was the spokesperson for the KCPD. "Then quit wasting my time with this bullshit and go do what I told you to do, you stubborn ass old Bitch!" I ordered.

Hon left out of the door with her black coat and pocketbook—off to retrieve my soon to be five hundred dollars. I felt like Cinderella getting revenge on the evil stepmother. While Hon was gone, I played my music loud so the whole block could hear it. I danced around the house as though I was Peter Pan and I had just conquered Captain Hook.

Three hours later Hon finally returned. "We're low on food. I'm going to the grocery store. Enjoy your trip, and say hello to Officer Johnson for me," she added.

"Kiss my ass, Bitch! I'm not telling him shit!" I said cruelly. I watched as Hon walked up the hill to the bus stop. When she was out of sight, I called a cab to take me to my friend May May's house. When I arrived, I went shopping to get more clothes and a travel bag to keep my new clothes in. We came back home and I went to the neighborhood grocery store and bought some food for dinner so everyone could eat. Now May May's family was huge. There was at least ten people living in the house. I told a "smooth lie" to May May's mother to justify my hefty cash flow—boasting that this was an allowance received from my mother's social security check.

When I returned to Hon's the next day, I went on a *"Let's Abuse the Hell Outta Hon Binge."* I continued to trick her into the basement and lock the door. I made demands for cash on top of the fifteen hundred a month using old faithful, the KCPD, the ultimate cash cow. Eventually, I had completely depleted Hon's saving account. It was drier than the Mohave Desert in summer. There was absolutely nothing left. Initially I didn't believe her and so I insisted she show me her bank statement.

"All I have is my social security benefits," she whined.

"Good," I said greedily. "Then you have *some* money!"

"Barely," she complained.

"When that check comes in," I told her, "Go to the bank and cash it and give the whole check to me for police protection," I ordered.

"But " she protested.

"If you don't, there will be *no* more private protection," I threatened. "And then you're open game for released criminals!"

This was a modern-day horror story in the making. The script had flipped and the abuser had become the abused. Within six months of Hon's savings running out and a host of unpaid pink notices and overdue bill notices, everything in the house was shut off.

Lights.

Gas.

Water.

And phone.

I would enter the house and Gussie would greet me with a new greeting, "Guess what the fuck happened to me this morning, you trifling bitch?" Hon asked with her I want to kick your ass tone in her voice. "I don't have any idea!" I snapped with attitude.

"I went to the motherfucking bathroom and I turn on the faucet and to my goddamn, motherfucking disbelief bitch, not a single drop of fucking water came out! I found the water bill notice, and it said that the cut off day was yesterday! Now why does your whorish ass think that happened?" Hon pressed, "I will tell you why bitch because you didn't pay the fucking motherfucking water bill, cunt! Now I can't wash my fat ass at all!" Hon growled with anger in her voice.

"Are you through with your colorful arrangements of words?" I asked almost laughing at her distraught anger. "No bitch, I happen not to be through. When is Officer Johnson going to get his dick out of his mouth and pay the goddamn bill so I can have my water turned the back on?" Hon spat with hatred in her voice. "And motherfucker what about the gas? There is no gas for me to cook, or take a hot fucking bath, that shit was turned off a couple days ago, you black goat!!! Why? I have never lived like this before!" Hon moaned. "You are a deep pain in the crack of my ass, you stupid-ass whore!!" Hon said sounding like a mad animal who needed to be put to sleep.

"Quit bitching old woman!" I insisted. "I'm sure Officer Johnson will look into it. Just have some fucking patience and do something to get your mind off of the unpaid bills," I said in such a mild mannered voice knowing that *Officer Johnson* wasn't looking into a motherfucking thing!

"Well," Hon began. "I would try and look at some television, but I can't Bitch because the cock-sucking electricity is off too, you fucking retard!!!" Hon said.

I walked to my bedroom and began to ignore Hon's rants and rave about the bills. Hell, I didn't care. I wasn't there most of the time anyway. I was staying with friends. I always had money so I always had friends. I had only come back for clothes. I could still hear Hon in the background cursing like a drunk in a bar who's mad that the bar is about to close. I just continued to ignore her and gathered my belongings. Shortly thereafter, I walked out of the house and on about my business leaving Hon hungry, funky and bored.

There was no food in the whole house left for Hon to eat. The cabinets were bare, the refrigerator was empty, the basement shelves were collecting dust, and Hon's weight was coming off like clothes on a nightclub stripper. Hon looked odd being so thin after weighing three hundred pounds all of her life. I think that she had gotten down to hundred and fifty pounds. Her dresses were hanging off of her like drapes on a window. Again I didn't care, it may sound coldblooded—but I went *all* out to get my revenge on this woman and there was no stopping me now. Anything that I could do without physically putting my hands on her I did. I locked her in the basement. Broke her in-half financially; and always made sure I put the fear of God in her to ensure she went to the bank and cashed her monthly social security check. Sometimes I even held her at gunpoint to intimidate her. I starved her out, and then ate in front of her just as she had done me.

On many occasions I would come home from a fast food restaurant with enough food for both of us to eat. I would sit down at the table and say, "Hey Hon, I brought some food home." Hon would come rushing into the kitchen like a starving animal. "Where in the fuck did you go to get the fast food from?" Hon asked.

"I went to Kentucky Fried chicken with Officer Johnson," I lied.

"Oh, well I guess that I have no choice in the matter … I don't particularly like fast food but I'm at the point where

I'm willing to eat it " she said with hesitation. So I got her a plate, and I placed a big helping of mash potatoes on her plate. "Now we have to say a prayer before our meal," I told Hon. When Hon closed her eyes to say a prayer I took the plate of potatoes back, and I placed them onto my plate. When Hon opened her eyes up from saying her prayer, her plate would be gone. "Goddammit where the fuck are the mash potatoes?" Hon asked in shock.

"You already ate them," I said.

"You are a motherfucking liar!" Hon said. "Let me have some goddamned chicken and potatoes, Bitch!" Hon insisted.

"Hell no bitch!" I'd shout. "I guess you forgot how you ate in front me when I was a child," I said. Hon rose up out of her chair and leaned towards me like she was about to do something.

"Sit your fat ass back down in that chair before I kick you back down!" I said emotionless. Hon looked into my eyes, and she saw that I was serious. So she quietly and slowly sat back in her chair. And there she stayed until I was too full to eat any more. The leftover chicken, macaroni and cheese, and potatoes I fed to Furious and Tinker. She watched the dogs get full while she sat there hungry as hell

When it was all said and done, I used her, verbally abused her, and took *everything* that she had—including her self-esteem. I made her as weak and vulnerable as I had been. It was an "eye for an eye."

I know that God has made me pay for my sins against her, but I hope she learned her lesson. Who knows? Maybe she didn't. Hon was as stubborn as a mule. She acted as though she knew everything. She tried to make you believe that her words were as solid as a gold bar at Fort Knox—and that you could believe everything that came from the gums of her mouth to your eardrums. I had to bring her down a peg or two. All the while I abused her, Gussie showed no remorse and never so much as looked into my eyes and ever uttered the words, "I'm sorry." I don't even know if it would have made a difference, and maybe when all is said and done, I'm no better than she was but I do know one thing with absolute certainty if I had it all over to do again would I make her suffer? Would I abuse her? Would I break her spirit? Empty her pockets and pocketbook? Trick her into a cigarette addiction? Lock her in the basement? Starve her? Bleed her of the comforts of gas, light, water and heat? Hold a gun to her head? And deplete what was left of her frazzled emotions? I answer this without shame and a one hundred percent unequivocal *yes*.

Chapter 24

The Jig is up

It was the summer of 1976. I was a fifteen year old bad ass living high on the hog off Hon's retirement. I only visited Hon during the daylight and on the first of every month. The rest of the time I juggled between May May, Patricia and Robin P's. I was having the time of my mother-loving life. I was finally independent, and I loved it. I bought myself a ten speed bike and a shitload of clothes and records that I couldn't listen to anymore because the electricity had been shut off.

I eventually got tired of walking around carrying a gun in my pocket at school; and with the bullies off my back, I wound up selling Hon's twenty-two revolver to a hoodlum boy who wanted it to commit crimes. He lived a couple of blocks behind my house in the neighborhood. I was glad that Hon could never use that gun on me again to threaten my life.

When everything in the house got shut off, Hon was one miserable wench. She complained about everything. "There's no fucking gas on, and I can't cook a motherfucking thing" she whined. "And what about the water, Bitch? I can't wash my ass because the water is turned off!" Hon said exasperated. "Well, I guess that you'll have to walk your fat ass around the house funky then, Huh?" I replied with pure joy. "There ain't no fucking food in the whole damn house to eat! The dogs are being fed, but I ain't!" she barked. "What kind of fucked up shit is that?"

"The dogs deserve to eat, bitch!" I said.

"Fuck! Everything is cut off because the bills were not paid! I thought that you said that Officer Johnson was going to pay the goddamn bills, Bitch" Hon yelled in anger. "I can't even see where the fuck I'm going because there ain't one single fucking light that works in the whole motherfucking house, bitch!" Hon bellowed. "I'm tired of this shit! When the sun goes down this house looks like a graveyard. Do you have anything to say, bitch? Are you going to solve this fucking problem or what?" she barked.

"Hell no! I'm not going to try and solve shit! I think things are fine just the way they are!" I said with a smile on my face. "I'm not hungry, I've bathed this morning, and I can turn the lights on at the hotel that I am staying in after the sun goes down." I dare not let Hon know that I had been staying with friends. She would be hotter than a tea kettle boiling water. Hon started pacing around the room with her hands on top of her head saying "Fuck! Fuck! Fuck" I can't take living like this anymore! I'm hungry bitch! You need to call Officer Johnson and ask him for some money to feed me with!" Hon ordered.

"Okay … oh wait a minute. I can't the phone is turned off!" I said sarcastically.

"Why you fucking smart-ass bubbled-eyed piece of shit!" Hon yelled. "If I had the strength, I would stomp your heart out through your asshole!" Hon threatened.

"Well, all I can say is that I'm a well-cleaned and a full bitch that ain't hungry … so I guess that you will have to starve to death before I would offer you any food, you old, sadistic, fat bitch!" I said as I stared Hon down in her eyes like a lion eyeing his prey.

Well every good thing comes to an end. And one day out of the blue, Hon broke.

Snapped.

Cracked.

I came home just like I did every day with the intention of grabbing a few clothes and hitting the road. When I walked into the house I greeted Hon with my customary, "Hello Hon!"

On the heels of my greeting, I was met with an ugly, two-eyed, funky monster who lived in the dark during the night but only because she didn't have lights. "Don't motherfucking say hello to me you black bitch!" Hon yelled with sobbing wrinkled eyes. "I'm sick and tired of you and your bullshit! If you don't leave my motherfucking house now and never come the fuck back, I will go over to Ms. Oliver's house and have her call the police and tell them how you are treating me!" Hon said in a voice that I knew that she meant business." Without protesting at all, I simply shrugged my shoulders. "Okay all right I'll leave," I said. "There's no need to talk to Ms. Oliver about anything or call the cops," I reassured her.

I knew the jig was up so I left peacefully. I knew that if Ms. Oliver got involved it would turn ugly. Ms. Oliver was our nosy next door neighbor who lived on the left side of us. She always had the belief that I was this sort of demon child and that I had voodoo powers that I would use on Hon to try and kill her. Where she got this hair-brained ideas I can't say, but all I knew in that moment was that my reign of power had just gone out like the lights in Hon's house.

Yikes!

But what about my money?

I turned and asked Hon. "So what about the protection money for the police?"

"I'll give you this last fifteen hundred dollars to give to Officer Johnson … and after that, I'll start paying the police myself, I don't need you to do a damn thing ever for me again! You are as dead to me as Sparky, you dirty, little Bitch!" Hon growled. As Hon went to retrieve the fifteen hundred dollars in cash, I couldn't help but wonder how much she had already told Ms. Oliver, if anything at all. I wasn't about to step in between Hon and Ms. Oliver, given that they both hated my guts right about now. As I stepped out the door, Hon yelled, "Here is the last goddamn fifteen hundred dollars, bitch! I hope you choke on it and die!" she said throwing the money down on the carpet. I knelt down and picked up the money without saying a word.

Once I had gathered it, I turned and walked out of Hon's door forever. I threw her house key at her and yelled. "I hate you too you selfish, old, mean Bitch! You always mistreated me, and now you can't deal with being on the receiving end! Well fuck you too!" was my final words.

As I walked away from Hon's house, I could see Ms. Oliver staring at me from her front porch. I continued walking until Hon and her house was out of my sight. As I walked toward the bus stop, I began to feel abandoned and unwanted.

Was I really going to be without Hon?
That crazy, fat ass, mean old Bitch?
Was it over for real?

I looked down at my last fifteen hundred dollars and for the first time thought about making it last. As I walked, my mind scattered with a host of random thoughts. I hated Hon for how she treated me, but to be kicked out and forbidden to return, had not been calculated into my plans. I felt both relieved and hurt. The revenge gig was up. It had been six years of torment and two years of payback. The equation didn't add up. I could have fucked with her for another four more years just in the name of calling it even Steven. *It wasn't fair,* I thought, but I couldn't dwell on the ifs, whys, and how comes. I had to deal with the "What now?" and more important, "Where the hell do I go from here?"

I walked to May May's house and explained my situation to her first. Then we both sat down in the living room so I could repeat the story to her mom. Luckily her mom said that it was ok for me to stay with them. I went to bed that night at May May's feeling relief that a burden was finally off of my shoulder. I didn't have to tell anymore lies to Hon. I didn't have to look at Hon's sour puss face anymore; and most of all, I didn't have to witness her decaying mind and body wither away like an autumn leaf from a tree.

It was a bittersweet moment for me. I wanted so much to leave her house, because deep down inside I was still afraid of her. But on the other hand I missed her. I know that sounds crazy, bizarre, outrageous, ridiculous and unimaginable, but Hon was the only mother I had ever known. Crazy as fuck … she was all I'd ever known. I didn't get sick pleasure out of watching her suffer, but I do think I turned myself off, numbing myself to her pain. In the beginning, back when I hustled my first $20 bucks I felt bad somewhere deep inside. But with the twenty in hand and snacks on the table, somehow I felt less, and less *bad.*

In the beginning, I never intended to force Hon to suffer so much, but it did give me some form of satisfaction to get my point across. It was almost as if to say, "See now you tell me how that feels?" All I ever wanted was her to know how bad I felt, how deeply I suffered and to say I'm sorry, Mary. Two words she never uttered. Creating unbearable suffering and taking away everything she loved that was the only way I knew how to communicate my message. I knew that she loved to eat and watch her TV. I felt traces of remorse once she was no longer my victim, but not enough to do anything any different if given the chance again.

During my stay at May May's house some of the neighborhood kids taught me how to shoplift. Since I wasn't trying to spend money like water anymore, stealing sounded like a pretty good idea to me. I was always a quick learner, so I picked up the scheme pretty fast. I bought a big black purse and went down to the neighborhood grocery, Millgram's, where I shoplifted items from that store for three weeks straight. I would steal things that my friends wanted and things that I fancied myself. But one day, my luck took a turn like an Indy five hundred race car driver on a race track. I had stolen some items, and I went to the checkout counter to buy a pack of gum, because I caught wind of the security officer following me in the aisles. I just wanted to get out of the store as quickly as I could in order not to get caught. After I bought the gum I was out of the store and off of their property; but one of my friends wanted a toy out of the gumball machines. I didn't want to go back, but I did. No sooner that I put the quarter into the machine and got the toy and was walking away, did I hear a voice behind me say, "Could you come with me?" I turned around to see a big, tall security guard. I also checked my peripheral vision and my friends had scattered like roaches when turning on a light.

"Damn," I thought.

I followed the security officer back to the store manager's office. The manager took my purse and he placed all of the stolen items onto the table. I begged him not to call the police on me, but he did. I waited around in the manager's office for two hours for the police to show up. I was handcuffed and crying like a baby. The police finally arrived, took my name down and escorted me to a white paddy wagon parked in front of the store. I was paraded around the store like the criminal that I was. The security officer took his handcuffs from around my wrists, so the officer could place his handcuffs on me.

How ironic was this! I was getting arrested by the same officers that I had lied to Hon about. The very same officers I was supposed to work with in the junior academy. Hon would have died if she had witnessed this travesty. I was led inside of the paddy wagon. There was no other offenders inside. I was the only perp that morning so I sat on the narrow wooden bench with my hands behind my back off to the downtown police station.

Chapter 25

Big Momma

I arrived at the downtown police station where I was escorted by the police officer to a detective's desk. I sat nervously while the officer took off my handcuffs.

"Would you like a soda, Mary?" the detective asked.

"No," I replied with tears in my eyes.

"You know what you did was wrong and you could go to juvenile hall for this offense," the detective informed me, but with empathy in his voice. I sat there in the chair not offering a reply. "Do you want to go to Juvenile Hall?" he asked.

"No I don't … I just want to go home," I said trying to be convincing.

"Well … I'll tell you what I'm going to do," he said sounding like he might have good news to tell me. 'I want you to call either your mother or father and have they come down to the station and sign you out" He said.

"Really?" I replied with hope in my weak little voice.

"Yes really. Would you like for me to call them?" He asked.

"No that's alright I can call my mother," I said. Now I knew that I couldn't call Gussie for two reasons: 1) her phone was disconnected and 2) she had just kicked me out of her house. So, I took the phone and I called up May May's mother. The detective wasn't paying close attention to me, because he was more concerned with some paperwork that was on his desk at the time. So I took advantage of his attention turned elsewhere to explain to May May's mom what I needed her to do. And in a voice no louder than a whisper I said, "Hello Ms. Emery this is Mary I'm in big trouble, and I need your help. I'm here at the downtown police station sitting at this detective's desk. I got caught shoplifting," I said in pure desperation.

"I know May May's sister told me what had happened," said Ms. Emery.

"I need you to play as though you are my mother, and come down and sign me out. The detective said that he would release me into my mother's custody instead of sending me down to juvenile hall," I said.

"Sure I can do that, let me speak to the detective Mary," Ms. Emery said.

I handed the phone over to the detective so they could work out my release. While they spoke I thought, God has my back once again. I was about to get out of another ordeal that could have changed my life forever. After a few minutes on the phone the detective hung up the phone, turned to me and said. "You mother is not feeling well today, so she is going to send your Uncle down here to pick you up." I knew that he was talking about Ms. Emery's brother and that was okay by me.

"Great!" I said. It was scary enough seeing all of these real criminals being put in temporary cells until they could either be bailed out or see a judge. All I know is that I wanted to leave this place of confinement. Soon I saw Ms. Emery's brother come in the precinct doors, and the detective waved him over with a hand gesture. He walked to the detective's desk and began signing some documents for my release. I started to feel happy again.

"Now I won't be seeing you back down here again will I?" the detective asked.

"Oh no sir" I assured him, "I've learned my lesson," I said meaning every single word. Ms. Emery's brother placed his arm around my shoulder, and we walked out of the police station. It felt good to feel the fresh air hit against my face and to see the sun shine bright in the sky. I was free once more. Needless to say that was my last time ever shoplifting again. Neither juvenile hall nor jail seemed like places that I ever wanted to visit again. Being imprisoned at Hon's all of my life was enough for me.

When we arrived back at May May's house, I thanked both her mother and her uncle for getting me out of that serious situation. Ms. Emery started asking me questions about my family, especially my mother. After a long conversation with her, Ms. Emery had remembered that she had worked as a CNA with my biological mother. Now Ms. Emery was still going to work five days a week working as a CNA. Ms. Emery asked me about my grandmother, who I only knew as "Big Momma" or Flossie. But Ms. Emery did some digging and she called up one of her co-workers who had also worked with my mom. And she told her that my grandmother's first name was Dorothy. She had remembered that my mother had always called her Dorothy when she would speak about her.

Wow!

Now we were getting closer to finding where my grandmother actually lived. I had stayed with May May's mother for about two months and my money was slowly dwindling down. And it soon became a burden to her mother to keep trying to feed all ten people who resided at the house. So one day Ms. Emery informed me that she had found my grandmother's phone number in the White Pages, and that she had called and spoke to her about my situation. Ms. Emery told me that my grandmother would be coming over tomorrow to pick me up so I could stay with her and my other siblings. I wasn't sure as to how I had felt about that reunion. I didn't know my grandmother and besides I resented her for allowing me to stay at Gussie's house without even trying to see me or take me away from there. I felt that she owed me because she had let me suffer at the hands of Hon.

The next day I woke up early after, all my real family was coming to take me with them. I was excited and a little overwhelmed by the whole idea. But I had no choice. I had to leave May May's house. It was about noon when my grandmother arrived and rang the doorbell. Ms. Emery answered the door and greeted my grandmother. I stared at her as though she was a complete stranger which she was. Then the silence broke as I heard Flossie say. "Come over and give your grandmother a hug." Without saying a word, I walked over and gave her a hug.

There was an empty hollow feeling that came over me. I didn't hate her, but I didn't love her either. Just because she was my blood relative did not give her carte blanche in my eyes. "Go and get your things so we can leave, your sister and brothers are anxious to see you," Grandmother said. I went the May May's bedroom and grabbed my belongings and clothes. I said goodbye to May May and her family. May May, my grandmother and I walked to Grandmother's two door station wagon and soon I was off to another place that I could call home.

Grandmother and I finally arrived at her house. No sooner that I stepped in I was bombarded with hugs from my three brothers and my sister. There in the living room sat Bumpy. I don't remember what his real name was but he was over Big Momma's house visiting. He was already seventeen and a senior in high school. But Big Momma told me that he had just been released from juvenile hall. Then there was William, the third oldest, Orlando who I believe was six and my sister Carmelita who was eight at the time that I had arrived at Big Momma's house. I still brought over my bad habits such as smoking cigarettes and my bad temper. I wasn't really prepared or ready to interact with all this affection that I was receiving. Grandmother showed me my room which was located in the attic. My sister and my baby brother began following me around like an assistant to a blind man. It got on my nerves sometimes. I was used to being alone and not having all of these intrusions in my space. It was definitely something that I had to get used to.

Grandmother fed me, and I ate like a pig. In fact I ate whole box of Kellogg's Corn Pops all by myself. I had been used to eating junk food … soda pop, chips and candy, not real food. I couldn't remember the last time that I had sat down and ate a bowl of cereal. Later, when Big Momma took me to the doctor, I was diagnosed as suffering from malnutrition. Big Momma asked me why Gussie had not been feeding me. I told her that I didn't know why. And Big Momma left it at that. Then she asked me. "Do you still have clothes at Gussies's that you need to retrieve?"

"Yes I do but she won't allow me to get them," I told Grandmother.

"Don't worry we can go over there tomorrow morning and get them" Grandmother insisted. "Tonight you just relax and get to know your siblings," Grandmother said with a twinkle in her eyes. "Sure thing Grandma. I'll do that" I said. So I went up to my room in the attic, and I got under my freshly laundered sheets and laid my head down on my fluffy pillow, and I thanked God for the mental peace that I had longed to have. I surrendered my mind that night and I had no worries or fears, no tears and most of all no bruises.

The next morning I was awakened by the aroma of pancakes, pork sausage, and eggs coming from the kitchen. Grandma had started early making a hearty breakfast for me and my siblings. I got out of bed and stretched my arms out wide like an eagle in flight over the Grand Canyon. I looked over at my alarm clock and had to turn the light because the clock wasn't one of those digital glow in the dark, it was a plain numeral one.

When I saw that it was only 4:00 am I thought that I must have read the time wrong. It was way too early to be awake, and as far as eating breakfast I didn't believe that my stomach was ready for such a big meal that early in the morning. My baby brother Orlando entered my room.

"Good morning Cookie," he called out to me. "Big Momma sent me to your room to get you up so you can eat breakfast with us." He said so eager and enthused.

"Why does Big Momma make breakfast so early?" I asked with a little irritation in my voice.

"Oh this is what Big Momma does all the times on the weekend," Orlando said with bright eyes and a Polaroid grin.

"I see" I responded. Even though my body said it's too early, go back to sleep—my stomach and tastes buds said get downstairs and get your grub on. It has been awhile since I was served a home cook meal. I had spent Hon's money eating at fast food joints and restaurants, so I was sure grateful to be able to sit down and enjoy a meal made with loving care. "Ok I will be down in a minute," I told Orlando. "Tell Big Momma that I'll be downstairs soon," I said with hunger hidden within my words.

"Okay Cookie, I will" Orlando said as he ran down the attic stairs from the excitement of eating breakfast with his big sister Cookie. I got myself ready and went downstairs to join my siblings for a decent breakfast at the kitchen table. Now big Momma had this big bulky cherry oak table in the kitchen. It had six chairs and looked to be made for royalty. It looked *very* majestic as it sat there in the kitchen making a bold statement. That was the first thing that you noticed when you walked into Big Momma's kitchen was that thick ass table.

When I arrived downstairs to the kitchen I was greeted by hugs and kisses from my siblings. Now this was something that was hard for me to swallow since I wasn't used to this kind of unconditional love that was a pure as salt water pearls from deep below the sea's surface. I felt the love and the happiness that had filled up the room for me. "Hello Cookie, I love you," said my baby sister Carmelita. "Well good morning to you Carmelita, I love you too," I said this time making sure that I looked her straight in her eyes so she would believe me. Carmelita could be so sensitive at times if she felt that you were not being honest with her in your conversations with her. She would cry easily like a thunderstorm produces rain, if she felt like you had hurt her feelings. And in a deep voice trying to sound older than his real age of fourteen was my brother who was the third oldest sibling. Of course he had to try and use his words carefully with strategic verbiage so he could sound cool. "Good Morning Sis, are you ready to have some breakfast with us and begin the day with power?" William said as though he was the man of the house. I replied back. "Of course I'm ready."

We all sat at the huge breakfast table as Big Momma passed out our servings of two pan cakes, two sausage, two eggs, and a glass of milk and orange juice. Big Momma then placed the white platter that held a large stack of pancakes in the middle of the table so we could help ourselves once our first serving had been annihilated. As I looked around the table I thought that this family was good, yes good. We were blood related, loved each other and most important we were there for each other. Finally a real family that was truly mine. After all of us had finished filling our bellies up with pancakes, we all took turns at excusing ourselves from the kitchen table. I was last. Big Momma made sure that we went in a proper order. The youngest ones' first and the oldest one last.

When I left the table I guess that I had acted as some sort of Diva, mind you that I never meant to that was never my intentions. Instead of getting washed up and dressed, I took my happy, full belly ass back to bed. I soon was awoken by the bellowing voice of Big Momma at the bottom of the stairs insisting me to come back downstairs. "Mary there is work needed to be done around this house!" Big Momma said as if she was really saying that there was a "catch" to eating her breakfast.

I was shocked that my siblings had forgot to mention this important detail to me earlier. "Ok I'll be right down!" I yelled back at Big Momma with resentment. I was now very leery of surprises that came with a clause. Come down and eat a good wholesome breakfast so I can then work you like farm mules afterwards. I reluctantly picked out the clothes that I was going to wear on that day, and I went downstairs and took a bath. I put on my clothes and I combed my hair. I was now ready to join the team who was my sister and my two brothers. They were already standing in the living room waiting for Big Momma's instructions. "Go get the mop bucket and fill it with water," she told William. "And Orlando you get the broom and dust pan for your sister Carmelita," she instructed him to do sounding like a drill sergeant at boot camp. Finally Big Momma barked out my instructions. "And Mary … you get the other mop bucket, fill it up with water and get some towels out of the linen closet so you can wash the windows." I wasn't impressed with having to wash the windows, mainly because Big Mommas windows were huge. They were bay windows and they looked and seemed like giant billboards.

After about four hours of working our fingers to the bone we all were finally through with our tasks. When big Momma inspected our work, I came up with a bad evaluation—that's because I did a half-assed job. I didn't feel that it was fair for Big Mommas to feed us so well, like cattle at a stockyard. I felt that we were ten minutes away from being slaughtered and sent to the store so our meat could be packaged and sold to the public for consumption. She had us work all the food off. Even though we did not have them back then, my bones and body felt like I had just finished an early workout at 24 Hour Fitness. Big Momma looked at my finished worked. The expression on her face had said it all without her even uttering a single word. "You call this clean child?" Big Momma scoffed at me. "Yes Ma'am," I said with exhaustion. Big Momma stood silent while giving a long glare, as if she was on the verge of deciding whether to knock me out or have me do it all over again. I was truly hoping that she would not choose the latter of the two choices.

Big Momma didn't say a word for at least a minute or more. She then stated. "Don't return to bed Mary ... we still have to go over to Gussie's house to get the rest of your belongings."

"Okay ... I won't."

As I walked away from Big Momma's intimidated stare I realized in that moment that Big Momma was the umpire at this game. And her long intrusive stares were signaling that I had my first strike. I was unaware that I was a player. Big Momma was the judge and jury; and I wasn't sure if I wanted to serve a life sentence of early morning cleaning each weekend. I felt like the criminal I had no lawyer, my bail was revoked, I didn't get credit for time served. Nor was

I even considered for an arraignment. Big Momma's house was her jurisdiction, and I couldn't ask for a dismissal for her misuse of authority, nor a mistrial, not even a change of venue. I knew because of my gut feeling that Big Momma was going have me in solitary confinement. And I was not going for that again. I felt that I had to be paroled, or come up with a plan for an escape from my blood related Flossie, Big Momma, Grandmother, whatever you might want to call her. But to me she was nothing but a big city, small town neighborhood warden.

Chapter 26

Hon We Meet Again

One day at Big Momma's house felt like a day in a place called *forever*. I had cleaned her house so much and for so long that I began to feel real muscles growing in my arms. All from one day's worth of work! I was sore and ready to take on the challenge of the day going to Hon's to get belongings. I wasn't enthused about seeing Gussie again but I did want all of the records, clothes and other items that I had bought with her money.

Wake up time was 6 a.m. on this day. I think it was against these people's religion to sleep in past 6. Holy hell! I rose from my bed, went downstairs and was greeted by the sunny day peeking back through big bay glass window. There was not a single cloud in sight as far as the eyes could see and nature was as alive as it could be. Birds were chirping loudly, and flowers were all blooming ready to be displayed as bouquets. I could see the neighbors passing by dressed in church attire. The men wore well-dressed tailored made suits and the women boasted matching skirt suits with big floppy wide hats, holding their children's hand leading them to their cars. The whole scene looked like an ABC Family Channel story.

Grandmother went and got my smaller siblings dressed and ready while William and I were left alone to dress ourselves. William, Carmelita and Orlando were going to be dropped off at my Aunt Eva's house while we were at Hon's. Big Momma made a big breakfast again waffles, oatmeal, eggs, toast and fried potatoes.

Back in the day most parents believed in serving big and hearty meals, that way children weren't complaining three hours later that they were hungry. Soon grandmother gathered all of us and began starting to verbally list things for my siblings to do and what not to do. "Now, William you are in charge of Orlando and Carmelita," said Big Momma. She assigned chores for them to do while they were over Aunt Eva's house.

"Carmelita you will wash your Aunt's dishes, and Orlando you will set the table and then take the dishes away after you all are finished eating," Big Momma suggested. Then Grandmother would instruct them on what not to do. "Now I don't want to come back and hear from your Aunt Eva that any of you kids misbehaved. You do what she tells you to do without any lip or back talk and offer to watch your baby cousin, Belincia!"

My brothers and sister all nodded in agreement with what Big Momma was reciting. They never uttered a word—just stood at attention waiting for more corporal orders to come down. I stood on the sidelines just witnessing this bizarre form of obedience. Maybe it was out of respect for Flossie that they acted that way, but to me it all seemed robotic. Grandmother always spoke firmly and stern, never raising her voice at you. It was definitely something new to me. I was always used to being yelled at and cursed out while Hon barked out orders. This was direct simplicity. Big Momma got her point across without embarrassing you. It seemed fake to me, but who was I?

Soon we all got into Big Momma's station wagon and headed off to Aunt Eva's house. Once there William, Orlando, and Carmelita got out of the car. They came around to the driver's side and gave Flossie a hug and a kiss on the cheek goodbye. I watched as they walked up the driveway to Aunt Eva's door. Aunt Eve came out waving her hands to Flossie as though she was trying to flag down a police car. She was so over dramatic with her emotions.

"Hello Mother!" Aunt Eva yelled out.

"Hi Eva!" Flossie replied back in a low but audible voice. "I'll be back to get them in a couple of hours," Flossie said assuring.

I continued to watch my siblings as they greeted Aunt Eva with hugs and kisses, as though they'd never seen her before. Even my Uncle Charles was giving Flossie an over-exaggerated wave as though he was the master of ceremonies at a beauty pageant. Everybody was so loveable and polite that it seemed so unreal. While sitting in the car I felt that I was watching an episode of the black Leave It to Beaver.

After all of The Price Is Right waving and blowing kisses through the air had been done and the show was over, Flossie pulled away from the curb and drove off. I was glad to leave that soap opera scene. On the way to Hon's house, Big Momma never said a word to me. It felt kind of awkward because I could read what she might be thinking. I began to feel as though she felt obligated to go to Gussie's to retrieve my belongings. She didn't really want to do it, and I could feel that through her deader than a doorknob silence towards me. No one really wanted to be around Hon, so I understood her feelings. In the wake of the silence, I took it upon myself to get the conversation going. "So Big Momma, do you really want to go over to Gussie to get my clothes, or are you doing it because you feel that you have to?" I asked just wanting to hear a sound other than my voice in my head shouting, *I'm bored!* Grandmother stopped at a red light, turned and looked at me and said. "Don't you think that it's a little too late for you to be asking me that question now, especially since we're halfway there?"

"No not really," I replied back.

"You still haven't given me an answer to my question, Big Momma," I said trying to force her to give me an answer. Grandmother turned again at me and said. "How I feel, or what I'm thinking is not of your concern young lady."

What a chicken ass answer to evade the question, I thought to myself. And with that, we both went back to the fresh calmness of silence.

I felt anxiety coming over me just thinking about seeing Hon again. It had been two months since she kicked me out. And I was hoping on a miracle when we arrived. Maybe she would realize that she had made me feel the same way I made her feel and that she would be ready to make amends with me, herself and God. But Gussie was too damn stubborn and mean-spirited to care about someone else's feelings. She was one of those people who were meant for damnation and hell. She was the real devil's daughter.

Upon arriving at Gussie's, Big Momma honked her horn to get her attention since she had no phone service. I saw the living room curtains move and Gussie peeking her head out of the window. Seconds later, she came flying out of the house and down the steps to the car like a 747 jet plane gunning down the runway. "And what the fuck are you doing over here at my house with that black Bitch in your car?" Gussie asked in her old usual callous voice.

"Gussie that is no way to speak to the child, and besides I brought her over to retrieve her clothes and other personal belongings," Grandmother said in a mild mannered voice.

"I didn't ask for no motherfucking rain," Hon shouted sarcastically at my grandmother. "So I don't want your pancake mix looking ass to do a rain dance at my house! You sorry excuse for a fucking Indian!"

Big Momma just shook her head without responding.

"Thank the fucking Lord anyway," Hon shouted. "I was getting ready to burn all of this motherfucking shit!"

"Gussie quit using the Lord's name in vain like that!" Flossie scolded.

"Fuck you, you make believe paper machete Indian! You came over to my goddamn house without a flea-bitten ass invitation whore!"

"Gussie can you please stop all of the cursing and let's just go and get the girl's clothes," Flossie said with compassion.

"Okay," Hon surrendered. "Fuck it! That bitch ain't getting any luggage from me to put her shit in!" Gussie replied exhaustingly. "That Bitch is getting what she deserves ... trash bags."

"Okay Gussie! Let's go and do this!" Flossie ordered.

As Flossie got out of the car to follow Hon into the house, I opened up the passenger door to get out too so

I could show Big Momma where my things were in the room. Just at the moment Hon swung back around and said. "Bitch you are not ever allowed in my house again!"

"All I want to do is retrieve my belongings," I said diplomatically to keep the peace.

"I don't give a fuck as to what you want to get! If you come any closer I will burn all of your good for nothing shit! You better let Flossie gather up your shit if you know what's best for you!" Hon said with a darkening rage.

"Fine!" I said as I opened the door and proceeded to enter and have a seat. I was just hoping that she would let me have all of my personal items. So I waited in the car quietly as Hon and Flossie gathered my life with Hon and placed it into big black Hefty lawn and leaf bags.

Soon I saw Hon and Big Momma coming out of the house with six large trash bags. I got out of the car and helped Big Momma load them into the back of the station wagon. After the last bag was inside of the car, I looked over at Hon and I saw this once a giant of a woman the same scoundrel who used to hurt me both on the inside and the outside— standing beside the car looking like someone who had just lost *everything*.

Actually, she did lose everything because I took it from her lie by lie and dollar by dollar.

Call us even.

I didn't feel guilty and I had no remorse while I stood there in front of her. She wasn't intimidating any more. She wasn't strong nor was she the woman I loved as a little child. Her words were no longer a threat, and for the first time in my life I saw her as I had seen myself as a child vulnerable, not sure of herself and weak.

I just stared at her and she stared at me. And without uttering a word we both locked into each other's eyes. And her eyes seemed to suggest, *Mary you've won. I give. You win.* Ironically, there was no trophy or award for winning this fight. I only got revenge, but in reflection, it was worth it. My deep thoughts were interrupted by Big Momma saying, "Let's go Mary we have everything that was yours in these bags. You can sort and go through them when you get back to the house"

"Okay Big Momma" I said with sadness in my heart.

I felt the urge to say goodbye to Gussie, to be civil, to acknowledge our life together. But that never happened because Gussie wouldn't give and neither would I. So, we would leave as we met strangers.

As I reached for the car door to get in Gussie spoke. I thought that she was going to tell me I'm sorry, but instead she asked. "Have you heard from Officer Johnson yet? I still have the protection money saved up " Now this was putting me on the spot. Big Momma was looking at me as to say what in the world is Gussie talking about; and Big Momma also was waiting for me to answer her back. Again I had to think quickly and on my feet. "No, I haven't but if you would like I can try and contact him if you want to give me the information."

"Hell no! I don't want you to contact him you fucking lame lazy bitch! Fuck you and your Goddamn grandmother!"

I shook my head, got in the car and we drove off. I thought to myself as we pulled off … *Gussie, you had one last chance to make it right with me and you blew it.* The next level of revenge will come from a higher power than me.

Chapter 27

Colorado Bound

It was exhausting dealing with Gussie, and I was glad that it was the very last time that I would see her. Big Momma never questioned me about what Gussie meant about the protection money, nor did I offer any information about it. I definitely didn't want Big Momma to discover my secrets, nor did I want my evil to come out in the light. I was just as bad as she was.

I realized that it seems that it's not the dark that people fear, but it's the light that scares us because we are there in the spotlight, so society can judge us, ridicule and sentence us to their determination of what's right and what's wrong. Not by the laws of the land, but by their own personal and moral conscience. We want to hide our dirt so no one can analyze it and come up with an alternative answer other than ours. We want to cling to it and protect our lies as a mother would protect her child. And I became one of those people who were hiding my secrets in the dark. Now both Gussie and I had secrets that were placed in this magical box that was never opened until this book was written.

Big Momma and I arrived home after stopping off at Aunt Eva's house to pick up William, Carmelita, and Orlando. We all helped and grabbed a trash bag from the car and took it upstairs to my room in the attic. After every bag was accounted for, I laid across my bed and decided that I wasn't going to mess with those bags today I was just going to try and chill and get to know my siblings. So I went downstairs to join them.

We laughed some, we played around some, and then I talked to them about our mother, and about how it was to live with Big Momma. Everybody had the same answer. Big Momma is "Awesome! We love her! She's the best!" For some odd reason my heart didn't agree. I still resented the fact that my siblings were allowed to live with Big Momma and I was left by the wayside to deal with Hon.

Big Momma was married to Grandpa Walter, but he was scarce around the house. He hardly spoke and you rarely saw him. He allowed Big Momma to be in charge and conduct conversations with me. When Aunt Eva came to visit, she spoke but was very reserved towards me. She just stared at me most of the time instead of sitting down and having real conversation. I felt like a piece of artwork on display at a museum when I was around her. They both treated me as though I was a specimen in a science project that they both needed to place under a microscope to really understand me. This was very irritating to me.

From the jump, I started getting in trouble with Big Momma. I was too big for my britches to be up under her tyrannical rule. First, I wanted to go to the store to get some cigarettes. I thought that I would do the right thing and ask Big Momma's permission.

"Big Momma, is it okay if I went to the store?" I asked.

"What are you going to the store for?" Big Momma inquired.

"If you really want to know, I want to buy some cigarettes," I said.

"Oh ... I don't allow any smoking in or around my house," Big Momma said as though she was laying down the law. To me that was not answering my question, so I ignored her reply and asked her again. "So does that mean that I can go to the store if I don't smoke in or around your house?"

"It means that I do not condone smoking for a fifteen year old child so the answer is no!" grandmother said in a low, but adamant voice. Well of course I didn't like nor accept that answer as gold. So I exited the living room, and I went outside on the porch. "Don't go outside of the yard, Mary!" Big Momma yelled. *That was it*!! Doesn't she know that I'm fifteen and that I have ridden the bus all the way downtown, to school and back? Who does she think that I am ... I'm certainly not a little child!

While outside I saw my baby brother riding his bike back and forth on the sidewalk. *Why is he outside the yard especially when he is younger than me?* I asked myself. Ahhhh then I had an idea pop in my head!

"Hey Orlando let me use your bike so I can ride up to the store!" I said in an intimidating voice.

"I don't know Big Momma told me to never let anyone ride my bike," he said with a quivering voice.

"Don't be a punk!" I scolded. "And besides I'm not just anybody, I'm your big sister that you haven't seen in years!" I replied trying to run a guilt trip on his little mind.

"Okay sis," he surrendered. "You can ride my bike, but come back quick because if Big Momma finds out that I let you ride my back, I'll get a whipping."

"Okay … I'll be back before Big Momma even knows that I left," I said reassuring Orlando. So Orlando handed me the bike, and I sped off to the store like I was running a triathlon race.

When I arrived at the store, I propped the bike up alongside the store wall and went inside to buy myself a couple packs of cigarettes and a Coke. I returned out of the store, got back on the bike and raced back to Big Momma's house. As I was pulling up to the house Orlando ran up to meet me at the bike. "Ooh Cookie you're in trouble with Big Momma!"

"Why is that Orlando? I asked. "What did you do?

"I'm sorry Cookie but Big Momma asked me where you were … at first I told her that I didn't know," he said crying. "Then Big Momma said that if I didn't tell her where you had gone she was going to give me a whipping, so I told her that you took my bike and went to the store," he said. "Big Momma was mad because she said she told you not to go," Orlando added.

"I got what I needed, and I'm not worried about Big Momma!" I said with my chest stuck out and hands on my hips. Soon Big Momma came to the screen door. "Cookie, Orlando said that you rode his bike to the store is that true?"

"Yes I did … and you already knew the question to that answer Big Momma," I smarted off.

"Don't you dare talk back to me like that girl? I will put you on punishment for not minding me. Do you hear me?" Big Momma asked with a slightly higher tone in her voice than usual. I didn't respond. I thought to myself ... hmmmm ... I've been beaten with brooms, mops, and skillets. I even had a gun pointed at my face and head and you think that I'm afraid of being placed on punishment.

Who gives a rat's ass!

I knew right then that Big Momma and I were going to clash. Big Momma showed a different side now instead of that heartwarming loving grandmother. She became the Drill Sergeant at boot camp, and all of us were enlisted when it came down to her strict rules and punishments. I knew that I was in trouble when I heard Big Momma shout. "Come in the house now Cookie, your punishment is going to start now!" She said. "You are grounded for a week!"

"Well I'm going to smoke me a cigarette first before I come inside" I said rebelliously. Big Momma stared at me as though I was an unwanted Jehovah's Witness standing in her yard. And while she was staring at me, I lit my cigarette and began to smoke. "Come in the house now Orlando, I don't want you out there while your sister is smoking!"

"Okay Big Momma, here I come," Orlando said as he waved to me goodbye.

When I finished taking my last puff of the cigarette I flicked it into the street and then I entered the house. Big Momma was in her rocking chair looking at me as though I had polio. "You didn't know that Orlando has asthma?" Big Momma asked.

"No I didn't ... how was I supposed to know that?" I said with anger. "I was living at Gussie's while he was living here," I added to my statement.

"Go to your room child, and don't come out unless you need to use the restroom or I call you down to eat!" Big Momma ordered.

I did as Big Momma requested and went up to my room.

But she wasn't done being mad at me just yet ...

While on punishment in my room, Carmelita and Orlando came up to the attic to visit me. "I'm sorry Cookie," Orlando said. "Yeah and he's telling the truth too " Carmelita said as she slurred the words because of her missing front teeth. I used to laugh and make fun at her when she would talk. Not in a mean way to hurt her feelings, but just in a fun way that would make her laugh and giggle. I was getting tired being cooped up in my room, and besides I was having a nicotine fit. I hadn't had a cigarette in so long I began to go into withdrawals. You smokers know what I'm talking about—irritability and inability to breathe. So I decided to break another rule. I lit up a cigarette in my room. I opened the window and I started smoking. I was a bad-ass back then.

Carmelita asked, "What are you doing, Cookie?"

"Smoking a cigarette," I replied back. "Do you want to try it?" I asked her.

"Yes I do," she said. So I told her to come over by the window and take the cigarette and inhale. When she did, she let out a cough that sounded as if her lungs were going to explode. "Be quiet! Do you want Big Momma to hear us?" I asked. Soon Orlando wanted a turn at smoking. "Let me do it, I promise that I won't cough like Carmelita did ..."

"No you can't," I told him. "You have asthma, it's not good for you to try and smoke." The little brat started to cry.

"But you let her smoke …" he whined. "You like her better than you do me," he said in a sobbing voice.

"That's not true Orlando," I said in a convincing but irritated voice. "Shut up and quit all that crying like a little bitch, come over here and take a puff if you want to," I told him. No sooner than Orlando took a puff of the cigarette, and he started coughing, did my older brother William show up in my room.

"What are you all doing up here?" William asked as though he was the man of the house. "Big Momma sent me up here to see what all the noise was about!" William said proudly. "Cookie … are you teaching Carmelita and Orlando to smoke cigarettes?" William asked shocked. Before I had a chance to answer him back the next words out of his mouth were … "I'm telling Big Momma that you are letting Carmelita and Orlando smoke in the house!"

I got off the bed and started to chase him, but William started running and skipping steps like he had performed this act many times before. I couldn't catch up to him before he ran in front of Big Momma spilling his guts out about what he had seen up in my room. And soon Carmelita and Orlando followed him down the stairs before Big Momma had a chance to call their names. Here it comes as I counted down. Five, four, three, two, one, zero. "C -o- o- k- i- e come downstairs right this instance!" Big Momma shouted from the bottom of the attic stairs.

"What Big Momma?" I shouted back down.

"Don't what me young lady come downstairs and see what I want!!" Big Momma insisted.

I slowly trudged down the attic stairs where I saw Big Momma at end of the stairs. She was wearing a long frown on her face that read disappointment and anger. "You are not about to come into my home and influence your sister and brothers with your filthy, nasty habits!" she warned with a stern face. "You have just added another two weeks to your punishment, since you are too old for a whipping!"

"I don't care about being on punishment" I said in a rebellious tone.

"Don't back talk me, before you make me raise my hand at you! Now go back to your room unless otherwise told to do elsewise!" Big Momma said in low keyed voice while gritting her teeth.

"Fine," I said stomping back up the attic stairs. But that wasn't the last time Big Momma would be angry with me that was still coming.

The last straw that broke the camel's back with Big Momma was when I got into a fight with William. We were both sitting out on the porch, while I was still on punishment. One afternoon on the swing, William started an argument with me. Now mind you I was still holding a grudge against him for ratting me out to Big Momma; so when he decided to kick me in my shin. I kicked him back, to which he responded by kicking me harder. At that point, I tried to kick his leg off from his knee, as if I was trying to make the game winning field goal. Big Momma heard the commotion on the porch and she came to the black screen door. "What is all the noise about out here? I'm trying watch TV!" Big Momma yelled. "Cookie started it Big Momma!" William insisted putting the blame on me."

"You're a goddamn liar!" I shouted back at him.

"That's it come inside the house now Cookie!" Big Momma said. "You sit right there in that chair!" I did as

I was told and I listened to what big Momma had to say. "I want you to know that I have spoken with your father, Homer, and I told him that you have been staying with me here." I just sat in silence waiting for the bomb to drop and explode. "He wrote me back and said that he wants you to come to Denver to live with him. He said that he will send you an airplane ticket to fly out there to live with him. What do you think about that?" Big Momma asked.

"What if I don't want to go?" I said in a sarcastic voice.

"Oh you're going," Big Momma said.

"Well if you already had your mind made up then why would you ask me what I thought about it?" I snapped back.

"There is no sense in talking with you Cookie! Go upstairs until it's time to eat!" she scolded.

I went to my room not showing any tears until I had reached my bed. Again this same picture was playing at the matinee, but this time at a different location.

Abandoned and Unwanted.

I had gotten tired of having a ticket to the live showing. I had only lived with Big Momma for two months and now it was time to go. What's next? I asked myself. I had a snitch for a brother and a grandmother who was ready to ship me off to my father. It felt as though my life was the theme song of the *Fresh Prince of Bel-Air*, just the lyrics were changed. Instead of saying you're moving to your Aunt and Uncle in Bel-Air, my song was "you're too big for your britches for me to scold so you're moving with your father in Colorado!"

I soon began to hate my family the more I got to know them. It seemed that every adult betrayed me. And once again I had to move on. My airline ticket arrived in the mail two weeks later. Inside of the envelope was a letter from my father about how excited he was that I was finally going to be living with him. The letter also read how much he loved me and how much of a great time we'll have. He ended the letter by writing, *"You'll fall in love with Denver, Colorado Love Daddy."*

My flight was scheduled for 8 p.m. Saturday night. I was going to miss my best friend Patricia, and my drinking partners, Vera and Robin P. and my dogs, Furious and Tinker. I packed up my things and stayed in my room reminiscing on my life, the ups, the downs and the heartache. I knew that I had said that I wanted to find a way to leave Big Momma's house, but I didn't want to be kicked out. I wanted to have this grand scheme that I came up with to resolve Big Momma's military standards.

That didn't work out.

Oh well

When the sun went down that day, Big Momma loaded my suitcases in the car with the help of my brothers Orlando, William and my sister, Carmelita. They all started to cry, but I didn't. I felt that they all had a part to play in me having to leave. I was the black sheep of the family. All of the siblings that were at Big Momma's house were children from my mother, but who had different fathers. While they were all staying at Big Momma's, I had to go. My siblings hugged me, told me that they loved me and then they waved good bye.

I thought that love was a lie and that it was just three words that were easy to say but harder to act upon especially when it came to me. I opened the car door of the station wagon, and I got in. Soon Big Momma was driving down the freeway speeding like a bat out of hell. She couldn't wait to put me on that plane.

Once there Big Momma had me check in and now it was just a waiting game. My heart was heavy, and I didn't want Big Momma hanging around any longer than she wanted to be. I felt like an egg without the yolk and egg whites. I was just a shell. As I sat in the chair at the airport next to Big Momma, I just wanted to separate myself from her as soon as possible. I didn't want to be anywhere near her. Soon the reservationist called out on the intercom the United Flight from Kansas City International to Denver, Colorado Stapleton Airport is now boarding passengers. Both Big Momma and I rose up from our chairs at the same time like two Jacks in the Box that you wind up. We looked at each other for a rigid moment—as though we were having the same thoughts at the same time *I can't wait for you to leave.*

"I hope that everything will work out all right living with your father," said Big Momma breaking the silence.

"Yeah I hope so too," I said.

Without even a hug Big Momma said, "Goodbye call me sometimes and let me know how things are going."

"Okay I will," I promised as I stood alone in the line waiting to board this enormous vehicle called a plane. I finally arrived to my seat and in a few minutes I was riding off into the clouds of the unknown future with my father. It had finally settled in I was Colorado Bound.

Chapter 28

Life with Daddy

Fall had arrived, and just like the season, I was on my way to a new life with Daddy. Twenty minutes outside of Denver, I looked out of the window of the plane and saw buildings that looked like colorful Lego blocks. The city lights were all lit up like Christmas time. The skyline was so remarkable that it reminded me of a carnival in space. I had psyched myself up to believing that going to another state was going start the healing process, but I knew I had to put forth effort if this relationship with my father had any chance of working. I decided while on the plane that I was going to make the best of this new relationship with my father. I had gone into Big Momma's house filled with resentment, but this time, I wanted to start off fresh and give my father a fair chance to be my father. I wasn't going to hold it against him for not asking me live with him sooner. I was going to make this a happy adventure. I was excited about traveling and seeing a new city, culture and environment.

The plane landed at 9 p.m. Denver time and we were welcomed by the pilot: *Welcome to Denver.* I waited a moment before exiting the plane. I sat back and took in the view, fresh air and the different kinds of people. When the line thinned out, I was able to exit the plane, and retrieve my six bags from baggage claim. I still had about forty dollars in my pocket from Hon's extortion money. Since I had so many bags, I had to get some assistance from one of the airport porters and pay for a cart to carry my luggage out of the terminal. And when I arrived, there he was … my father, Homer. He was waiting for me in the lobby of the United Airlines terminal.

He stood there leaning against the wall wearing a brown plaid suit coat, a tan pair of dress slacks, a dark brown rustic turtleneck sweater and some brown shiny shoes. He was grinning ear to ear. My father was a very thin, dark-skinned man about average height. He loved to wear his dark Stevie Wonder shades. That's what I called them because they were so big and every time he would wear them he looked like he was blind. In a way, my daddy reminded me of a broke down Sammy Davis Jr.

"Hello baby! Come give Daddy a great big ole hug!" he said as he rushed towards me as though he was a contestant for the Price Is Right. "Hi Daddy," I said sounding like a daddy's girl already. When we finally reached each other we gave a great big bear hug to one another. "Turn around and let Daddy take a look at you!" he said with joy in his voice. "You were just a little baby in diapers, and the next time that I saw you, you were walking and talking. Now look how big you've gotten! You look just like your mother, sweetheart," Dad said without taking a break to breathe.

"Thank you Dad," I said graciously.

I found out soon enough that Dad cursed just as bad, or even worse, than Hon did because the next words that came out of his mouth was. "Fuck! Are all those fucking bags yours?"

"Yes Daddy they're all mine," I responded. "The great big one holds my records and then the other suitcases have my clothes in them," I said.

"Goddamn! You packed as though you were going to fucking bum fuck Egypt!" he said in a nasty tone. "Do you expect me to lift the motherfucking bags in the goddamn car? I have a bad back when I got injured in the military! Fuck! Shit! What the fuck am I supposed to do with all of these motherfucking bags, baby girl?" He said while have a pacing tantrum. People began to stare at us like we were husband and wife. I was so embarrassed. He was ranting and raving like a total maniac.

I thought to myself I had just left one moron to travel and live with another lunatic. This can't be real. "Calm down Daddy ... we can get another porter to carry my luggage to your car," I said thinking that I had solved the problem of his anxiety.

"That service costs and Daddy didn't bring any money to pay for shit like that!" My father said as though this was an *extreme* hardship.

"It's all right I have some money I can pay for it," I said to ease the tension.

"Really?" Dad asked with a surprised voice. "Okay then," he added.

I called a porter over to assist with the bags and soon all of my bags were tucked neatly in the trunk. The ones that couldn't fit were placed in the back seat of daddy's car. We got in the car and were off to explore Denver, really just to meet dad's friends.

Dad droved this white, two-door winged car that had two red stripes that went on both the sides of the driver and passenger doors. I figured out quickly that my father was really cheap when he would turn the damn car off when he was stopped at a red light.

"Dad, why did you turn the car off at the stop light?" I asked.

"Oh I turned off the ignition because gas is too high, and I like to conserve it when I can," he said like the cheap skate that he was. Turning the car off at every other traffic signal was getting on my nerves, but not enough for me to continue to complain about it. On the ride to some unknown part of the world my father would start giving me historical facts according to him about the state of Colorado. "You know baby girl the sun shines in Denver three hundred days out of the year. And did you know that the directions of North, South, East, and West are the opposites from Kansa City?"

He would recite information as though he was a history professor. I quietly listened to his rambles like an infant listening to a bedtime story. While driving he showed me the state capitol, and the Lowry Air Force Base. It was nice to have a change of scenery and to be with someone who I felt safe with. In this moment, I didn't have a care in the world.

We soon pulled up to one of my father's old friends house by the nickname of Big Jim. Dad and I came over unexpected, but Dad didn't care. We got out of the car and Dad knocked on Big Jim's door. "Hey Jim! It's Homer!

Come open the door!" I saw someone pull the living room curtains back to take a peek outside. Then a bright porch light came beaming on above us. The door opened and this tall black man with a deep voice answered back. "Hey there Homer, it's kind of late man for you to be visiting," the big burly man said to my father. "Yeah I know. But my daughter just arrived at the airport, and I went to pick her up. I just wanted you and your family to meet her!" dad said as though I was a newborn infant. "Oh sure come on in," Big Jim insisted.

"This is my daughter, Mary and this is my friend Jim," my father said.

"Hello, it's nice to meet you," I answered back.

"Wow Homer! She is beautiful!" Big Jim said as he gave me a looking over.

"Yeah I know! She looks just like her mother. Hey Jim where's your wife? I hope that she hasn't went to bed yet!" Dad said enthusiastically.

"No she hasn't, let me go get her. Hey Baby!" Jim shouted. "Homer's here and he wants you to come and meet his daughter!" Jim explained.

Soon this short, jolly polite woman enters the room with her hair in curlers. "Hello Homer and who is this beautiful doll?" she asked.

"Oh this is my daughter Mary. Say hello to Jim's wife, honey," Dad said.

"Hello" I said blushing at all the attention there were giving me.

We all sat down at the living room table and I watched as my father, Jim and his wife laughed and talked. Big Jim offered Dad a beer while his wife sipped on a glass of wine.

Big Jim went to the refrigerator and handed me a soda. I was grateful, but I looked at the beer like a cat looking at Meow Mix. I wanted one too, but I dare not let Daddy know that I drink, not after he had spoken so highly of me. I didn't want to do anything that would put a blemish on his belief of who I was. He made me sound as though I was this pure and innocent teenager who was so righteous by all means. In his eyes I was the perfect daughter, and for now I wanted to stay that way.

After a couple of hours and the adults were beginning to feel a buzz from drinking, my father decided to ask, "You know since I've been staying over at my ex-wife's place and I don't quite yet have my own place, I was wondering if you both wouldn't mind if Mary could spend the night?" Good move daddy, I thought to myself. Wait until the liquor has affected their thought process and then blow their minds with a question that they couldn't refuse. How could they tell their good friend "no?" After all, Homer had just got his daughter after thirteen years of being without her.

I could probably learn a few things from this cheap bastard. "Of course she can Homer," Jim said with a big alligator smile. "Is it all right with you too?" Homer asked Jim's wife.

"Oh yes it is," she said in a soft warm voice. "You will have to sleep on the couch and I'll get you something to sleep in tonight," she said to me.

"Okay," I said feeling sleepy from the flight.

"Oh … have you eaten anything since your plane ride?" Jim's wife asked me.

"No I haven't," I said hoping that meant she was going to feed me.

"Are you hungry darling?" she asked.

"Yes ma'am," I said in a hurry.

"Okay … I'll fix you a peanut butter and jelly sandwich," she said courteously.

"Me too!" my father interjected. "I haven't had anything to eat either since picking her up from the airport!" he added as though she was a waitress taking his order.

"Okay … that's two peanut butter and jelly sandwiches coming right up!" Jim's wife said playfully.

She disappeared into the kitchen and soon returned with a tray that had two peanut butter sandwiches cut in a precise and perfect triangle with a cold glass of milk.

"Thank you," I said as I happily enjoyed the taste of this sandwich. I felt like I was eating caviar because of the pleasant hospitality.

"You are quite welcome dear," she said cheerfully.

My father took his sandwich and scoffed it down like a vacuum cleaner on full power. The laughter was interrupted by my father's smacking as he ate. At the table, I noticed that he only had two teeth on the bottom one of each side of his mouth. He looked like a bull dog while he ate his food. I was getting annoyed from all of the clicking and sucking sounds that he made with his teeth while he ate. I just wanted him to hurry up and finish his food.

When we had finished eating, Jim's wife took our plates and the tray and went into kitchen. There she washed, rinsed and set them in the drainer to dry. I followed her to the bedroom to retrieve a pair of pajamas. She showed me where the bathroom was and gave me a towel and wash cloth. I changed out of my clothes and I returned to the living room where I saw Daddy heading out the door. "Okay darling,

Daddy will be back in the morning, to take you over my ex-wife's apartment so you can meet her," he said with some underlining disgust in his voice.

"Okay Daddy, I'll see you in the morning," I said.

He gave me a bear hug and kissed me on top of my forehead. He thanked both Jim and his wife for allowing me to stay in their home and then he left out the door and into the night. As I fell asleep that night, I thought maybe Denver wasn't going to be so bad after all.

The next morning Daddy arrived at Jim's house after noon. He entered the house with that bull dog grin. I had already taken a bath, eaten breakfast, and Jim's wife was just finishing up my hair. She had French braided my hair so I wouldn't have to worry about messing with it each day. That hairstyle would last a good three days before I needed a touch up.

"Look at my little girl! She looks like a young lady!"

"Thanks Daddy!" I said again eating up his compliments as though they were a box of Russell Stover's chocolate candies.

"Are you ready to go with Daddy and meet his ex-wife?" he asked.

"Yeah" Sure" I said. "Daddy what about my hair? Do you like it? Big Jim's wife French braided it for me," I said as if I was getting ready to attend a glamour shoot.

"Yeah, it's beautiful Honey," daddy said as he tried to hurry out of Jim's house.

As we approached the car, I saw Big Jim run to the porch. "Call me later Homer!" he said as if he was dad's prom date. "Okay I will!" Homer replied.

When we got in the car Daddy turned to me and said, "Daddy's ex-wife is sort of mean that's why we're divorced" he said as though he was schooling me on her." Daddy had turned on the radio and there in the car he had brought up another irritating flaw of his: singing. The man couldn't sing worth crap. He was all off tune and again I heard that damn clicking of those two teeth in his head. I stared out the window, not uttering a word hoping that the song would soon be over as he bobbed his head from side to side to the music.

For a moment he looked and acted like Ray Charles. And of course he was sporting those Blue Blockers, window-shield looking sunglasses on his face. At my father's ex-wife apartment I soon breathed a sigh of relief. The music was over and Dad was now wearing a serious expression on his face—like he was preparing himself to face her like I used to do with Hon. Then next thing my father did was he proceeded to open the trunk of the car. That's where he kept his stash of alcohol. He brought out a pint of Vodka and he opened it. And he then turned the bottle up and drank it like a runner who was dehydrated and was drinking water. He drank until it was half empty. "Now I'm ready to face this fat mean Bitch!" he said as though the Vodka was some sort of miracle drink that gave him courage. He then went to the glass security door and rang the buzzer to her apartment.

"Who is it?" a voice on the speaker said.

"It's Homer, and I have my daughter with me," he said. There was silence which remained until Daddy rang the buzzer again. "What do you want Homer? Again the voice asked. "Idella quit playing games and let me in! I want you to meet my daughter!" my father said demanding entry into the apartment.

After another moment of silence the door buzzed for us to come in. We climbed up the stairs to the second floor and down the hall to her apartment where Dad reluctantly knocked on her door. I heard the chain being taken off the door, and then the latch and a lock was opened. There the door stood half-way opened. My father reached and pushed the door back so we could enter the apartment. That's where I saw this tall Big Bird figure of a woman with a short cropped hair cut sitting on the couch looking as though she was mad at the world and at my father.

"That's no way to act towards me Idella," Dad said. "It's a motherfucking shame that you always got to act like a fucking bitch towards me!" daddy shouted.

"And what is your damn point Homer? I know that you didn't drive all the way over here to tell me about my attitude!" Idella said in a voice that was deeper than my father's.

"I want you to straighten up your fucked up attitude and meet my daughter that's what the fuck I want you to do!" Daddy said. "Fine then," Idella said as she stood up from the couch. When I got a good look at her I knew that if Godzilla had a daughter she would have been it. "I'm Idella" She said. "And you are whom?" she asked in a firm voice that had the correct annunciation.

"My name is Mary. I'm Homer's daughter," I said proudly.

"I know that shit already. And believe me there are many other things to be proud of than this drunk who you call your daddy," she said without any remorse. I didn't appreciate her talking bad about my father, but I didn't let on to my distaste of her behavior.

"I need you to do me a favor Idella," Daddy said in a needing way.

"Hell no Homer! I'm all out of doing favors for you!" she said as she continued to eyeball me while talking to him. "Please Idella, I need to you to let Mary and I stay the night. She just came to Denver on a plane from Missouri," dad said.

"I don't care if she came from Jamaica. She can't stay here and neither can you as a matter of fact. Can you comprehend the words divorce, you dumb drunk?" Idella asked harshly.

"Bitch I ain't dumb. I might be a fucking drunk, but I ain't dumb," he said defending himself. To me he was dumb for admitting that he was a drunk!

"Goddamn it Bitch let us spend the night! It's not like you have anywhere to go. Don't nobody want your lurch ass any way!" dad said.

For a moment I thought that I was back at Hon's house the way these two were going at each other. After about an hour of arguing, Idella finally gave in to my dad's request. "Don't expect me to feed her … she is your damn daughter!" Idella said.

"Fine Bitch I got some money, you probably ate all the food in the house up anyway," Dad said.

"And don't think that you are going to slither your black ass into my bed either Homer," Idella warned my father.

"There ain't no goddamn room in the bed anyway when you get in it," insulted Homer. "You are the only bitch that I know that needs the driveway to iron your fucking clothes."

Now, that was a good insult, I thought. You go dad. I was his cheering section. I knew at that moment that I didn't like this bitch myself. I busted up laughing. I noticed that the more that he drank that night the funnier he got. Later that evening, Dad and I went to the store and bought us two chicken pot pies and two coke colas, and a pint of vodka. We came back home and ate our food and we went to sleep on the two big sofas that aligned the living room of Idella's house. As I drifted off to sleep I thought about two things 1) What other adventures and characters does my journey of Denver and my father have in store for me; 2) Who in the hell names their daughter Idella? No one but Godzilla!

Chapter 29

House to House

After spending the night at Idella's apartment, Dad and I got up that morning and got ready to face a new day. "What's for breakfast Idella? Dad asked. "Whatever you bought and that's nothing! You haven't bought any food since you've started staying over here!" Idella barked at my father.

"Well can you go in the kitchen and fix some breakfast for me and my daughter anyway?" Dad asked. "You need to start acting like a woman and get in the kitchen where women are supposed to be," Dad said.

"No ... I need to be kicking you and your daughter's ass out of my apartment," Idella said in a forceful voice. I knew that Idella didn't like me much, but what I didn't know was what her reasons for not liking me were. Was it because she hated my father and any kids that he had happened to spawn were disliked, or was it because she just didn't like me for general purposes? Whatever her reasons were, I didn't want to stay and find out. "Let's go Daddy, we can get breakfast somewhere else," I said after getting tired of their back and forth debate.

"Baby girl don't interrupt Daddy when he's trying to talk. Women are to allow the men to finish talking first," Daddy instructed as though I had really committed a taboo. Without a word I looked at him as though he was speaking to someone else.

"Look here woman even though I am your ex-husband, I'm telling you to take your fat ass into the kitchen and fix me and my daughter breakfast now!" Dad ordered. "I want some eggs, bacon, toast and pork chops!" Dad recited as if he was sitting down at a booth at Denny's.

"You are about to make me lose my religion, Homer! I will cuss you out if you don't get the hell out of my house! You really don't want me to embarrass you in front of your daughter do you?" Idella challenged.

"I will slap the ever loving cow shit out of your ass if you even try to embarrass me in front of my child," Homer said as he paced the floor back and forth as if he was delivering a powerful Sunday sermon to the congregation.

"Fuck you, Homer! Do I need to get out my baseball bat?" Idella threatened.

"You know Bitch I don't need to eat none of your goddamn food! And neither do me and my daughter needs to be in your house!" daddy said in a cowardly voice. I thought that Daddy was the man of the house when he was talking all that shit—and when Idella mentioned the baseball bat—he decided that it was time to leave. Idella wore the pants in that household for sure.

"Let's go get the hell away from her baby girl!" Dad said.

"Ok goodbye Idella," I said.

"Good riddance to both of you!" Idella said as she turned away and walked into her bedroom. Dad and I walked out and down the stairs to his car parked outside on the street.

Once inside the car, daddy started flapping his jaws. "Fuck that Bitch! She didn't want to mess with me! I held back because I didn't want you to see Daddy act like a fool! Boy that Bitch was lucky I tell you," Dad said as a cowardly boast.

"Yeah of course she was Dad …" I responded in disbelief of his manhood. "Dad where are we going to eat at?" I asked. 'What about IHOP, or Denny's?" I suggested.

"No baby girl … there is no reason to go out and eat when there are women I know who can cook for us. As long as God makes women and kitchens … man will always have a place to eat," dad said as if he was quoting from the Bible. "We are going over to my play aunt's house today. I call them Ruth and Bunny," dad said as if he was taking me on a field trip.

"Okay," I said.

When we arrived at Ruth's and Aunt Bunny's house, neither one of them were happy to see to us. In fact, they both looked shock by our unannounced arrival. Neither one of them said anything for about a minute or two. Then I heard someone from behind the screen door say. "Fuck! its Homer act like we're not home!" the other voice responded. "I can't! I opened the door already and they both can see me!"

"Well this ought to be fun, and he has some floozy with him too!" I heard someone say but I really couldn't see who was talking at the time. "Well just don't stand there, he knows that we are home because you answered the damn door ... let his ass in!" the other voice said with disappointment.

I began to wonder what my father had done to these people for them to have such an attitude towards him. Standing at the door with Ruth was Aunt Bunny, and the first words out of Ruth's mouth was, "Homer do you have my money that you owe me?"

"Damn can't you say hello first?" Daddy asked. "I tell you I can't stand an ignorant ass woman! You need to show some respect to a man when you see one," daddy said as he walked past Ruth and into the kitchen. "Ruth get in here and make me and my daughter some breakfast!" Dad ordered.

"Who the hell is she? Does she have a name, Homer?" Ruth asked.

"Of course she does it's Mary," Dad answered sarcastically.

"Well hello there Mary. As you already know my name is Ruth, and this is my sister Bunny," Ruth said.

"Hello Ruth and Bunny. Are you really related to my father?" I inquired.

"Hell no we're not related to that imbecile!" Ruth replied quickly.

"God forbid that we would be related, to tell you the truth I can't stand your father!" aunt Bunny proclaimed.

"Oh okay," I replied. Then Ruth went into the kitchen and started fixing Father and me some breakfast. While cooking breakfast, Ruth asked my dad. "Homer, is Mary in school and if so what school is she attending?"

"Damn Ruth! She just got in a couple of nights ago from Kansas City!" "You need to read your medicine bottles and make sure that you are taking the right amount before you start asking dumb ass questions like that!" Dad replied as he laughed at her statement. "Well it was only a question Homer, you don't have to be so critical!" Ruth said out of embarrassment.

"I might even try to home school her," Homer said.

"Not with the brains God gave you Homer, she would be dumb as a bag of rocks if you ended up being her teacher," Aunt Bunny said while laughing. "What would be the name of the school Homer?" The Dumb Ass Academy," Aunt Bunny said in a sarcastic tone.

"Fuck! You old sick ass bitches! I don't see neither one of you with any degrees hanging on your walls! You both have a lot of damn nerve to be talking bad about me!" Daddy said in an angry tone.

"You know Homer … you are one ignorant ass excuse for a man," Aunt Bunny said.

"Just shut the hell up and go to sleep! Why don't you take enough medication so you can overdose in bed? At least we would have some fucking peace and quiet!" my dad shouted back at Aunt Bunny.

"And why don't you kiss my ass, and go to hell!" Aunt Bunny said.

"Your ass is so flat I would have squint to see it, Bitch!" Daddy replied.

"Now stop it you two let's not behave this way in front Mary," said Ruth. "Now Bunny you go ahead and go to your room and I'll bring your breakfast into your bedroom when it's ready."

"Well all right but you better tell Homer to stop fucking with me," Aunt Bunny said as she lit a cigarette and walked into her bedroom.

"Get out of here you ugly Bitch!" my father shouted at Bunny.

"Homer what did I just say?" Ruth scolded my father.

I began to wonder if my father had anyone who liked him besides Big Jim and his wife. Soon breakfast was done and we all sat down at the kitchen table to eat. Aunt Ruth had left the kitchen to go to aunt Bunny's bedroom. Aunt Ruth was carrying a tray in both hands which held Aunt Bunny's breakfast on it. When Aunt Ruth returned to the kitchen she let out a suffocating gasp. "Homer, I know that you are not eating before anyone has said their prayers are you?"

"What?" Dad responded like the jerk that he was. "If the Lord wanted you to say a prayer every time you sat down to eat … the food would have it labeled on the boxes. On a carton of eggs … Warning don't eat these eggs before you say grace, after they have been cooked!" Dad said jokingly.

"That's not funny Homer!" Ruth scolded. "And I wish you wouldn't make fun of the Lord or saying grace. This is a God fearing house," Aunt Ruth said in a serious voice.

"Well why do they call it saying grace? Why couldn't it be called saying Larry or saying Richard? It's always a woman who fuck shit up," Dad said. "You can't eat your fucking food because of a bitch who wants you to pray first. And now we got to repent to God so we can go to heaven because the bitch bit into an apple! I bet that bitch Eve didn't say grace or Beverly when she ate that apple and went to tell

Adam. No she didn't because the Bitch was hungry just like me!" Dad said as though he was there watching Eve.

"Shut up talking like that Homer" Aunt Ruth said raising her voice. "You need to ask God to forgive you and you need to say grace before you take another bite of my food.

"Fuck! Fine!" This toast needs some butter and jelly, thank you Lord for filling up my belly! How was that Ruth?" Dad asked sarcastically.

Ruth didn't say a word, but rolled her eyes at him. Then she looked at me as if to say you sweet poor innocent child. Her look reminded me of look that the church congregation gives the neighborhood hoe when she comes to services. You know the look of damnation and that your soul already has a reservation to hell.

I also thought that my father was a chauvinistic pig who really had issues with women. Finally after the crude remarks had stopped and we all had finished our meal. Dad got up from the kitchen table and said. "Well it's time to have a cigarette." Now that's what I wanted to hear. I hadn't smoked a cigarette since I had left Big Momma's house. I didn't know what my dad's response would be about smoking, but I guess that I was going to find out soon enough. I talked myself into asking him if I could have one of his cigarettes. "Dad, can I get one of your cigarettes?" I asked hoping that he would not debate the issue.

"You smoke baby girl?" Daddy asked proudly.

"Yes I do," I replied.

"That's my girl, why of course you can have one of Daddy's cigarette," Daddy responded. Daddy reached in his same old plaid jacket pocket that he wore when he met me at the airport and pulled out some non-filtered Pall Malls cigarettes and gave me one. "You want a light baby girl? Daddy asked.

"Yes please," I said with joy that he didn't complain about me smoking.

"Okay," Daddy said. And we both spent some bonding time with each other over a Pall Mall cigarette. Now those non-filtered Pall Malls were some of the nastiest cigarettes I had ever smoked. All you tasted was the strong taste of pure tobacco. I was used to smoking menthol cigarettes such as Kools, or even Salem's; but these tasted as though I was smoking dirt right from the ground. They were awful, but I didn't have any money to buy myself a pack, since I had to spend my money buying chicken pot pies and soda for the both of us when I stayed at dad's ex-wife, Idella's apartment.

"Homer you don't mind that girl smoking cigarettes at such an early age?" Aunt Ruth asked in a hasty voice.

"No Bitch! I don't mind! That's my daughter and I'm raising her, not you … so stay out of my business." After we had finished our cigarettes, Daddy pulled out a pint of Vodka from his other jacket pocket. He opened it and turned it up as though he was playing a trumpet. He didn't come up for air until it was half gone.

"I guess you're going to let her drink too, huh Homer?" Ruth challenged.

"I guess it's time for me to go. Oh by the way, can Mary spend the night at your house tonight? I'm still looking for a place for both of us to live!" Daddy exclaimed.

"Yes I guess so Homer there's not much for a young girl her age to do over here though," Aunt Ruth said.

"That's okay ... just make sure that you feed her lunch and make some for me and save it until I come back," Homer said as an order. Again Aunt Ruth looked at him with disgust. Dad then rose from the chair. "Goodbye baby girl, Daddy will be back later on tonight to check on you," he said as he pinched my cheek. And he left out the door and entered his car and drove off. I watched as he slowly disappeared down the street. I went back into the kitchen where Aunt Ruth was there standing, and staring at me. "Let's wash the dishes, Mary. I'll wash and you dry."

"Okay," I said politely. After the dishes had been washed, rinsed and put away I asked Aunt Ruth if I could watch TV. "Yes you can but the only TV that we have is in Bunny's room. You'll need to ask her yourself if you can watch it with her." I knocked on aunt Bunny's door and said. "Can I watch TV with you Aunt Bunny?

"What? I thought that you had left with your crazy father I guess so, but you got to be quiet so I can hear the TV," she said.

"Okay," I agreed. I then sat in the chair and silently watched her boring TV show with her as time slithered along like a snail on the beach. I was bored out of my mind when I heard the doorbell ring. I got up from the chair in Bunny's room and ran to the living room, just to see who it was. "Don't answer my door! You don't live here!" Aunt Ruth scolded me. So I stepped aside and I allowed her to answer her own door, even though I was cursing her out in my head.

"Hello Aunt Ruth," said a woman who had two boys with her who repeated the greeting.

"Hi there who are you?" The older woman said with a smile on her face as big as the sun. "My name is Mary," I said.

"This is Homer's daughter," Ruth interjected.

"Oh really, I remember that he told me that you were coming out to Denver soon. My name is Judy and these are my two sons, Butch and Kenny." Both boys said hello to me and ran into the kitchen. I was happy because one of the boys seemed to be close to my age. I was just happy to see some younger people in the house because Ruth and Bunny were like two old women living in a convalescent home. I was completely bored to my bones before they had arrived.

The boys wanted something to snack on and so Ruth scurried into kitchen to get their request. I sat in the living room with their mother Judy. Now Judy was a fair skinned, tall, black woman who had dyed her hair a strawberry blonde. She had an upbeat, hip, and cool demeanor about herself—like someone you'd love to hang out with. She also had those big pretty brown eyes and if she ever dyed her hair black, she would have resembled Diana Ross, I thought to myself. She wore some cool ass clothes with some Ray Ban designer sunglasses. I sat down in the chair next her wanting to know more about her.

"So you're from Kansas City?" she asked me.

"Yes I am. I've been here for a couple of days now," I said with enthusiasm.

"Have you gotten a chance to explore some of the places here yet?" she asked.

"Not really, but I have met my father's friends Jim and his wife and my dad's ex-wife, Idella," I explained.

"Oh you mean Lurch!" Judy laughed. "Yes, I met her too. She's mean as hell, isn't she?" Judy laughed and said.

"Yes she is, and she does look like Lurch on the Addams family." Judy had me cracking up talking about Idella. Finally I was having some fun in this mortuary. I thought.

"Where are you and your father staying at? Judy asked.

"Nowhere yet he's still looking for a place for us to live," I said.

"You must be kidding! Homer brought you all the way out here and he doesn't even have a place for you both to stay?" Judy said with astonishment in her voice. "Well I don't put anything pass that leaching scoundrel," Judy said. Wow! I thought does anyone ever have nice things to say about the man that I was about to live with known as Daddy?

While I was still enjoying Judy's company, Aunt Bunny and Ruth walked into the living room. Soon all three women were discussing and comparing notes about my father right there in front of me as though I had somehow evaporated into thin air. They laughed, made fun of him and joked as though he was going to be the headline article in tomorrow's newspaper. I quietly stepped out of the room without being noticed. I guess that's what I get hanging around grown folk's conversations.

I went into the kitchen where Butch and Kenny were. They had finished eating the snacks that Aunt Ruth had fixed for them. "Hey you want to go and play outside in the back yard?" Butch asked me.

"Yeah let's go!" I said wanting to be anywhere else other than the living room.

Now Aunt Ruth's home was a one level ranch style home and every room was spacious. The kitchen had these sliding glass patio doors that gave us quick access to the backyard. Both Bunny and Ruth didn't have a lot of furniture which made the house seem roomy. Now the furniture that they did have was new, but it had such an ancient décor about it. Some of the chairs and the sofa looked like it may have been previously owned by King Arthur. Their home wasn't fancy but it was cozy.

Ruth was still working as a nurse at a hospital and her sister Bunny had retired from being a nurse. It seemed that back then a career at the hospital was the job most women had—except for Judy she had her own business. She was a hairdresser, and her shop was located on Colfax Street in Denver.

I remembered wanting to own my own business just as she did, but soon that thought was diminished. I just wanted to wrestle and play with Butch and Kenny. Soon it was lunch time and we all sat down at the kitchen table, even Aunt Bunny joined us to eat lunch. I saw Aunt Ruth prepare my father's plate and put saran wrap on top of the plate and she placed on the counter. After Judy had finished her meal she decided that it was time for her and the boys to leave. "Oh you're leaving now …" I said with sadness. I didn't want them to leave.

"Yes I have some errands to do," Judy said.

"Can we stay here and play with Mary while you do your errands, Mom?" Butch asked.

"Please!!" the boys and I begged.

"I don't see why not. I'll pick you boys back up when I have finished running around," she said.

"Cool!" we all said as we went back to talking and playing as if we had no worries in the world. Before we had known it, it was time to have dinner and Aunt Ruth had us all wash up and sit down to eat. When the boys and I finished our meal we sat in the living room waiting for Judy's return. Aunt Ruth cleaned up the kitchen and she started to run her bath for that night. "I hope that your father comes back before I go to bed … that's if he comes back," Ruth said. "Bunny and I go to bed at 8 p.m. sharp!" she insisted. Needless to say both my daddy and Judy arrived back to Aunt Ruth's house at the same time.

Judy grabbed her boys but not before my dad asked her if I could spend the night at her house the next day. She agreed. So I spent the night at Aunt Ruth and Bunny's, then at Judy's house, and at another woman's house I had just met who went by the name of Aunt Francis. She was Homer's real-life sibling. And just like the others, she didn't care too much for me or my father. She was a short brown skinned black woman who was a real snob. She thought that since she was a real estate agent and was making good money that her shit didn't stink. Well her whole attitude stank to the high heavens if you asked me. I didn't want to visit her because she always wanted me to entertain my cousin Roger. Roger had Cerebral Palsy and as a fifteen year old kid, I didn't need this.

Eventually, I returned to Big Jim and his wife's house where I received both good news and bad news. The good news was Daddy had found us a place to live. The bad news was given to my dad by Jim and his wife. "Homer, your daughter has been using our telephone to call long distance to Kansas City. And let me tell you that phone bill was high to the tune of $300!"

Ouch!

I'd gotten homesick and missed talking to my friends so when I asked Jim's wife if I could use the phone she said yes without inquiring who I was calling. My dad was so mad at me that night he left and he didn't reappear until the next morning to give me a piece of his mind about that phone bill. I just knew that baby girl was in trouble, but how much. I was going to find out real soon.

Chapter 30

Idaho Springs, Colorado

That morning was just like any other precious Colorado day. When I opened my bedroom window, I felt the crisp and clean air on my face. There was a slight breeze that came along which brought some seconds of relief from the hot sun. The clouds were thick and shaped in the forms of big cotton balls in the sky. My hypnotic view of nature's paradises quickly vanished and the day became chaotic with all of the drama coming from my father about Jim's phone bill.

"Mary, bring your goddamn ass out of that bedroom!" I heard my father yell from the living room. I was no longer his baby girl. Now, I had a name.

"I'm coming Daddy," I said reluctantly.

When I arrived in the living room I saw my father there standing with one hand on his hip and the other one holding the bill. I hadn't had a chance to wash up and put on my clothes before he had arrived. So there I was standing in the living room, half asleep in my pajamas.

"What the fuck is this, Mary? Can you please in God's name tell me what the fuck is this?" Dad asked repeating this phrase one more time just in case I didn't hear him the first two times.

"It's a bill Daddy," I replied sarcastically even though I knew exactly that it was Jim's phone bill.

"I know that shit already you fucking smart ass! I want to know why there are three hundred dollars in long distance calls charged to it from Denver to Kansas City?"

"That's because I missed talking with my friends back home. I asked Jim's wife if I could have permission to use her telephone, and she said *yes*," I said throwing the blame back on Jim's wife instead of me.

My father turned and looked at Jim's wife and said. "How could you let her use the phone she has only been here a week? She don't know no goddamn body here in Colorado! You're just as dumb as she is!"

"Don't you talk to me like that, Homer! I thought about asking her who was she going to call at first, but then I thought that she was calling you so I let her use the phone. So, you need to stop fussing at me," Jim's wife said back to Homer.

"Jim are you going to allow Homer to speak to me in that tone of voice?" Jim's wife asked.

"Well baby … Homer does have a good point," Jim said as he scurried out to the back door to do some pretend work on the yard. *What a coward* I thought to myself. Jim ran and disappeared instead of standing up against my father. What a complete chump.

"Boy you can't leave a simple minded woman and a smart ass teenager together," Daddy said. "I'm surprised you two geniuses didn't burn the house down. Now, back to you Mary," Daddy said angrily. "Fuck! How do you expect Daddy to pay for this motherfucking big ass phone bill? What in the fuck did you talk about that would cost 300 hundred dollars?"

I remained silent.

"Can you tell that I am so goddamn mad at you?" Daddy asked as he paced back and forth and shook his head.

"Yes daddy," I replied. "I can see that you are very mad."

"I could just knock the shit out of you for doing such a dumb ass thing! I only get a fixed income every month and now I got to give half of it to Jim to pay for the fucking phone bill! My God! That is money out of my motherfucking pocket!! Shit! Fuck! Damn it to hell! Why?" my father cried out in despair.

I wanted to laugh at the way he was ranting, raving and pacing the floor. He had reminded me of a confused lab rat trying to make his way through a maze. "Daddy got to sit down, rest and have a cigarette," he said as he placed his head in his hands.

He sat down and he lit up a cigarette and still was complaining about having to pay the bill. "Fuck your friends in Kansas City! You are gone from there so just act like they died or something! Don't call them motherfuckers no more!" Daddy said.

"All right Daddy I won't," I promised

"Do you think you could write each of the friends that you called and tell them to ask their momma's for one hundred and fifty dollars each to pay for the phone bill?" Dad asked as if that was a real remedy.

"Dad I only called three friends and the bill is only three hundred dollars. That would be an extra one hundred and fifty dollars you're asking for," I replied.

"I know that shit!" he yelled. "The other one hundred fifty would be for me!"

Dad then went out to the back yard and called out Jim's name. "Hey Jim! Let's go and get ourselves a beer and get away from these silly ass women!"

"Oh okay Homer you got some money?" Jim asked hastily.

"Hell no man I don't have no motherfucking money! I asked you so you can buy us both some beers!" Dad said with a tone of entitlement.

"Oh okay right Homer let's go," Jim said as he grabbed his wallet.

Now it mid-morning and these two went to have some beers. I don't even think that my father had eaten anything yet for breakfast. So I was left there with Jim's wife to watch TV and await their return. The day was going by so slow and Jim's wife had nothing to say to me at all. She fixed me breakfast and lunch and by the time my father and Jim returned home it was late in the evening and she started to serve dinner.

When Homer and Jim walked in the door the first words out of his mouth were insulting and rude. "Ah it's about time that your woman does start doing the things that God put her on the Earth to do! Cook, clean, fuck, and produce babies! That's all women are good for … anything else they will fuck it up!" Both he and Jim laughed at my father's comment. But Jim's wife stared both my father and Jim down, as her eyes promised Jim *you just wait till Homer leaves.* And her sharp silence deafened the laughter that dad and Jim shared.

After dinner Daddy said to Jim, "Hey man … I need for you to let my daughter stay just for two more nights, I'm working on getting us an apartment and I just need two more days."

"Sure Homer that's no problem man," Jim recited.

Those were two of the slowest days of my life. I found myself in another boring routine. Wake up, wash up and dress up. Then eat breakfast and watch TV. Dad would run in and out of the house sometimes he would arrive back to eat lunch with me and then the other day he only came back for to have dinner.

I was anxious about finally getting our apartment that Dad had so proudly boasted about. I couldn't wait for him to come in and say those magic words. We have a two bedroom apartment. So I waited and waited. And on the second night Daddy came in with a fifth of vodka a carton of cigarettes, and the good news that I had been waiting for since I had arrived in Denver. "Baby girl daddy got us an apartment and we will be leaving tomorrow morning to move into it!" Daddy announced with a chuckle.

"Yes!" I shouted.

That night we celebrated the new apartment. I had to keep my excitement zipped up like an overnight bag, so I wouldn't look like I was being ungrateful to Jim or his wife for having a place to rest my head. While the adults had liquor, wine, and pizza I was in the bedroom watching TV with my soda and a slice of pizza. Daddy even gave me a pack of his nasty ass Pall Mall non filtered cigarettes from the carton he had just bought. After I ate and washed my plate out, I went to put on my pajamas. I went to bed dreaming about our new place.

The next morning I awakened early. When I walked into the living room, no one was up. As I looked around the living room, I saw that the fifth of vodka was empty laying on its side near the couch that my father was sprawled out on snoring. There were beer cans and two empty wine bottles sitting on the table along with six empty beer cans looking like an unkempt bar.

Damn lushes.

I went back to my room and played the waiting game. I had to wait for someone to wake up before I could do anything else. And I waited from early morning to the mid-afternoon. I even fell back to sleep myself waiting on these drunks to wake up and take care of business. Finally, late in the afternoon I heard my father waking up. I rushed out of the room and into the living room, "Daddy are you up?" I asked trying not to be annoying, but wanting to get his full attention. "Hell no! I ain't up I just have to use the bathroom!" he said in a groggy drunken voice. I waited for him to come out of the bathroom. "Daddy, how long do you think that it will be before you're up?" I asked.

"Damn baby girl! Give your father a chance to shit, shower and shave before you ask that!" he said sternly. Shortly thereafter, I heard Big Jim get up and then next his wife.

Okay, I thought to myself. Life is beginning to happen now. Let's all get in gear and get rolling. Well of course everyone else was on a different time schedule than me. Jim and his wife had to have their morning coffee. My father had to have his morning booze and coffee. I was so hyped up at seeing the new place I didn't want any breakfast this morning; I just wanted to go. Finally after all of the yawning, stretching, and hangover ailments were addressed, my father decided to get ready to leave. "Hey Jim you got some aspirins that I can take? I have a splitting headache," said Homer.

"Yeah Homer, they're in the medicine cabinet," Jim replied.

"Thanks man!" Daddy said. Soon both Daddy and I said our *thank you's* and *goodbyes* and we headed off to the car. Daddy placed my small bag in the trunk and we were ready to go to our own place. We rode off into the sunset. Daddy said that he wanted to get there before the sun went down so he was speeding down the highway like a bat out of hell. I felt good knowing that finally Daddy and I were going to get a chance to bond and know each other. I was ready and I had hoped that he was ready too.

We were driving for what seemed to be a long, long time. When I began to see the city starting to disappear in the rear view mirror and the mountains getting closer I asked my father. "Daddy where are we going exactly, and how long will it be before we get there?"

"We are going to Idaho Springs, Colorado, baby girl!" Daddy said proudly. "And it is only a thirty minute drive from Denver!"

"Oh we're leaving Denver. But why Daddy?" I asked.

"Because you can't learn anything in black schools, the white schools are better for a black girl like yourself," he said as though he had experienced this theory.

"Really?" I asked. "Did you graduate from a black school daddy?

"No and that is why I don't want you going to a black school. When I was growing up I was only allowed to go to the seventh grade and I was forced to drop out," he said.

"Why?" I asked him thinking that I was going to get a reasonable answer.

"I'll tell you why baby girl," Dad said as he cleared his throat. "I was kicked out of school because I was the smartest kid in the whole school and the principle and all of the teachers were jealous of me!"

"What? Are you serious?" I asked.

"Yes! Your father is a genius! When I tried to go back to school the principle had all of the doors locked even the main entrance to the lobby was locked. They were afraid of Daddy's intelligence," he said. I knew all of subjects before they tried to teach me. I was showing the teachers how to do it," Dad said as he gave me a look to see if I was buying this bullshit. "Did you go to college? I asked. "No because the white man wanted me to enlist in the service instead," he said. At this point I didn't want to ask him why, but he told me anyway.

"My grade point average was 4.00 in the seventh grade and when I enrolled into college and went to attend … the whole damn college had moved from the previous address that I enrolled at!" he said without cracking a smile.

"The college moved without telling you? I asked.

"Yes right after I enrolled, I went to start my classes and when I arrived the motherfucking school was a goddamn parking lot! That's the fucking truth! And after that since the board of education was jealous of my intelligence too, they had the military to send me a draft letter to enlist in the Army so I did. Daddy served the United States motherfucking service and boy was it a battle zone when I enlisted."

"Did you fight in a war Daddy and how long were you in for?" I asked like a complete idiot.

"Fuck no I didn't fight in no motherfucking war, I wanted to but I pulled my back out just when they was about to ship me over to the war. Daddy got hurt in the line of duty. I even received a purple heart from Richard Nixon." My father interrupted his story by asking me to look in his black bag and grab him a bottle of aspirins.

"Daddy didn't you take two aspirins at Jim's?" I asked.

"Hell no baby girl I took the whole damn bottle! He can afford to buy some more."

I thought to myself not only is my father a liar he's also a thief. When I opened the black bag there they were a whole bottle of Excedrin's. "Daddy when Jim told you where the aspirins were what did you tell him?" My father started to grin and then he said. "Oh I told Jim that he was out of aspirins while I took them and put them in my pocket."

I didn't want to hear any more of his scattered brained lies, so I stayed quiet for the rest of our trip. On the ride there I noticed that the air was getting even thinner and my ears began to stop up as we were going higher and higher in altitude. I looked at the foothills and saw different kinds of trees. There were evergreens, aspens, and spruce trees everywhere alongside the mountain. Daddy said that we were climbing up to six thousand feet. I saw ranches with horses and cows running freely. I saw buffalos and people on top of tall mountains hang-gliding off of them.

The road to Idaho Springs was narrow and winding, and soon I began to see people riding on horses on the street.

"We have arrived Baby girl!" Daddy announced. I looked up and saw a huge sign that read *Welcome to Idaho Springs Colorado*.

A few blocks down was our apartment. Daddy pulled up in front of this two story house. At first I thought that my father had bought us a house. I should have known better with his cheap ass. After all he just stole a bottle aspirins from his so-called best friend then drove thirty two miles to come to Idaho Springs. I felt as though we were the poverty stricken Bonnie and Clyde.

We pulled up to a two story, vintage blue house that was trimmed in white with a big front yard and a gray mailbox. We got out of the car and walked up the steps of the front door. Daddy pulled out the keys and opened the door. There was a hallway that led to a community kitchen where there was an electric stove, refrigerator and a table.

"Our room is upstairs baby girl," Daddy said. We both climbed the stairs to the second floor and our apartment was on the right. When Daddy opened the door my dream started to burn and crash like a race car where the driver had lost control. I looked around and all I saw was a room with an old beat up pleather couch a refrigerator, and a small coat closet, a table and a window facing the street. The other room had a full-sized bed, a closet, and a dresser with a window that looked out onto the streets. The bathroom was across the hall. "Daddy are we at the right address?" I asked in disappointment. "Yes we are baby girl! This is my castle and your palace!" Daddy said proudly. "Now let's go and get all of your fucking bags that you brought out here," he said.

It was a long way to be carrying all of my bags from the car to the second floor, so I took my time and I took one bag at a time—of course while my father sat on the couch and started drinking his fresh bottle of vodka. "Are you going to help me Daddy? I asked.

"Hell no!" he said. "No one told you to bring all of those motherfucking bags here from Kansas City. I only have two bags ... and besides Daddy's back is hurting so I can't help," he justified.

I was cursing him out in my head while I struggled to retrieve all six of my bags from the car to our room. It took me a while, but I finally got all of my bags upstairs. "Tomorrow I will enroll you into school. Listen, make sure you take home economics so you can start cooking for daddy," he said with a smirk on his face.

Is this what I have to look forward to? There wasn't even a television in the room, just Daddy's old record player and his old ancient records.

"What's for dinner Daddy?" I asked.

"Daddy bought you your favorite meal for both of us chicken pot pies and coke cola."

Oh boy I said to myself. *Here we go again with them damn pot pies!*

Chapter 31

A Cheap Date with Daddy

After dinner both my father and I retired to bed. He got the pull out sofa and me the full-sized bed. We rose at 6 a.m. the next morning. It was Monday and the beginning of the rest of my life. Dad was taking me to Idaho Springs to register for school. In the back of my mind, I worried whether I would be able to transfer into the tenth grade because of all my ditch days back in Missouri.

I got washed up and dressed by 7:00. Now it was time for breakfast. When I returned to our room my father was not there. I figured that he had not gone far since he was there when I went to take my bath. I went to my room and I sat on the edge of my bed waiting for my father's return to the room. I was a bit nervous about returning to school especially a new school and an all-white school. Hell I was in an all-white town. There was only one other black man there and he called himself a cowboy. He was the first and only black cowboy I ever met. He didn't live too far from our boarding house and we met him last night while we were moving in.

My thoughts were soon interrupted by the sounds of keys opening our room door. It was my father and he had bags in his hands. I was hoping that it was breakfast. I wanted pancakes, sausage and eggs this morning. But of course it wasn't. "Hey baby girl! Help Daddy with these bags," he said as he struggled to hold them.

"Sure Daddy" I replied as I took two bags at a time. He kept a hold of the third small bag. The first thing Daddy did was open up the small brown paper bag and he brought up a pint of vodka and he commenced to turning it up until it was half gone. "Ooh wee that shit is good!" Daddy exclaimed wiping his mouth off.

"Daddy isn't kind of early for you to be drinking? I asked. "You haven't had anything to eat yet, you need something in your stomach first," I said as though he was really going to take heed of my words.

"Don't you ever question me about shit, woman! I am the man of this house and whatever the fuck I do you better agree with it and don't say a fucking word!" he said angrily. "I got you some breakfast. Are you hungry?" he asked, flipping it and becoming jovial again.

"Yes I am," I said. "Did you get any eggs and pancake mix?"

"Hell no I didn't get any pancake mix and eggs! The Bitch at the checkout counter, wouldn't let me buy two eggs out of the dozen, so I left them there on the counter. Those damn eggs are expensive and we don't need twelve when it's just you and me anyway! And fuck! That pancake mix shit is too damn hard to make! I would have to get two boxes of that shit so we both could have a pancake each!"

Oh God! I thought. *This man is dumber that a cement block.*

"But I did get us some more chicken and beef pot pies, and some Shasta Colas." The pot pies were ten for a dollar and the sodas were 75 cents for a six pack so I bought two. Then I got a carton of cigarettes for me and two six packs of beer baby girl! Daddy really knows how to budget money!" My father replied as if he'd done something spectacular. I couldn't believe that he had found a liquor store that was opened at 7 a.m. in this little town. But for sure he did. My dad could find a liquor store after an earthquake. My last thought for this morning was that this day needed to end soon so I could go back to bed. After my father drank three beers and downed the rest of the pint of vodka he was ready to heat up two pot pies and serve two iced filled glasses of Shasta Colas.

After we ate we were off to register me at the high school, which was only a ten minute drive from the house. I was hoping the teachers wouldn't notice that my father had been drinking all morning. Before we entered inside of the school, my father took a handful of Altoids mints to kill the smell of the booze.

Welcome to Misfits U.S.A. It was official.

The school was so beautiful boasting of architecture that looked to be more Greek than American. The exterior was built with massive stones of gray and black granite. The doors were made of fine wood, the handles brass and the soaring windows were all spotless.

As we toured the school I noticed that all of the classes were small about fifteen students per class. Everything seemed to be in perfect order with the exception of the oddness of human stares as the students glared at my father and I like aliens as we walked past them. There were mean stares, confused stares, and just simple rude stares given to us as we walked around. Some students dropped the books that they were carrying when they saw us. Whispering started to happen, then came the pointing of fingers in our directions and loud laughter.

What's so funny? I asked myself.

Maybe it was the way my father was dressed. He called himself trying to fit in. So that morning he wore a beige turtle neck sweater, a beige matching suit coat with pants and to top it all off he had some tan colored cowboy boots with a scarf around his neck as though he was wearing an ascot. He did remind me of the black Thurston Howell the third on Gilligan's Island. Even though my father was nowhere near being rich and was not sophisticated in the least, he always believed he could play the part. That he could make you believe that he was both worldly sophisticated and somewhat rich. All a person really had to do was ask him to pay for something and then they'd see the real truth of my father.

After the tour we returned home. Dad went straight to the refrigerator and opened another beer, and he reached in the bag and pulled out another brand new bottle of vodka and started drinking. I went straight to my bedroom but not before dad called me back out.

"Mary come in here … I want you to sit down so I can go over Daddy's rules with you." Now I knew that this discussion was coming, but I had other things that I wanted to discuss like school supplies. "First of all Daddy is going to drive you to school and pick you up from school," he said sometimes slurring his words.

"Okay," I said flashbacking to Hon's days of driving me back and forth to school in the bat car when I was in elementary.

"Second of all you do not talk to any of the neighbors nor the landlord, the teachers, or the principal about what goes on in this house," he said barking out his orders. Now this brought back red flags to me—because those were the same exact words that Hon said when she was hiding the fact that she was torturing me. I quickly dismissed that thought because I just knew that God wouldn't let that situation happen to me twice. And besides I knew that I was in a safe place with daddy.

My father kept on with his rules to be followed. "You will not have any visitors over here whether I am at home with you or not. You will not date any boys as long as you are staying under my roof. You will come home after school and do your homework. You will take your baths in the evening, after you have finished eating dinner. And you will not be allowed to go over anybody's house from that school unless Daddy says that it's okay. Do you understand all of my rules?" He asked me all buzzed up on the alcohol. I was so glad that he had finally finished giving me the rundown of all of his rules that I quickly answered.

"Yes of course, I understand all of your rules. Daddy can I ask you a question?" I asked in a daddy's girl voice.

"Sure baby girl … what is it?" Daddy asked now completely drunk.

"Can we get a TV, because it's kind of boring without one?"

"Fuck no! Do you think that Daddy is made of money and besides a TV is what I call an idiot box? You can't learn a damn thing from watching motherfucking TV!" My father said with a tone in his voice that said that question can be dismissed and never asked again. "Besides baby girl, I have a project in mind that will certainly keep you busy. You won't want to watch TV after doing this little project for daddy," he said wearing a sideways smirk.

"Oh really? What is this project daddy?" I asked out of curiosity. "We will discuss this more after dinner baby girl. But now it's time to have some lunch, I'm hungry as hell!" My father said quickly changing the subject.

"What's for lunch, Daddy?" I asked as though I didn't already know.

"Well Daddy's going to change it up a little. This afternoon we will be having beef pot pies! You know they have turkey pot pies too at the store! Daddy's going to have to buy some of them too!" he said with joy.

Uggggh!

"Daddy can I have some water instead of the soda"? I asked. "Why of course you can." When the pot pies were done, Daddy placed them on the table along with his beer and bottle of vodka and my cup of water.

After lunch Daddy took me in his car and we rode down to the Safeway supermarket where he stocked piled on pot pies and Shasta soda, beer, and vodka. After all of the liquor that he had consumed I was wondering how he was still walking straight and most importantly how was he able to drive his car without getting pulled over by the cops. After returning from the store, Dad put up the pot pies, soda and beer into the refrigerator, but left his fifth of vodka on the table. After having two more beers, my father was out like a light. He fell asleep snoring on the couch in the living room. Since there was no TV in the room I too went to my bedroom and fell asleep. I wasn't allowed to close my door to my bedroom at all even though my bedroom was less than six feet from where my father slept.

When I woke up it was dark outside and the street light were blaring in my window. I rose up to see that my father standing over my bed just staring at me. I thought for a moment this is again another scene from Hon's drama. "You need to eat because it is getting late! You also need to take a bath before you go to bed."

"Okay Daddy," I replied. I sat down at the table to a steaming hot turkey pot pie and a can of beer. This time daddy had no conversation for me, so we both sat quietly and ate our dinner. After eating I got up and went to my room to retrieve my pajamas and to go to the hallway to the bathroom which had the bath tub, sink and toilet that the second floor residents had to share. I looked back just before I opened the restroom door to that my father was right on my heels following me into the bathroom. "Oh do you need to use the restroom first, Daddy?" I asked. "You can go ahead of me if you need to," I said with a cautious tone in my voice.

"No that's all right. I am going in with you. There are a bunch of men who live on this floor and I'm not about to let anyone of them hurt you," He insisted.

Chapter 32

911: A Crisis in Colorado

I had my breakfast with Daddy this morning like usual, Shasta cola and a Swanson's chicken pot pie. After breakfast, we loaded ourselves into his car for the five minute drive to school. When we pulled up, Daddy kissed me on my lips and said, "I'll see you soon baby girl, Daddy can't hardly wait until you are back in my arms again. I love you."

"Yeah I love you too," I said.

As I walked up the curvy pathway to the school, all that I could feel was filthy ... even though I had taken a bath. I didn't want to go back to Homer and pot pies, but again I had no choice. I put on my game face and walked into the school with my head held high. That attitude soon changed when I met up with a group of girls and one girl asked me. "What the hell are you doing at our school? Why don't you go back to Africa?"

This comment made me angry but I had to bite my tongue, because there was four of them and only one of me. I ignored them and kept walking. When I found my first classroom there was a piece of paper in my seat that read,

"We don't want you and your nigger father here!" Everyone in class looked suspicious, but there was no one in that room that pleaded guilty to being the author of the note.

I made it through class that day feeling like a broken toy. The rest of the day was uneventful. At day's end, my father came to the school to pick me up and take me home.

The only time that I had a break from my father, was when Judy would request that I spend the weekend down in Denver at her house to visit with her two sons, Butch and Kenny. I enjoyed those getaways because it took my mind off of all the pain that I was hiding inside.

Every time my father drove me into Denver, I remember this long stretch of steep highway from Idaho Springs to Denver. But when Daddy would reach the top, it was downhill almost all the way into Denver. Dad would wait until he had reached the very top of the hill, then he'd cut off the ignition and coast all the way down the highway. We were going so fast, we'd pass up cars that still had their engine on! I was terrified at first, but eventually I got used to this idiot way of driving.

There once was a time when both my Dad and I were on our way to Denver to see Big Jim, and I had gotten so depressed, that I had completely given up again on life, God and me. So while my father was coasting down this stretch of highway I suddenly grabbed the steering wheel ready to end my life and his. He couldn't call me enough Bitches to change my mind about killing the both of us on that day. Every time my father would snatch my hand off of the steering wheel, I would immediately grab a hold of it again. The car was started heading for a small cliff and my father hit me in the face and grabbed the wheel and steered it back onto the highway lane. "What the fuck are you trying to do bitch? Kill the both of us?" he asked while sweat started forming above his brow.

I just sat in the passenger seat not shedding a tear. I then left the steering wheel alone and we were able to make into Denver unscathed. Daddy decided that the trip to Denver was over so he headed the car back towards home. When we arrived back at our room in Idaho Springs, my father made me undress and he beat me with his fists for messing with the steering wheel. He beat me until I was black and blue on my back and legs.

I returned to school the following day where my worst enemies were waiting for me. These two girls wanted to kick my ass bad. They would give me dirty looks and offer racial slurs to me on a daily. I was so tired of being fought at in school and then going home receiving abuse from my father that I was so ready to end it all.

The next morning Dad and I got up as usual and commenced doing our routine. We ate breakfast and then he drove me to school where he opened mouth kissed me and patted me on my ass as I got out of his car. Then he said. "Daddy loves you baby." I nodded my head without returning a glance or word back to him.

As I walked up the sidewalk towards the school I saw Jo. Now Jo was a cigarette smoking, beer drinking girl who loved to fight. She was very much a tomboy. She came up to me and what I thought was going to be an altercation turned out to become a good friendship. Jo had her entourage that she ran with and soon all of us was in this clique. Finally I had made some friends at this school and it took me about a month. I told Jo and her friends about the two girls and some other students who were giving me a hard time at school. Jo told me that whenever I needed her and the other girls just let her know and that they would help me fight those girls. I was thrilled to have an ally on my side. I just wished that she could have helped me fight my father.

Well luckily that day at school the two girls didn't get a chance to fight me. When school had let out my father was right there in the school parking lot waiting for me. When the girls saw my father they backed off and went in separate directions. "Are those two girls friends of yours?" my father asked. "No they wanted to fight me, but when they saw you they decided to change their minds," I said.

"Fuck those two little bitches and anyone else who tries to mess with my daughter. My father said as though he was protesting for a civil rights breach. "Tomorrow before you leave out for school, I want to give you Daddy's 45 so you can blow those bitches head off if they try and mess with you again."

"Ok Daddy," I said. I couldn't actually believe that he really wanted me to use the gun against these girls. But then I remembered that I had used Hon's gun to scare off my menacing attackers back then. But I never intended to actually shoot somebody, that's why the gun was never loaded with bullets. I asked myself, "Were dad and I so different after all?" I finally came to the conclusion that we were nothing alike. We just shared the same DNA blood line. My mother didn't even put his name on my birth certificate, so we shared nothing in common. How sad but true. My father was still a stranger to me in both my mind and my spirit.

On that following weekend my father took me to an outdoors firing range where he let me fire off the gun at paper targets. Now I wasn't very good at shooting and the gun was so big it was hard for me to hold it. The gun also had a strong kick-back when it was fired. We had spent the whole afternoon at the firing range. Afterwards, we drove down to Denver where we went to a gun shop where my father bought a box of hollow point bullets for it. On that Sunday he had me practice shooting the gun again, but this time in an open field in Idaho Springs further up the mountain in a secluded area. The thought ran across my mind plenty of times to just turn the gun on him and shoot him dead. But I guess God wouldn't allow me to take that risk. The next morning which was a Monday, and before we left out of our boarding room, Daddy reached inside of his black gun bag and pulled out his favorite pearl handled 45 caliber revolver. "I want you to put this gun in your bag and take it to school with you and when you arrive at school you give it to the principal to hold for you until school is out. When school lets out you go back to the principal's office and get the gun … and if those girls mess with you then you take their fucking lives! Aim for their hearts or their heads and empty the gun barrel into their bodies!" My father instructed me. He then drank his pint of vodka and we headed out the door so he could take me to school.

When I arrived at school dad kissed me and told me to have a pleasant day at school. I didn't know how pleasant the day was really going to be. I was confused about what to do with the gun in my bag. So I did as my father had suggested and went to the principal's office. I reached inside my school book bag and I pulled out the pearl handled 45 revolver and asked the principal to hold it for me until school was out. Well needless to say that all hell broke loose at Misfits USA High School on that morning. The principal's face was pale from fear. I guess he thought that I was going to shoot him. He asked me where did I get this gun and who had given it to me. I told him the truth … that my father gave it to me so I could use it to kill these girls who have been messing with me. The principal requested I remain in his office. When he returned he had one of the counselors with him and they both sat down and talked to me about my father and the gun.

At that meeting that's when every hidden emotion came out all at once. I started to cry uncontrollably. I told the principal and the counselor everything about what my father had said, and done to me since we've moved to Idaho Springs. I showed them the bruises that were on my back and my legs. I spoke about his arsenal of weapons that he used to threaten me with. I even told about the open mouth kisses and the pats on my rear end that my father so gladly gave and anticipated on doing each day. I was soon emotionally drained with both relief and fear. I just didn't know what was going to happen to me now.

The principal calmly asked me if I wanted to return home to my father and my answer was no. This was the biggest thing that ever happened in this town, we have never had to deal with this kind of emergency situation the principal explained. After my reply the principal got on the telephone and before I knew it the Sherriff, the Deputies, and the town Fire Department were coming in the principal's office to talk to me. I repeated my story to the Sherriff, the Deputies, and the Firemen. The principal handed over the

45 revolver to the Sherriff. Then the Sherriff made a phone call on the principal's phone. When he hung up the receiver he explained that Idaho Springs didn't have a social worker there in that county, so he had to contact the Department of Children's Social Services in Denver to have one come up to the school to talk to me.

While I was waiting for the social worker to arrive the Firemen and the Sherriff went and got me breakfast, a real breakfast. About an hour had passed and the social worker arrived. She entered the office and sat her briefcase down and we started to talk. She had insisted that everybody leave the office so we could talk alone. She was a very hip and cool social worker, and I liked talking to her. She wasn't the straight-laced, by the book, employee who was filled up with conversations of boredom who worked for the state. She treated me with respect, and most important, she had a good sense of humor. She made me feel at ease with my situation and this horrific incident, and I appreciated her for that.

After I explained my story to her she informed me that she and the Sherriff would have a talk with my father and see what he had to say. I was soon whisked out of the principal's office and into the Sherriff's SUV and I was taken to his house to stay while he and the worker talked to my dad. After the visitation with my father, the Sherriff and my social worker returned to the house. The social worker informed me that both she and the Sherriff had spoken with my father at his room. She told me that neither the sheriff nor any of the deputies had seized my father's weapons of machetes and guns. I couldn't understand why he was allowed to keep these weapons. There were a lot of things in life that I didn't understand and my father was definitely on that list.

I stayed at the Sherriff's house for about a week. He and his wife had two children and a newborn infant son who stayed up at night crying; and this situation wasn't the best fit for me or them. So I ended up being placed with a new foster parent who lived in Idaho Springs too. She was a single white woman who appeared to be upset when she realized that I was black. Needless to say that this placement didn't work out either. My Social Worker later told me that she had found me a placement in Denver and that she thought I would like. It was going to be with this single divorced white woman who lived with her stepdaughter who happened to be black too. Like the fact that the stepdaughter was black was really going to make a difference or was going to have such a great impact on me. I still felt angry and unwanted; and as far as living with someone who had a black stepdaughter wasn't really going to make a big change of my mindset of people.

So the social worker and I started the 30 minute drive into Denver. We stopped by a McDonald's and grabbed a bite to eat, and then we headed off for our initial interview with the new foster parent. On the drive there I remembered that I felt happy about returning back to Denver, but nervous about the meet and greet of yet another person who would judge me. I had no chance to sit down with her first and explain myself to her. As far as I know I was just words on a piece of paper to her that she interpreted as having some mental psychological flaws that doctors had diagnosed without even speaking to me personally. I was a subject now that belonged to the state of Colorado, and that was uneasy for me to accept; because I still was a human, living, and breathing, person who had feelings, hopes and dreams. I had issues that needed to be addressed, not symptoms that needed to be diagnosed and cured.

When we arrived in Denver we drove to an area of town that was called Park Hill. It was a very clean neighborhood that was filled with children and the sense of family. We parked in front of this red brick duplex and got out and knocked on the door. Her house was the duplex on the left which I later learned that she was the owner of both houses. We were greeted by the medium height, jovial, white woman who offered her a seat in the living room. After our brief conversation with her, my social worker informed me that the Sherriff would be bringing my clothes and luggage down later. So this would be the place that I would stay at and wait until the custody hearing trial date was set. The trial wasn't going to happen for two weeks so this gave me some time to get acquainted with the woman that I knew as Gigi. Later that day I met her stepdaughter Sharon. She was the same age as me and was born the in the same year that I was. That was one cool connection that we both shared, and we got along just fine.

I was told that we would be sharing a room together which was something that I had to adjust to since I was used to having my own room. I guess that I couldn't be diva and request such a ridiculous accommodations from the woman, who also worked as a social worker herself. After dinner the Sherriff had arrived with my suitcases, clothing and my precious record collections. I was happy to have my belongings. These were remnants of my past and present. I needed these things not only because they were my necessities but they were a part of me; reminders of my schemes, lies and my suffering. These things were the only items that I had that made me feel secure and that I could identify with. They were a part of my past and my life that I knew and had experienced. And I wasn't about to let them go, at least no time soon.

During my first week staying with Gigi I had visits from my social worker and my guardian lawyer. He prepped me on what my testimony was going to be and how the prosecution's reactions were going to be like at trial. We ended up having several sessions to get me ready for trial. My lawyer also informed me that only a judge will be hearing my case instead of a jury, which was fine by me, the less people that I would have to tell my story the better. The lawyer asked me if I was aware of the six thousand dollars check that my father had cashed, which was the allotment that was left of my mother's social security benefits after being split between my siblings. I told him that I had known nothing about that money. My dad had never mentioned this to me. I knew that my father was a lying drunk and petty thief, but now he was an untrustworthy scoundrel. More negative traits that were added onto his moral and ethical resume.

Soon the trial date had arrived, Gigi took some time off from her job to take me to court. I met both my attorney and my social worker there. This was the first time that I had ever set foot inside of a courtroom. I always wanted to stay out of this legal world even though criminal law had fascinated me with its process and the fact was based on who told the most believable story backed up with facts of evidence. I looked around the courtroom and I caught a glimpse of my father when he entered. The arrogant jack-ass had the nerve to bring a loaded gun inside of the courtroom, which the bailiff confiscated. He then walked over to me, and I just screamed out loud. The judge who was already seated at the bench ordered my father to take a seat and not to engage with any conversation with me.

My father and everyone else who attend the trial took their seats and the trial then began. I was the first one called to the stand. My lawyer asked me questions that he had prepped me on and I began to explain my ordeal to many strangers including the serious looking judge. After my testimony I was soon cross-examined by my father's attorney. Each time I spoke to the attorney, the anger in my voice slipped out like water slipping through a small hole. I was finally asked to step down from the stand and then it was my father's turn to spew his lies and twist the truth to suit him. I was appalled by some of his testimony. And in regards to my mother's social security benefits he said that he spent the money on me, even though he couldn't prove that any money was spent on me. Because it wasn't unless he was trying to say that he bought six thousand dollars' worth of Shasta soda and pot pies on me. Then came the time where the judge was about to make his ruling. The whole trial only took a week and the judge was ready.

In regards to my social security benefits the judge stated that those benefits were so supposed to be held for me until I was eighteen; but since my father was able to arrange to get the money, it was just a sad situation that he himself could not undo nor could he request that the social security department reissue me another check. The judge did rule in my favor in regards to the custody issue.

He granted sole custody to my foster mother, Gigi, and he added that my father had no rights to any visitations and that I was now a ward of the state. After this statement court was adjourned and the bailiff gave my father his gun back, and we were all free to leave the courtroom. But before I reached the hallway my father had caught up with me and he stopped me and said. "Bitch, I will kill you for making me go through this shit. Do you hear me? A daughter is not supposed to go against her father, especially to the police. You are a fucking rat. If I ever catch you alone and by yourself, I will kill you!" His words frightened me and had haunted me for a few years. I looked at him with nothing but a blank stare. I didn't show the heartache and disappointment that I was feeling on my face. Again I wore a game face. I walked passed him and waited for the social worker, my lawyer, and Gigi to step out of the courtroom.

I thanked the lawyer and the social worker for the time and help that they had given me. I was even blessed by getting a chance to talk and thank the judge who presided on my case. He apologized about what had happened to me, and he wished that he could have done more about what my father had done to me; but that his hands were tied because of the law. He wished me well and then he left to prepare for the next upcoming case, then Gigi walked out and asked if I was ready to go home. I said yes and wondered if this was really going to be a home for me, not physically but emotionally. I needed some security in my life. The present was filled with uncertainties and the unknown. As I thought back upon my life, I had realized that I had to reinvent myself after my abuse with Hon and now again with my father's unorthodox behavior. I wondered when I would be done with the finished prototype.

I came to the realization that when you are finally finished building the foundation and structure of your soul then you are dead. Life always rebuilds itself and humans are no different. The subject matter and themes stay the same such as flowers, trees, and nature but the structure, the location, and the foundations all change so a new and different one can be born to exist with the others. Now I was on my way home with Gigi to exist in this new life in Denver in Park Hill. Was I ready? Was I able? I asked myself. I had to become ready whether I wanted to or not. Only god knew my grief and my intentions but no one knew me.

Chapter 33

Free at Last

On the verge of my sixteenth birthday, I felt so alone. I had to re-group and pull myself together and not dwell on what could have been. I kept in touch with Judy and her two sons. Their family had kept the insanity at bay with their odd ball kind of humor. Now since the trial and my ordeal with my father was over, I began to live a new life. This was the life of a foster child in Denver. It wasn't exciting, but I had to make the best of it. I still held on to my past with resentment and anger. I didn't feel that I had deserved to go through all of the turmoil that I did. I didn't understand why God allowed me to suffer so much and be raised as an object instead of a child.

My life as a foster child is not really much to tell. I stayed with Gigi for two years until I was emancipated out of her home at the age of seventeen. I had registered at a new school in Denver and I stayed at South High School until my senior year, then dropped out and went to a vocational school to get my GED. I had my very first job at Reiver's restaurant on Gaylord Street near my high school. I was hired as dishwasher and I became the best damn dishwasher I could be. The minimum wage back then was $2.65. And with the money that I had earned, I bought clothes and more records, especially my girl Natalie Cole. Even when things got bad for me and I was feeling pretty low, Natalie always came through with bringing a smile upon my face. I continued to buy Ms. Cole's albums as I got older; in fact her song *Keep Smiling* which is on her self-named Natalie album saved my life when I was determined to end my life for good after my father's trial. And her song *Annie Mae* was a song about my life and how close I came to becoming a prostitute. She saved my life with her words. God even blessed me by given me an opportunity to meet her in person while I was in Denver.

At eighteen I met and began dating this sweet guy named Robert. He was seven years older than me when we started dating. We dated for six years. He was a true gentleman--one who I was not ready for. And I realized that now he will always be in my heart as a good man. I had moved in with him to escape having to live with Gigi. After living with Robert off and on I was finally able to get my own apartment. Also at eighteen I enlisted in the Army for six years as a reserve. I only went to the Army so that I could get half of my college tuition paid. I was stationed at Fort Dix, New Jersey for my basic training and Fort Belvoir, West Virginia for my AIT schooling. Our base in West Virginia wasn't that far from the Quantico base. That base taught enlisted personnel to work for the FBI and other government agencies. I ended up only staying five months because I wasn't given all of the information about my enlistment by my recruiter. I found out that only full-time enlisted personnel were allowed to participate in that college program, not reserve personnel. So I requested to be discharged from the Army. The Staff Sergeant wanted to give me a dishonorable one for wanting to leave early. But after a brief intense debate, I was able to walk out of his office with an honorable discharge.

I had many jobs, but I loved the criminal justice system. So I enrolled at Metropolitan State College and took two years of Criminal Justice courses. I had wanted to become a trial lawyer; like a prosecutor and then a judge. I got distracted from school with my relationship with Robert, so I stopped going. I soon got interested in comedy, mainly because people had been telling me all of my life that I had missed my calling and that I should do stand-up. So I did. I went and signed up for the amateur night at the Comedy Works on Larimer Square in downtown Denver. Judy's son, Butch, went with me that night and I bombed; mainly because I had stage fright.

But I was determined to sign up again. In fact, I signed up on three more different occasions and the third time was the charm. That night, I made the audience laugh. And all that I needed was the sound of applause and laughter to encourage me to try and make it a career. I had caught the stage bug and I was going for it.

Well needless to say I didn't get hired so I ended up getting my guard card, and I began working security to pay my bills. I had my first car at twenty-five. I remember that it was a four door Buick Skylark that Robert co-signed for me. The car was kind of run down as far as the engine, so I had to let it go. I didn't mind driving, but it scared me to death to try and drive in Denver's winters. I'm the kind of person who likes to be driven or chauffeured instead of having to deal with the stress of driving.

During the time that I lived in Denver, I ended up losing a lot of my belongings, either by bad relationships that didn't work out, or by so-called friends stealing or throwing away your shit. So I let it go and promised myself that I would get those material things again, only this time it would be bigger and better than before. After spending about fifteen years living in Denver, I got bored and tired of all the blizzards that the winter snows would bring. So I had my sights set on Los Angeles.

I loved being at home and watching all of those music videos that showed the hot sun and the cool beaches. Yes I knew that I had to go there. Besides I felt that if I was going to make it big time then I had to go to Hollywood. So I quit my job and I took my money and I bought a one-way greyhound bus ticket to Los Angeles.

I didn't know a soul out there. I didn't care one bit about that. In fact that never deterred me from my dream to live, work, and find an apartment in Los Angeles. I couldn't wait to get out there and go to the beach and mingle with the people. And besides it was sunny in the month of January. Now that was my kind of city.

The year was 1986 and I was twenty-five years old and knew that I had wanted more out of life. Whatever good it had to offer me, I was going to get in line for it. I had made my New Year's resolution to go to Los Angeles, California. I knew that there had to be more out there than just Kansas City, Missouri, and Denver, Colorado. And I wanted to pursue my comedy career. So I packed my bags and left one early afternoon. It was a twenty-four hour ride from Denver to Los Angeles. We had a short layover in Las Vegas, which I thought was gorgeous. I soon arrived in Los Angeles. At that time the greyhound station was located on Sixth and Los Angeles Street. The first thing that I did was I found a motel to stay at. And you know it had to be on the famous Sunset strip. I adventured around LA on my own and I found the Laugh Factory and The Comedy Store. And I signed up for both of them for different nights. I thought to myself, here I am in Los Angeles drama-free, carefree, and most of all Free at Last. I didn't have to worry about Hon, my father, or any relatives. I felt like a bird that was in flight to a new world where no one knew my past and no one knew me. Now I was signing up on their lists to do amateur stand-up on a weekly basis while paying for my motel room and making sure that I ate every night. It started to get real expensive. The little bit of money that I had was starting to vanish.

Soon I found myself not being able to eat or pay for my motel room. So I asked around to see where I could stay next. I didn't have a job and knew no one there. Some people on the streets told me that I would have to go to skid row and go to a shelter. A shelter? What the hell was that, I thought to myself. I never heard about shelters until I came out to Los Angeles.

I know that the name didn't sound right, but I had no choice now. I had just enough money left for a bus fare to get me downtown to this so-called skid row neighborhood. So here I was in this big city, broke, hungry, and eager to find another place to sleep, eat and rest my head.

Once I reached the skid row area I came across a black man who asked if I needed help. So I took a chance and I explained to him that I was from out of town and my money had run out. And I needed a place to stay. This man who he had introduced himself to me as Tony, was more than happy to escort me to a shelter. In fact, he lived there too. So I followed him down to this shelter hoping that no harm would come to me. He explained to me what I had to say and do in order to be accepted at the shelter. I did as he had instructed me to do and presto I had a bed, got fed a meal twice a day and I had two years to stay. Wow! I thought. California is the bomb. I had never heard of anyone staying somewhere for no rent and they feed you too. I was ecstatic. Of course Tony followed me around like a puppy dog, but he always had some good advice when it came to making some money. He told me about a vocational school that was located on 4th and Broadway that I could enroll in a class and receive $5,000 from a student loan. And of course, how did Tony know this information? Because he also attended there. He was becoming a dental assistant. So we walked up to the school, and a couple of the faculty members by the name of Sharnett and Ruby helped me qualify for the student loan. You know that I had signed up for security so I could get my guard card. I ended up receiving at $2,800 in cash in a sixth month period. That student loan soon became a monkey on my back that I am still trying to get off.

Later and while attending the California Institute, Tony and I decided to date each other. At first it was kind of cool, but then it got to be really scary because to my surprise, Tony smoked crack cocaine. Now I had never heard of this drug before and smoking a pipe, I was so naïve that I thought that they meant a tobacco pipe that people used to smoke when I was a child. Tony got mean after he took a hit from the pipe. And if he didn't have a pipe, he would make one out of a soda can and a piece chore boy Brillo pad that he used for a screen. When I was around him, I would pretend to inhale the smoke from the crack pipe. So I never got hooked. When Tony made the statement that he was going to kill me if I tried to leave him, I waited until we walked to school together and I told everyone at the school what he had said. Yes, I put him the spot!

On that same day I had missed my morning security class so I went and attended the afternoon course. And to my surprise this gorgeous looking, charismatic, and suave black man walked in and I couldn't take my eyes off of him. He was the finest man that I had ever seen in my life besides those men that they hire to play on soap operas. He was teaching the security class. He introduced himself as Mr. Tate. He wore a tailored made suite with a white shirt and a t-shirt underneath his dress shirt; which I thought was so professional. This man was sharper than a carving knife. He had beautiful white pearly teeth with a smile that made you want to make love to him in an instance. He wore his jet black curly hair neatly cut close to his head and he had a well-manicured and trimmed mustache. I found out that he was mixed with black and Spanish. He was too fine to be real. He spoke soft and sexy. I couldn't even concentrate on my studies because I was so busy fantasizing about him. I changed my morning class to the afternoon, just so I could have him as my instructor. I found out quickly that I had another side to me that was foreign ... it was called a hoe.

He told the classroom that he was an LAPD Officer. I thought he was the man of my dreams. I was in love with this man. I loved him like I had never loved a man before in my life. I didn't think that I could even love a man after so many had mistreated me. But I did. I had found a way for us to talk and get closer. After a few months we both went our separate ways, not because I wanted to, but because he didn't feel the same way I did. This broke my poor little heart. It took me some time but I got over him and I had promised myself to never love another man that much and that hard. It was way too much of a heartache for me to bear and handle. So we said goodbye and I was forced to move on. I had lost contact with him, until I happened to look him up on Facebook and there he was. Still fine! I sent him a friend request and he accepted. We don't write to each other but, I know where I can find him when I want to reminisce about the good old days.

Chapter 34

A Gift from God

My life in California was filled with working and fulfilling my goal to get an apartment in Los Angeles. I was soon able to do that. As my future unfolded ... the remaining members of my family fell apart. After I told my grandmother about what my father had done to me in Colorado, she no longer allowed me to speak to my brothers and sister again. I learned later while I was residing at Gigi's that my baby brother, Orlando, had died by drowning in a friend's pool. I haven't spoken to my siblings in more than thirty years.

Do I miss them? The answer is no because I don't even know them.

Now Gussie, otherwise known as Hon, died from cancer in 1977 alone on her living room floor. At the time of her death, she was still without gas, lights, a telephone and heat. She was still saving *all* of her money for Officer Johnson.

My father died also in the early eighties of Cirrhosis of the liver and brain cancer. I never did go and visit him while he was lying on his death bed. Not even when his doctor called me at home and begged me to come. In those days, I found no forgiveness in my heart for him. Not even on his deathbed.

Over the years, I lost contact with Patricia and my favorite gym teacher, Ms. Simmons, but I do hope that they are doing well. I would imagine by now that both sets of grandparents on both parents' sides are deceased. And as far as my Aunt Eva and my aunt Francis, I also assume that they too are gone.

I am just so happy that God made me such a strong person so I didn't lose my mind, nor did I start using dangerous and harmful drugs. Even though I had liked to drink I am thankful that I didn't grow up to become an alcohol, such as my dad.

While I was out here residing in California I tried to become famous by doing stand-up comedy on stage. I appeared at the Comedy Store, the Laugh Factory, the Savoy and Pig N Whistle. Needless to say that my stint with comedy never panned out, so I spent the next seven years working, and saving up my money. I finally ended up getting a nice one bedroom apartment, which I loved.

I spent six years in my beautiful apartment and I saw many tenants come and go. And during those six years I was quite content in going to work, paying my bills, and keeping a roof over my head. And then tragedy struck, I ended up losing my job and I could not pay my rent. I panicked. The last place that I didn't want to go back to was Skid Row. I had tried everything possible to try and keep my place. But nothing came through that allowed me to keep it. I even tried to stay with friends, but no one offered.

Ultimately, I had no choice but to go back to a shelter, which I was in twelve years ago. So, I humbled myself and made the trip down there once again. I remember asking God, why did I have to lose everything that I had worked so hard to get?. And why did I have return back down to the Skid Row area. I was indeed hurt, mad, and disappointed with myself and life once again. I had thought that I had beat the odds and that I was on my way up not down. And again I felt hopeless as hell. But during my stay at the shelter, I met many people homeless and staff that had changed my life for the better.

In one transitional shelter that is located in the heart of Skid Row, I saw a flyer posted in the hall about this author coming down to our facility. Now we have been mandated to attend these wellness groups and other meetings which used to bore the hell out of me. I sure didn't want to go to another mandatory meeting, besides my time there was almost up. I had better things to do like look for a place to stay. I was only allowed to stay there for six months and I was now in my fifth month there. And no matter how I tried to get out of this meeting my case manager just wouldn't let me. In fact she threatened that if I didn't attend this meeting then my stay was going to be cut short and I would have to find another place to stay sooner. So on the day of the meeting my case manager informed me that this meeting was going to be a six week session. I thought oh my God, I got to find a way out. But of course it was my luck that the meetings were on Fridays a day that I didn't have to be at work.

The first meeting was held on the first floor conference; where about fifty women had shown up because of being threatened. By the third week the attendees had dwindled down to fifteen women. So her sessions were held in our women's dayroom. This did make it more up close and personal and I guess cozy too. This woman was a well-established author by the name of Darnella Ford.

She has written several books such as Crave, Finding Me, Rising, Choke and Naked Love. The program that she was presenting was called *Journey to Worthy*. And it was filled with many tips on how to think and love yourself. She always would open the meeting up with what she called words of inspiration, which I found to be very cool. She was a cool person too. She was very approachable and she didn't mind a good honest debate. After her inspiring speech I got enough gall to ask her since she was a writer and all; would she be willing to tell me if I had natural raw talent to become a writer. She said that she would be happy to give her professional opinion regarding the talent that I felt that I had possessed. Of course she gave me the chance to write an outline of ten topics and a prologue, which was a short paragraph that explains what the book is about. She taught me that.

After reading my prologue she was impressed and she decided that I did have a natural talent for writing. And she has helped me from the beginning of writing the book, to the very end to get my book published. If it hadn't been for her inspiration and sharing her knowledge about how to write a book … this book would still be a dream instead of an actual publication. And I do believe that she was a gift from God. I love and respect her dearly. I really learned a lot from her about writing a book. I found out quickly that it wasn't as easy as I thought it would be. She taught me that it was a process and I that needed to be patience in order to grow as a writer.

We have laughed and we have cried together. That's what true friends do and they don't hesitate or think twice about how they interact with each other. Friendship is not rehearsed nor is it scripted. Darnella is as pure and wholesome as a friend can be. She let me fly. And I will always be grateful to her for that. I appreciate her time that she spent on editing the book with love. I do feel that her program really brings out the talent that a person has no matter what it may be.

Journey to Worthy has helped me and I am sure that it could help many others to live the life that they were born to live. Journey to Worthy gave me my dreams back. So after reading my book, I do suggest that you should check out this program Journey to Worthy and see what it can do for you for living a better life.

I thank God that I was forced to go to her sessions by my case manager. It helped me so much that I want to pass it on to others. You can go to journeytoworthy.org and learn more about this program and Ms. Ford.

I may not ever forget how I was treated as a child and I don't feel that God intended me to. But I refuse to dwell on the sorrow to where it starts to jeopardize my mental well-being. As far as forgiveness I have let some of it go and I have forgiven some people … only because they knew nothing about me.

I remain a work in progress.

We all are.

I now know that I have a journey that is calling me toward bigger and better things in my life. I am ready, willing, and able to take my journey with a clean, spiritual mind in order for me to be blessed in abundance.

I do hope that my story can help someone. Find someone that you can trust and talk to them. Somebody's got to listen. It doesn't matter what you may be going through, a bad relationship, abusive parents, abusive adults, or even your siblings. ***There is still enough love in the world and help is not so far away.***

I hope that my readers have enjoyed my book and felt the emotions that I had felt. I want to end this chapter by saying thank you and may you be blessed with love.

Chapter 35

Epilogue

I have learned many valuable lessons about myself after writing this memoir. Mainly to love myself so I can maturely accept love back. I learned that I am not her alone I many friends and loved ones who care about me in many different ways. I had to delve into my inner self and be honest with myself in order to heal and change my outlook on life. I was afraid to be me, because I spent so much time loving someone else better than I loved myself. I owe myself some kindness and compassion after all these people are no longer in my life. I am learning to be dependent on me for the very first time.

Mary Ross

Conclusion

In conclusion I would like to leave you with a solution that you can use in your everday life. No matter what trauma or tribulation that you have suffered as a child or may be living through now. Check your attitude. Find a place in your mind to meditate and have the courage to feel, deal, and heal as a friend requested that I do. I have beaten myself up for years over what people had said or the way that they treated me. I kept playing the scene over and over in my head until I started believing the worst of me. You can't allow this to happen. You must meditate on good thought and good times, you must be will to take a chance on yourself, and most of all you must be ready to heal. Award winning author Darnella Ford said it best. "We hurt ourselves when we love ourselves the least"

Resources

Website Journeytoworthy.org
Email her at darnella@journeytoworthy.org

Printed in the United States
By Bookmasters